VOICES FROM THE

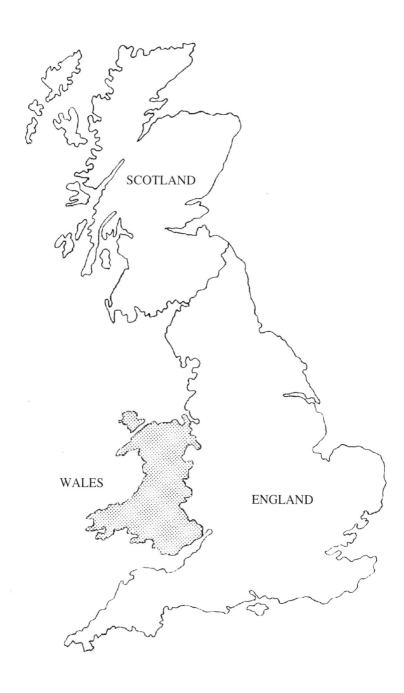

VOICES FROM THE WELSH REVIVAL

An anthology of testimonies, reports,
and eyewitness statements from
Wales's year of blessing, 1904–05

Brynmor P. Jones

EVANGELICAL PRESS OF WALES

Cover design by
Rhiain M. Davies (Cain)
based on an oil painting
by J. Glyn Jones

Published by the Evangelical Press of Wales
Bryntirion, Bridgend, Mid Glamorgan, CF31 4DX, Wales, UK
Printed in Wales by Bridgend Print Centre, Bridgend

Contents

To the honoured memory of Dr J. Edwin Orr, Professor of Revival History, a humble generous scholar who, in his last years, personally urged many of us to do whatever we could to complete the work he had begun.

Foreword

This book contains primary evidence of what happened in the 1904–5 Revival. Rev. Brynmor Jones has done an immense amount of researching in order to gather the material which he presents in this account. Though it has been a labour of love for him, he has placed us in his debt by his efforts in this and a previous volume entitled *The King's Champions*. Reading this book will not only take us back to the beginning of this century but also to what God can do suddenly and gloriously for his church. Nothing is more needed than that as we approach a new millennium.

Whilst certain events and incidents are recorded in this volume, we have here more than a historical narrative. It is a chronicle of experiences. In being asked to write this foreword, it was suggested to me by the author that I might comment on the prominence of this experimental aspect. I am glad to do that because, while experiences can be superficial or spurious, it is not possible to have a revival without them. Why is that? It is because, in a time of revival, true religion comes to flower.

True religion, which is 'the life of God in the soul of man' and is 'more than notion', includes human feelings in its scope and subjects them to its sanctifying influence. It focuses them on the Lord Jesus Christ, who died for sinners, and integrates them with the understanding and conduct. In any genuine revival these experiences are intensified and enlarged. They are heightened towards God in adoring praise, deepened within in terms of contrition, trust and delight, and extended to the family of God and lost mankind.

It is such experiences that we read of in this book. Time and again people refer to what they felt, heard or saw. In all these descriptions, the reality of the heavenly world is attested and also the witnessing ministry of the Holy Spirit. In regenerating, he discloses that world of truth and life and causes an unbeliever to see it and enter (John 3:3,5). In reviving, he clarifies, assures and edifies by disclosing even more of the glory of the Saviour to the church and also in the world (John 16:13-15; 8-11).

May these accounts contribute to bringing about an even greater outpouring of the Spirit to the glory of the Lord Jesus Christ! That is the kind of 'new age' which we really need. It will arrest the moral decline and dehumanization in our society; it will dignify human beings by humbling them as sinners and recreating them in the image of Christ; and it will purge and empower the church for its missionary task in the world.

HYWEL R. JONES
London Theological Seminary

Author's Preface

Although appearing after two of the other books in the series, this book is intended as the first of five books whose common aim is to show the mercies of our God, the transforming love of our Saviour, and the power of the Holy Spirit, as displayed during and after revival. Its sequel is the enlarged edition of *The King's Champions* (1986), which deals with the nurture and protection of the 'children of the revival'. The third book (1989) traces the rise of the Welsh Keswick Movement centred upon the Llandrindod Convention. A fourth book, currently in preparation, will provide a complete account of Evan Roberts's revival and post-revival ministries which finally ended in 1930-33. One task then remains, namely that of tracing the linkage between the revival and the hundred gospel halls and missions scattered around Wales, including those where pentecostalist influences and trends first appeared five years after the revival.

An anthology of eyewitness accounts must necessarily have parallel and even repetitive material; it is not a straightforward, unswerving story. The 'voices' are not those of scholars, church statesmen or top-rank journalists, but of local correspondents and reporters, ministers and visiting preachers, and those active converts who gave their stories, in some cases many years later. The result is a wealth of reports, testimonies, letters and diaries, which provide an in-depth study of the very different revival experiences, including some of rejection. They are the final proof that a national awakening or revival is far different from crusades, missions and renewal meetings. As Evan Roberts said, 'Revival is a movement of the Spirit of God and is to be owned by men; Mission is Man's work which is to be owned by the Spirit of God.'

The stories in the main sections are offered to Christians everywhere who now long for another day when the Lord will visit the nations. May the reading of the reports and testimonies cause us to cry to him with even greater urgency. It is hoped that the last three chapters, on 'Resisting the Spirit', 'Grieving the Spirit' and 'Quenching the Spirit', will give us the knowledge needed to detect and rebuke the great sower of tares whose name is Satan, our accuser and adversary. To quote Evan Roberts again, 'In the hour and power of God in revival, the tempter appears to be present, but he is present as a counterfeiter. He is always mixing his workings with the workings of God.'

ACKNOWLEDGEMENTS: Thanks are due to many: first of all to friends such as the Rev. James Walters, Mr Oswald Penry and Rev. Courtenay B. Harris who pointed me to various sources. The same is true also of librarian-archivists at Caernarfon, Dolgellau, Mold, Haverfordwest, Swansea and Aberystwyth, who helped to recover forgotten documents. Thanks are also due to owners of copyright material for their permission to reproduce it here.

I am grateful to Mr Ken Jackson of Cardiff for hours spent in recovering and re-recording the converts' testimonies, and to Professor R. Geraint Gruffydd, Rev. Owen Milton, and Rev. and Mrs Glyn Davies for helping, amongst other things, with difficult translation work.

The Rev. J. Elwyn Davies, Mr Alan Francis and Mr Meurig Thomas gave much encouragement in the early stages. Thanks are due to the English Literature Committee of the Evangelical Press of Wales for accepting the book for publication and for their constructive criticisms, and to the staff of the Evangelical Press of Wales for carrying through the publication of a very substantial book. I am also grateful to the Rev. Hywel Jones for his perceptive preface which shows what lies at the heart of all true revival. The eyewitnesses cannot be thanked until we all meet in the Glory.

PROLOGUE

Ride in triumph, blessèd Jesus,
   Gird Thou on Thine armour bright;
Neither earth can stand before Thee,
   Nor proud hell with all its might;
At Thy Name, so great and glorious,
   All Thy foes withdraw in fear;
Filled with awe is all creation
   When Thou, Christ of God, art near.

William Williams, Pantycelyn (1717-91);
tr. by William Edwards (1848-1929)

PROLOGUE
The First Voices of the Awakening

'Until the spirit be poured upon us from on high'
(Isaiah 32:15)

Much energy has been wasted in trying to trace the source of the Welsh Revival of 1904–5. Suggestions have included social ferment, educational change, cultural confusions, and even the use of new preaching styles. Jessie Penn-Lewis was sure it came from the world-wide 'chains of prayer', whereas R. B. Jones saw it as a kind of 'holiness' movement and F. B. Meyer claimed it as a spiritual child of Keswick teaching. Welsh Presbyterian writers linked it with their Forward Movement, while Baptists saw strong links with the infant Christian Endeavour. In recent Pentecostalist books and magazine articles, the events in Wales are seen as parallel with signs and wonders throughout the world. Historian Dr J. Edwin Orr always felt it had opened the gates to a spiritual leap forward. No explanation has convinced or will convince everyone. The earliest signs of revival, however, appeared not in a church or movement, but in the secret experiences of men upon whom the Lord had already laid his hand and whom the Holy Spirit now touched with coals from the altar. Therefore our first duty and need are to hear and study the testimonies of those who were awakened.

In this context one must give due honour to those quiet, preliminary evidences of a more general nature in West Wales. The first-fruits were the 'conventions to deepen the spiritual life of the church'. Did not the Spirit prompt several West Wales Presbyterian ministers and others to feel a deep need for these? It was their working party, approved by the district presbytery, which called on W. W. Lewis and D. M. Saunders for help. These men were commended as 'wholly consecrated men soaked in the life of Christ'. On 31 December 1903 they held a small convention at New Quay in Cardiganshire that taught the way of cleansing

13

and yielding and receiving full assurance. This call deeply impressed Florrie Evans, who will feature later, along with other young members of the New Quay churches, who were set on fire to witness. On 30 June 1904 there began a second conference at Aberaeron where Keswick-type teaching was given. There was a late September conference at Blaenannerch at which Seth Joshua spoke, during which John Thickens first noticed 'a young man sitting opposite us in obvious distress while Mr. Joshua was speaking . . . a young neurotic man—that is neurotic in our opinion'.[1] The young Evan Roberts had not yet heard the final call, but the three conferences bore fruit in numerous rural missions and fervent group meetings, as will be seen.

To a lesser extent there were little conferences of revival seekers who were ministering further to the east in the Glamorganshire villages and townships of Pen-coed, Aberdare, Dowlais, the Rhondda Valley, etc. These included a group of pastors who had been directly influenced by their meetings with Dr F. B. Meyer.[2] Finally there were small, hardly noticeable stirrings in a few North Wales churches. All this points to some general pattern of Holy Spirit activity as he began to come in power.

Nevertheless, our chief concern here is with the experiences of a few men. Listening to their testimonies we may well note a strong family resemblance, because each is broken before he is filled:

Suddenly there came to me an indelible consciousness of the amazing holiness of God like a purifying fire—like a fiery river flowing out from the throne, and I in the midst as if reclining on it. I do not know whether it were in the body or out of it, but the fire percolated through my whole nature. I remember the thoughts which gripped me. 'The Holiness of God, and I still alive in the midst of the stream. One cannot die here.' When I recovered consciousness of my earthly surroundings, I was amazed to find that the pain which for years I had been enduring constantly had vanished, and I slept that night like a healthy little child.

(W. S. Jones)[3]

Six of us went [to Llandrindod], and Dr Meyer fulfilled his promise. He came to talk with us in our lodgings, and a heavenly dawn broke on the souls of some of us. Heavenly light drove away the black darkness! . . . We saw clearly that sanctification was the work of God, and that He begins the work in the will. All we had to do was to be willing for the Lord to sanctify us. We saw that the willing also was of God. The King won the castle of man-soul that week in the case of some of us . . . The particular intent of Dr Meyer's ministry was to use every evangelical persuasion he knew to bring the will to open the gates so that the King of Glory might come in.

(O. M. Owen)[4]

It was on Friday that Dr F. B. Meyer came to us according to his promise. He said to each one of us, 'What is it that *you* want?' I told him, 'I don't know for certain but one thing I do know—I want the Holy Spirit.' [Then he said,] 'You want the Spirit; well then, take hold of Him. I see you are like the Jews waiting for a sign. Yet all you need to do is to take hold of the Spirit whom He has given to you.' A new world opened up for me. Now I saw it. I went home on Saturday and took the service as usual without telling anyone. Next Sunday I still said nothing, yet they somehow knew that there was a new man in the pulpit.

(R. B. Jones)[5]

I felt the *Holy Spirit* like a deluge of light causing my whole nature to tremble; I saw *Jesus Christ*—and my nature became as a small drop at his feet; and I saw *my self*—and I despised it!

(J. T. Job)[6]

In an afternoon meeting, which was addressed by Mrs. Penn-Lewis, God's train filled the temple, and when she asked us at the close to bow our heads, and for everyone who accepted Christ as Lord to say, 'Yes, Lord,' after a hard struggle I was helped to do so . . . As far as I can recall, the most I expected was some help to overcome my bad temper . . . but instead of that I was baptised with streams of life-giving, cleansing, transforming power for about half an hour, that made me feel clean and healthy and joyous to the very depths of my being.

(E. Keri Evans)[7]

By divine providence these men were going to be at hand when scores of perplexed, ordinary chapel folk experienced these floods of light and power but could not understand the meaning of such events. The pattern thus becomes clearer. Each of these men becomes deeply dissatisfied and aware of his own need; then each is brought to the hour of surrender to the power of the Holy Spirit; and finally each one emerges as a humbler, purer person, fit now to be a channel of revival. Two other examples are Seth Joshua and W. W. Lewis, who were far closer geographically to Evan Roberts and his fellow witnesses, and were destined to be used by the Lord to bring them also to be broken and remoulded.

15

Long before 1904 the evangelist Seth Joshua had learned to loathe the forces of sin which had kept him a slave for years. The Spirit of God convicted and crushed him, and then cleansed and filled him. He longed to see his countrymen similarly saved. His son, Dr Peter Joshua, told a Cardiff visitor to a Christian Businessmen's Breakfast in Chicago that he had lived in Grangetown, Cardiff, when a boy. Then he told a story about him mitching school one day and going to Sophia Gardens with a jam jar to see if he could catch some tiddlers. He spotted his father walking in the park, and ran to hide behind some bushes:

> As he came near I was frightened as I heard that he was crying (something I thought never my Dad would ever do) and as he went by he was saying, 'Please God, give me Wales', and kept saying this as long as I could hear him. After a while I ran back home, and while I had to explain to mother that I had mitched school, I asked her what was wrong with Dad, and told her that I had heard him crying and saying 'Give me Wales.' She ruffled my hair and said, 'You'll understand one day.' God never gave Wales to my Dad, although he gave him many souls, but one day when he was preaching when he made an appeal Evan Roberts was the only one who stood to his feet and trusted the Saviour. God never gave Wales to my Dad, but he gave Wales to Evan Roberts.[8]

The exact turning-point in W. W. Lewis's spiritual history is not known, but those who heard him at the West Wales conventions understood that some astonishing power had changed a cool, schoolmasterish person into a bold and passionate pleader.[9] At the Blaenannerch convention he preached obedience and consecration until men felt as if lightning-struck:

> This mighty man was clothed with power from above, and we were summoned by him to an exacting judgment. We doubt if he were clothed with such power in any other meeting in his life. It was not a case of 'hwyl' [fervour in the pulpit], but of flash after flash on our consciences until each of us turned into a terror to himself. We saw ourselves in the light of the judgment of the last day.[10]

Some of those flashes pierced the soul of Joseph Jenkins of New Quay—yet another member of this group of transformed preachers. A very earnest young minister, he was already sitting in judgment on his own ministry. He and his friend felt keenly that they were not fully consecrated, even though they seemed to be fruitful in their ministry. Possibly from R. B. Jones, who had spent his holiday at New Quay, Joseph

16

Jenkins had heard of the wonderful experiences of those who went to the first Welsh Keswick convention. When he invited W. W. Lewis to his local convention, he knew that he was one man who could help him. In this kind of turmoil, he heard conference addresses by W. W. Lewis and J. M. Saunders on consecration and assurance, and then the wonderful testimonies. It was these testimonies more than anything else that overwhelmed him. John Thickens could write of these meetings:

> There were in these meetings no sounds of triumphant joy; indeed, we sang but very little, because these were hours of heart-searching, and their chief effect upon us was to create within us a longing to know Christ's love, or a longing for God in Christ to satisfy us with something—something for which we had no name.[11]

Days of reading, praying and struggling followed, before the vision of the cross gave Joseph Jenkins peace at last:

> [On his knees that memorable night, he refused] to loose his grip on his Lord until He had blessed him, and indeed he was blessed for he was clothed with strength from above, and he knew it. And then, when he rose up to take his seat a strange blue flame took hold of him until he was almost completely covered. It rose, as far as he could gather, from the floor of the room and billowed up, encircling him. It retreated and returned a second time, and then retreated and returned again, but he did not know its meaning then any more than he did a quarter of a century afterwards, but he connected its outward manifestation with the pure communion that had existed between him and his God.[12]

After such a glorious foretaste of revival, Joseph Jenkins found he too could preach with freedom and authority, and it was that spirit which shone through his February sermon on 'This is the victory' (1 John 5:4), which did strange things to some of his own congregation. Soon the Lord would send him to many a church in West and North Wales which needed that same consuming flame.[13]

The few contemporary accounts of Evan Roberts's childhood and youth show that he was already a complex personality. The Member of Parliament, D. R. Grenfell, his boyhood friend, and Tudor Rees tell of a normal, healthy lad who played rough games on the river beaches at Bwlchymynydd, rescued two from drowning, ran errands for his mother, worked obediently but not brilliantly at the National School in Upper Loughor and eventually went to help his father work the pumps in the colliery and manage his huge garden.

Another picture is of a slender young collier with piercing eyes, a lovely smile, a clean, upright look, and 'some signs of idealism and clean values'.[14] This youth was chosen to be a Sunday school secretary and then leader of the young people's groups where already the youths were taught to 'take part as moved by the Spirit'. The members of Moriah Chapel valued his gifts and readily agreed to help him prepare for full-time ministry even though he was in his mid-twenties.

Next there is D. M. Phillips's portrait of a man who studied serious religious books, learned to play the organ, communed with God as he walked; a man who knelt for hours in silent worship and took part in chapel meetings—always waiting for the day when the Spirit would come.

Finally there is that other picture of the mature student at Newcastle Emlyn who puzzled his friends, worried the landladies, and angered the tutor as the study of academic things became a torment to him and he escaped gladly into the evangelistic missions of Seth Joshua and others.[15]

Our only concern in this chapter on the divine preparation is to report some of his spiritual battles. Between his fifteenth birthday and his final weeks at Newcastle Emlyn, Evan Roberts passed through more than one experience of testing and chastening. Moments of joy and clear vision alternated with times of depression and dryness. Let him speak for himself out of autobiographical notes recorded by various people:

> For a long, long time I was much troubled in my soul and my heart by thinking over the failure of Christianity. Oh! it seemed such a failure—such a failure—and I prayed and prayed, but nothing seemed to give me any relief. But one night, after I had been in great distress praying about this, I went to sleep, and at one o'clock in the morning suddenly I was waked up out of my sleep, and I found myself, with unspeakable joy and awe, in the very presence of the Almighty God. And for the space of four hours I was privileged to speak face to face with Him as a man speaks face to face with a friend . . . And it was not only that morning, but every morning for three or four months. Always I enjoyed four hours of that wonderful communion with God. I cannot describe it. I felt it, and it seemed to change all my nature, and I saw things in a different light, and I knew that God was going to work in the land.[16]

Some years later there came another period when he no longer experienced these divine visits and he was convinced that he would fail his examinations and that he was not really called to the ministry. But then came a second time of blessing at the start of his student life and another vision of the Lord's presence. The strange wrestling with study books developed into a time of great testing. He tells of a day when he obeyed the Spirit by rushing without his topcoat to some meeting 'to pray for the girls of New Quay to have strength'. Yet once again:

> 'Tuesday night . . . I felt awfully hard. I looked at the cross without feeling anything. I wept bitterly because of my hardness of heart; but I did not weep because of Christ. I loved the Father and the Holy Spirit, but did not love the Son.
>
> 'Wednesday, before going to Blaenanerch, I felt like a *flint*, and told that to Mr. Williams the guard, whom I met in Miss Phillips's shop. I felt as if every feeling had been swept from my bosom . . . I wanted to speak to Miss Phillips about her religious condition. I said to her *"I'll pray for you, you pray for me,"* and in a moment the tears filled her eyes. I do not remember what happened from this time on Wednesday, more than that I had something wonderful about 3.30 p.m. . . .'

The girls from New Quay did their best to persuade him to stay at Blaenanerch until the morrow, but he would not hear of that. Having failed to influence him, 'Well,' said they 'we have nothing to do.' 'No,' replied he, 'neither have I anything to do, but wait for the fire to descend. The altar is built, and the wood upon it, and the sacrifice only waiting for the fire to come down.'[17]

Such was his condition on the day in September 1904 when he went in a wagon to Blaenannerch, with the students singing and Seth Joshua praying that God would find an Elisha and break him in. In the account he gave of his experience that day, which was widely circulated,[18] Evan said he had felt some living energy or force entering his bosom till it held his breath and made his legs tremble—and that this increased steadily during the prayers. Someone who was a witness of this crisis and often told the story to Welsh friends was M. P. Morgan, the pastor of the Blaenannerch church:

> It was a fine day and there was a great assembling, with contingent after contingent from different districts in south Cardiganshire, and in their midst a goodly number from Newcastle Emlyn, students and others in sympathy with the movement. I remember well I was sitting behind the Rev. Seth Joshua when he was praying and in his prayer he was pleading with the Lord to bend us . . . With that, I heard a noise as though something had fallen. In addition there was some whispering and I felt very displeased that someone was disturbing the meeting. I opened my eyes and the first thing I saw was Evan Roberts fallen down in a pew

19

nearby, and Mrs Mona Davies, New Quay, and others wiping his sweat which was pouring out.[19]

The first days after this personal surrender or 'bending', Evan Roberts was freed from all that deadness that had troubled him, and he was able to send cheerful letters home to his brother Dan telling him that he felt courageous in Christ, joyful and healthy. Yet he was still very moody, and his friend Sidney Evans testified that although the great crisis of 'bending to the Spirit' was over, he was still waiting upon the Lord for a definite plan. Evan and Sidney were now engaged in planning evangelistic missions and seeking the guidance of the Holy Spirit, because they were convinced that 'the wheels of the gospel are to be turning rapidly before long. The night is beginning to vanish and the dawn extending gradually but certainly.' They had been praying for about one hundred thousand souls for Christ and a vision Evan Roberts experienced confirmed to them that this number would be converted.[20] Letters to the family spoke of serious study preparation and showed no sign of the intense strain that made him pray half the night. He was now on the eve of the calling.

For that final, great voice of command which sent him on his way, we turn from Evan Roberts's own testimony, well publicized in books, to two vivid, personal, eyewitness accounts—from Ann Phillips and from Rachel Phillips, both of whom were present in the Newcastle Emlyn chapel when the last struggle began on the last Sunday in October 1904. The veteran Presbyterian minister, Evan Phillips, preached that evening from those fateful words, 'Father, the hour is come; glorify thy Son, that thy Son also may glorify thee' (John 17:1). The hour, indeed, had come for a man and for a nation.

1. Rachel Phillips's story of Sunday, 30 October 1904:

Roberts sat Sunday morning in a pew close to me . . . There was some silent influence in the service touching the strings of the heart. I could not restrain from weeping throughout the service, and the people, especially the young, felt this influence. I could not see the face of Roberts; those who could see it told me that his face was shining, his countenance was changing, and appeared as if under a wonderful influence. When going out, and before going down the steps of the gallery he stood and looked at us, saying—'Well, what a meeting! O dear! the place is full of the influence of the Holy Spirit! O! I felt it coming over me like a breeze.' When descending the steps, the world came in and troubled me, and I said to Roberts, 'How can I go home; my eyes are red because of weeping in the service.' His answer was, 'Never mind; do not be ashamed to show that you feel. Come home.'[21]

It seems that Evan Roberts also attended the young people's prayer meeting that afternoon and stayed in a half-sitting posture, shedding tears and repeating over and over, 'Glorify Thy Son.' He went to the Phillips's house for tea but kept on sighing and then asked for a house prayer meeting. The girls said they had to go to a singing practice, but Rachel confessed that the real reason was fear that Evan's constant praying would do him much harm. 'What burdened us was care for his mental condition.'

It was in this strange state that Evan went up into the students' pew for the Sunday evening service and heard almost nothing because he was seeing only the people in Loughor chapels and was hearing the Spirit say, 'You must go.' After the service he went to Evan Phillips to be assured that this was a heavenly vision, not a deception. The wise pastor told him, 'No, no! The devil does not give such thoughts. It was the voice of the Holy Spirit.' At once Evan Roberts knew he must obey.

2. Ann Phillips's story of Sunday, 30 October 1904:

Sunday evening, after coming home, and Roberts with us, we found ourselves in a great prayer meeting in the house; and this was Roberts's prayer:—'O Lord, I am willing to shed my blood for Thy Son'. His words burned our bosoms, and we felt that he was shedding his blood, as it were, for Jesus at the time. When departing for his lodgings, he told us that he was going home on the morrow, because of the vision in the service and the call of the Spirit. We were not at all willing for him to go. There was such a charm in his company, and such divine fervour characterised him, that attracted us all.[22]

Before Evan Roberts catches that morning train, let us pause a moment and consider how wonderfully the Lord had prepared all things. Men of good counsel were being made humble and holy. The chosen messenger was being broken, moulded and filled. At the same time, in towns and villages far and near, the faithful were praying, 'Revive thy work in the midst of the years.' The Holy Spirit was already providing the men and the means for the miracle which was about to begin.

Let us pray that the Lord once more in our day will turn away his wrath, cancel his just sentence and give us a double portion of his forgiving, restoring love. Is it so surprising that the Spirit of God had worked quietly and simultaneously within movements, churches, prayer groups, chosen helpers, and in the one hidden messenger? Are not these ways prescribed in the Word of God? In the next chapters we will meet the people of a hundred towns whose hearts the Lord had prepared for the day of awakening.

I. PROCLAMATION

Here is love, vast as the ocean,
    Loving-kindness as the flood,
When the Prince of Life, our ransom,
    Shed for us His precious blood:
Who His love will not remember?
    Who can cease to sing His praise?
He can never be forgotten
    Thro' heav'n's everlasting days.

On the Mount of Crucifixion
    Fountains opened deep and wide;
Through the floodgates of God's mercy
    Flowed a vast and gracious tide;
Grace and love, like mighty rivers,
    Poured incessant from above;
And heaven's peace and perfect justice
    Kissed a guilty world in love.

William Rees ('Gwilym Hiraethog'; 1802-83);
tr. by William Edwards (1848-1929)

1

The Herald Stands Forth
at Loughor

'Stand in the gate of the Lord's house . . . and say,
Hear the word of the Lord, all ye . . . that enter in
at these gates to worship the Lord'
(Jeremiah 7:2)

On Monday morning, 31 October 1904, about the same time as fellow students were returning to Newcastle Emlyn from their weekend 'appoints', Evan Roberts was seated in a train going the other way towards Carmarthen. He had stopped at the Post Office to scribble a 'word in haste' to Florrie Evans telling her how and when he had been given his orders from the Holy Spirit by means of a vision. Now in the railway carriage he wrote a further letter to a prayer partner, Miss Nellie Ceredig Evans of Cardigan, informing her that this strange action was by command of the Holy Spirit, and that he had to obey:

> The main object of this note is to ask you and your friends to pray for us. I ask you, in the name of the Saviour, to be bold at the throne of grace, and oh! endeavour to impress this indelibly on the mind of your friends . . .
>
> I pray God that He will ere long pour His Spirit abundantly upon your young people . . .
>
> Please excuse the *lead* [pencil] and *writing*. This has been written while the train was in motion from Newcastle-Emlyn to Pencader.[1]

Changing trains at Carmarthen he felt an impulse to preach in the open air to fellow travellers concerning the need to consider the state of their souls. He felt a wave of happiness carrying him towards Loughor, although his unannounced arrival there caused a flutter or two in the nest. Mary Roberts, his sister, told Aneirin Talfan Davies:

> Mam thought that perhaps he had been preaching somewhere on Sunday and was calling on his way back, but he explained that his purpose

was to come here for the week. He had experienced very remarkable blessing and had come home to lead the young people [of Moriah Chapel] into the same experience . . . When Evan came home, Dan was lying on the couch looking very disheartened. Evan could not understand what was wrong, and then Dan told him that he was losing his sight . . . and that a Llanelli specialist had told him there was no hope . . . [Evan] turned towards Dan and said, 'You shall have your sight— the Lord has need of you.' Suddenly Dan regained his sight. A sort of miracle happened, and when he went to see the specialist, he marvelled, unable to understand what had happened.[2]

Mary Roberts also told Aneirin Talfan Davies that when her brother asked the minister and deacons of his chapel to permit him to have a special young people's meeting where he could deliver his message, they gave their consent at once. It was very unusual to allow a mere student to do this and not even to ask why he was absent in term-time from school. But the pastor was deeply impressed and the senior deacons respected the young messenger. Of course some members were suspicious and Evan's letters imply some strong doubts within the family also. He felt keen anguish when the Spirit was not obeyed quickly enough, but soon the letters are filled with great joy:

DEAR WILLIAMS,
    I do not know how to begin writing in the midst of this divine fire. The whole place has been moved, and my heart burns within me with the Holy Spirit . . . Oh! my dear Williams, this is a wonderful and awful week . . . What a service last night! The girls and the women shouting aloud, having forgotten themselves. Over thirty were baptised by the Holy Spirit. My dear boy, there's a band of workers! . . . The people come to us from a long distance. I am thankful that Christ through the Holy Spirit draws people to Him.[3]

DEAR ELSIE,
    . . . This has been a blessed week. I have been very busy. Off from morning till late at night. We never go to bed this week till about one or two in the morning . . . The great feature of this work is that people are being awakened, and learning to *obey*. Those who have been with religion have had quite a new and blessed experience. They never thought what joy there was in an open confession of Christ. Young people from the Independents and Baptists come to these meetings. Of course, I cannot stop them, and I do not want to stop them. I should like very much if

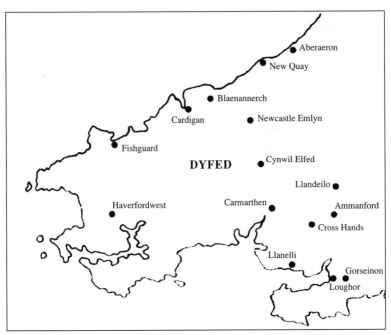

Revival centres and other places mentioned in South-west Wales

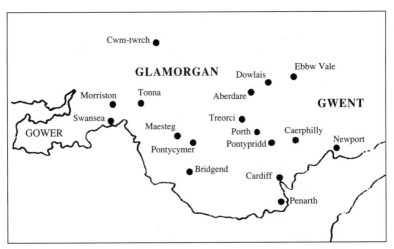

Revival centres and other places mentioned in South-east Wales

the Spirit was to descend on other denominations. I called these meetings for young people; but old people flock with us. Again, we cannot resist these coming.[4]

Those young people included Rhys and John Penry, a Mr Webb, and a slip of a girl named Hannah Hughes. Decades later their testimonies were recorded at Moriah Chapel, Loughor, by the then minister, James H. Walters.

The first surprising fact that emerges from these testimonies is that the revival in Loughor did not spring out of a total wilderness. Rhys Penry said that 'things were blooming' at his church (Bryn-teg Chapel), and that young people were going on Sunday morning at 9.30 to pray, 'but we were desirous of something else—something extraordinary'. John Penry mentioned seeing godly old people who were converted in 1859 now sharing their simple faith with a group of youths who came to weeknight meetings to meet God *before* the revival. Mr Webb of Gorseinon pointed out that they had built Seion Newydd Chapel three years before the revival because the congregation was already growing quickly. Each meeting there had been a blessing even before a certain night when 'God the Holy Spirit took possession':

> Many were at the same time crying to God for mercy. No one did speak about the revival, but the Holy Spirit filled the place with almighty convicting power . . . There was no one present who could lead to the Saviour, but the Holy Spirit glorified the Son by showing them Jesus Christ who was able to save to the uttermost.[5]

The same picture of preparedness is painted by John Powell Parry of Ruabon, who said that revival would have been impossible without real spiritual discipline. And J. Ellis Jones could tell us that what was needed was a richer experience of salvation and assurance.[6]

This is the climate in which Evan Roberts delivered the messages whose effect on the young men and women is told here.

1. Testimony of Rhys Penry

[Although things were blooming in our church] I was not satisfied with my moral and spiritual state—many times praying for something more. I wanted to be better. I remember a Sunday morning when we were praying in the young people's meeting and I could not express myself except through the hymn:

O! Iesu mawr, rho d' anian bur . . .
[Oh! great Jesus, give your pure nature.]

I was praying that morning, not just reciting the verse . . .

There was an old woman known to us all as Mari Tu Hwnt ['Mary Beyond']. Now two girls were on the way to a Saturday night oratorio practice in Bryn-teg Chapel [on 5 November] when Mari met them in the road and said, 'Do you know about these remarkable meetings in Moriah? Since Evan Roberts came back, they are extraordinary meetings.' Meanwhile Evan Roberts had met Thomas Shepherd, who played the organ for our oratorio practices, and had spoken earnestly to him, and he told us about the Moriah meeting. After practice we young people were minded to go down . . . It was about nine so we pushed into the gallery so as not to disturb the meeting. We felt there was something different about this meeting. Then Evan asked, 'Is there anyone here ready to confess Christ?' I was debating up in the gallery and I said to myself I could stand up to confess since I had been faithful to all the chapel meetings and was morally upright . . . I did stand up to confess Christ, and immediately I was under conviction, especially of smoking . . .

They decided to invite Evan Roberts to Bryn-teg Chapel on Wednesday evening, and he agreed to come. I had been working the afternoon shift on Wednesday from 2 p.m. to 10 p.m., and as I came home from work there was a crowd out on the road, and a great crowd going down from the top towards the Police Station . . . I asked them why all the people were out at this time on the roadside like this. They told me to run home as quickly as possible and have a bath and go back to Bryn-teg. There are remarkable happenings at Bryn-teg . . . I was back in Bryn-teg by 11 p.m . . .

When I arrived there one of my friends said, 'Come on in, Rhys, lad' . . . I was in the meeting until after midnight. No one had announced this meeting yet the crowds had packed the place. Many people who hadn't spoken to each other for years were reconciled. A policeman came up from Gorseinon to see what was happening and he was saved in the meeting. There were others who didn't understand what was going on, and had left their pints in the pubs and come up to see . . .

On Thursday the new chapel was full to overflowing . . . I came under conviction in the meeting and Evan Roberts came up to me and asked what was the matter. I said, 'I don't know', and he said, 'Come on your knees.' So we prayed . . . We went home at about four to half past. My father was at Evan Roberts's side in the meeting. At the end a reporter came up to Evan and asked, 'What can I put in the *Western*

Mail.' Instead of answering him, Evan prayed, 'O Lord, save the reporter'—and he was saved and went home. Yes, those were strange meetings: Penyrheol and Gorseinon were filled with the Spirit of God ... People had to run to the meetings, being made conscious of God. The roads were packed and everyone crowded into Bryn-teg every night for weeks.

On the Sunday afternoon, 13 November 1904, the chapel was over-flowing and the meeting going on with no preaching (Evan had gone) and people standing up to testify and confess Jesus Christ. Suddenly I saw—I was awake and conscious of everything—I felt Jesus coming to me and I was going to him (very much like John Bunyan), and as He came towards me—He was on the cross—He moved His hand and pushed me away. 'If God has deserted me,' [I thought,] 'only a lost state awaits me.' That thought was too terrible to bear and I stood up and said, 'Dear friends, God has departed from me; I have no hope; only total loss awaits me; pray for me.' It made no difference to me how many people heard me. Well, the only one I knew nearby who could pray for me was my brother John, but John was in the same condition. It was extraordinary. People said, 'Rhys, if you are lost, where are we others?', for conviction had gone through the congregation.[7]

2. Testimony of John Penry

This starts at the point where the group went to Moriah about nine o'clock on 5 November and went up into the gallery, finding that that Saturday night meeting was packed. They heard Evan Roberts speak from his open Bible on 'the white horse striding through the land, that is Jesus and his gospel is going to triumph in this land and we will see wonderful things happening'. Now John comes to the first turning-point:

> On Sunday night after the service and singing practice in Bryn-teg, we went down to Moriah at 9.30 and the place was overflowing. Evan Roberts was there. This meeting had started after the minister had closed the first meeting. After taking charge of the meeting, Evan Roberts went from seat to seat and asking everyone personally whether they were willing to stand up and confess Jesus Christ. He started at the pulpit on the right hand. I had a seat next to the door and he came to the seat and said, 'Will you stand up to confess?' 'Yes,' I said, and I stood on my feet. I said to myself, 'Why can't I? I am religious!' I stood up to confess; I was not ashamed—but not everyone stood. It was now about eleven o'clock and Evan went back to the big seat and said, 'We are

going to finish this meeting now for there are children here and some want to go home to their children. But I want those who can stay to stay, and after everyone who has to go has gone out, we'll close the doors. No one shall come in or go out.' The majority went out till there were about fifty young people left under forty years of age.

The doors were locked and he asked us to gather in the seats in front of the big seat and said, 'We are not going to leave this meeting tonight till the Holy Spirit is poured out. I want you each one to pray this short prayer, "O Lord, send the Holy Spirit now, for Jesus Christ's sake."' We began and went from each to each until all had prayed. 'The Holy Spirit has not come,' Evan Roberts said, 'so we must ask again.' We prayed again all the way round. 'Well,' he said, 'the Holy Spirit still has not come. We are not leaving this meeting tonight until the Holy Spirit has descended. We will start again.' And as we came to halfway down the second row of chairs a young woman broke out into tears, calling on the Lord. Then someone was praying elsewhere, and then another was sighing and weeping profusely. 'That's it,' said Evan Roberts, 'the Holy Spirit has come. We can now go home from the meeting happy and rejoicing.' Afterwards he went up to the sighing and weeping ones. Everyone had been dealt with by 2 or 3 a.m.

I am sorry to say I wasn't able to be in the Bryn-teg meetings the following week, on Tuesday and Wednesday evenings, because I was in work. But when I was in work I could see the chapel, and there was much excitement among the night-shift workers. They were going out every now and again to see if the lights were still on in Bryn-teg Chapel. We all of us went out in turns and there was a real stirring up of the tin-works because the ungodly were fearful and amazed to see lights in the chapel at three and four and five in the morning. It was 5.30 a.m. before the lights went out. My father was at that meeting until 5.30 a.m. My father, a man of great piety before the revival, stayed throughout all the meetings and never wanted to go home . . .

On Saturday night I went down to Moriah into a chapel which was full of people gathering in crowds and flocking in from everywhere. The first converts were there testifying to the work of grace in their hearts. Evan was walking up and down the aisles from seat to seat and talking with people. At last he came to me and said, 'How are you tonight?' 'Oh! rather hard so far.' 'There we are, that's all right,' said Evan.

On Sunday morning I went as usual to the 9.30 a.m. meeting at Bryn-teg, but this Sunday there was no preacher. Mr Stephens had been obliged to stop preaching because the people who had been saved and

31

sanctified during the week wanted to take the meeting themselves . . . [There was no Sunday school that afternoon, but rather another revival meeting. At that meeting] I had a vision of Jesus hanging on the cross. My head was in my hands and I was in tears for about an hour. My sister had been blessed that week and she said, 'John, come on your knees here. Pray.' I went on my knees and prayed, 'God be merciful to me a sinner.' Sin had come home! As God sees sin, not as we see it. I rose to my feet. That's all! That's all! The tears stopped and joy came in. That night before going to the meeting I went to the bottom of the garden to pray, asking God to be in the meeting that night. As soon as the meeting started, I went to the big seat to try to tell what God had done for me that afternoon, but other people were queuing up to speak from the big seat and there was no opportunity for me to speak, yet I did tell them what happened that afternoon. I said, 'Look here! I went through a wonderful experience this afternoon. I saw myself as a great sinner and, you know, Jesus Christ has forgiven my sin and I love Him with all my heart. My heart was like flint, now it is like a lake of water. The Lord has done great things.' You know, the glory of the Lord and the joy of the Lord came into my life to such a degree as to be indescribable, until I felt I was a new man in body, soul and spirit. The only verse that came to me at that time was, 'Put off thy shoes from off thy feet, for the place whereon thou standest is holy ground.'[8]

3. Testimony of Hannah Hughes

This is a homely story from one who was then just a teenage girl, yet who came under the blessing in that very first week. She gives much the same picture of the first nights as do the Penry brothers and some of Evan Roberts's letters, but this time it is a girl's way of looking at things, so we have a fresh insight:

Evan Roberts was in a preparatory school intending to enter the ministry, but he received this call . . . He had had a message to come to the young people of Moriah. He came of course. He answered the call. I was in that meeting, the usual prayer-meeting, but after that ended, Mr Jones said that Mr Evan Roberts wanted to speak with the young people. I thought that I was too young. I saw someone younger than I going out and he said, 'You are young enough to stay.' I thought, 'If she can stay I can stay.' We all went to the front, about sixteen of us. He asked us to confess Jesus Christ as our Saviour. The thing was entirely new to me. I did not understand it, but I accepted everything from him because I looked up to him as a boy out of the ordinary, and he meant everything he said . . . The meeting went on until 10.30 p.m. and there was much concern in our house because I had not arrived home. I went with the other girls to the house across the road to tell their mother where we had been and what had happened. My mother came over to ask if I was there, and Mrs John said, 'It gives me the shivers.'

The following day there was a meeting in Pisgah . . . We had a remarkable meeting there with a number taking part . . . That meeting continued until 10.30 p.m. My mother could not understand why these meetings continued so long, and what the young man had to say to us all the time. 'Well, come and see,' I said, 'but remember the meeting is for the young people.' 'Young people or not,' she said, 'I'll be there to-morrow night' . . .

Soon the big showers came of course, with people crying for forgiveness, making up old quarrels, paying their debts. It was a pleasure to hear the children singing hymns on their way to school. The pubs were emptied. The whole community was changed. You realized that God took a personal interest in you. I think it was the confession that you took Jesus Christ as your personal Saviour. That came to your mind all the time, that we had an interest in heaven.[9]

All these personal testimonies were about responses to Evan Roberts's fourfold call: to confess Christ publicly and openly; to give full obedience to the Holy Spirit in order to be filled with the Spirit; to confess known sins; and to put away all doubtful things. It was during those weeks that Evan taught the fast-growing congregations to say the prayer which he had first given to the young people, 'Send the Spirit now for Jesus' sake.' On 6 and 7 November, as he spoke of confession, the scene was astonishing—ministers and deacons, veteran members and youths, groaning and sighing and weeping. Then the people at Moriah Chapel were brought to their knees on 10 and 11 November by a command to remove the wrong habits and wrong relationships and bad feelings from their lives. D. M. Phillips records an amazing scene:

Some were on their knees for a long time, unable to utter a word, owing to their soul's distress and agony. Others did their best to help, and lead them out of their pitiful state. Some fell helplessly under the powerful, divine influence, and others cried groaningly . . . In the deacons' pew behold Evan Roberts with the perspiration streaming down his face, and praying in divine agony for God to glorify His Son, and save sinners. The ministers looked surprisingly at the scenes, and only one of them had the courage to utter a word in the great commotion.[10]

It is when we read these marvellous experiences of humble converts that we begin to understand why the news spread like wildfire so that the railway stations and lodgings became very crowded. Little wonder, too, that as soon as Evan Roberts was persuaded to visit other Loughor and Gorseinon chapels, the people flocked in from all the villages. In such informal meetings young people learned how to praise, testify, and go out joyfully into the villages for miles around. In some cases the converts had travelled from far away and simply took back the message and confirmed it with their own testimony. Two Ammanford students, W. A. Jenkins and D. G. Thomas, witnessed to their fellow students and spoke at Bethany Chapel, Ammanford, which also became eager for the blessing. A note of theirs to Evan Roberts speaks of joy, assurance and power.[11]

Once again we turn to Mr Webb's personal impressions of the vital weeks at Gorseinon when the converts prepared themselves for guidance:

> How remarkable that we would be at meetings all through the night, then return home about 5 a.m. so as to be at work by 6 a.m! Every dinner hour, directly on the one o'clock hooter, dozens would wend their way to the carpenter's shop to praise and thank God for his free gift of salvation through his matchless grace. It was as the psalmist wrote, 'As the hart panteth after the water brooks, so panteth my soul after thee.' To seek the living God and to know more about Jesus came before meals and sleep.[12]

Of course there was some criticism and resistance in the remaining days before Evan Roberts began his larger work. Jessie Davies, who once lived next door to the Roberts family, said that her father would not go along to revival meetings and that her own employer, like other businessmen, looked upon the exciting events as short-lived.[13] In a letter to a friend dated 11 November 1904 Evan Roberts spoke about prejudice against the movement but defended himself, 'I have to say strange things; I have to open my mouth and speak out . . . I am bound to speak the truth, be the cost what it may.'[14]

As the news of revival spread far and wide it became inevitable that someone from afar off would send a call to 'come over into Macedonia'. The precise circumstances of the invitation to Evan Roberts to hold meetings at Trecynon, Aberdare, on Sunday, 13 November 1904, which led to further remarkable meetings at Pontycymer, near Bridgend, later that week, and which marked the beginnings of the revival in the South Wales valleys, were so unusual that Evan Roberts and Sidney Evans and others recognized it as the guiding hand of the Spirit of God.[15] In the next chapter there will be many opportunities to see how the Holy Spirit went before Evan Roberts, and produced strange and wonderful effects on people's lives in each of the teeming industrial valleys of South Wales. However, before moving on, we note the account of a meeting at Loughor given by a *Llanelly Mercury* journalist. It is a sincere and undoctored account. The editor himself, Brinley Evans, was so much in tune with events that Evan Roberts gladly gave him an interview.

> He has the eyes of an enthusiast and the tenacity of purpose and strength of will of which martyrs are made. He also believes thoroughly in himself not as a preacher or an orator, but as a humble instrument guided and led by a higher Power . . . Disdaining the tricks of the pulpit beater, he speaks straight out to the heart in simple language. He tells the 'old, old story' as he would to a child, and instead of striking terror into the hearts of his audience, he wins them over by appealing to the conscience and all that is best in man. At later stages of his meetings, however, when the air is charged with electricity, Mr Roberts himself becomes powerfully moved, and walks up and down the aisles of the chapel in a state of ecstatic fervour.

During the interview the editor of the *Mercury* noted that:

> there were traces in his deathly white face of severe mental strain. The long vigils of the week had evidently told on him, and the more so as he had been able to sleep but little . . . He walked up and down the little room with a restlessness that told of a brain ever at work. At times he would break out into singing snatches of hymns.

When it was suggested that he might be taxing himself too much he replied:

> No, no; I am not. The Holy Ghost will sustain me. I was converted 13 years ago, and I have been praying for the Holy Ghost ever since, and now it has come. Oh! it is glorious. What I want is for the people to know the joy of religion . . . It should be the happiest thing in life. Our fathers—thank God for them—were saintly men, but they were gloomy and melancholy, as though their religion was a sore trial to the flesh. What they missed was the joy of the Lord. They got into a groove and we must now get out of it.

There follows the account of a meeting held at Bryn-teg Chapel, Loughor, on Thursday night and Friday morning, 10-11 November 1904:

Thursday's meeting did not conclude until 4.30 o'clock on Friday morning while the meeting on Saturday night lasted until 5.00 o'clock on Sunday . . . Everything here was left to the spontaneous impulse of the moment. The preacher . . . walked up and down the aisles—open Bible in hand—exhorting one, encouraging another, and kneeling with a third to implore a blessing from the throne of grace.

A young woman rose to give out a hymn which was sung with deep earnestness. While it was being sung, several people dropped down in their seats as if they had been struck, and commenced crying for pardon. Then from another part of the chapel could be heard the resonant voice of a young man reading a portion of a Scripture. While this was in progress, from the gallery came an impassioned prayer from a woman crying aloud that she had repented of her ways, and was determined to live a better life henceforward. All this time Mr. Roberts went in and out among the congregation offering kindly words of advice to kneeling penitents. He would ask them if they believed, the reply in one instance being, 'No, I would like to believe, but I can't. Pray for me.' Then the preacher would ask the audience to join him in the following prayer: 'Anfon yr Ysbryd yn awr, er mwyn Iesu Grist, Amen' ('Send the Holy Spirit now, for Jesus Christ's sake, Amen.')

This prayer would be repeated about a dozen times by all present, when the would-be convert would suddenly rise and declare in triumph, 'Thank God, I have now received salvation. Never again will I walk in the way of sinners.' This declaration would create a new excitement, and the congregation would joyously sing:–

> *Diolch iddo, diolch iddo*
> *Byth am gofio llwch y llawr.*

> [Thanks be to Him, thanks be to Him,
> For ever remembering the dust of earth.]

I suppose this occurred scores of times during the nine hours over which the meeting was protracted. A very pathetic feature of the proceedings was the anxiety of many present for the spiritual welfare of members of their families. One woman was heartbroken for her husband, who was given to drink. She implored the prayers of the congregation in his behalf. The story told by another young woman drew tears to all eyes. She said that her mother was dead, and that her father had given way to sin, so that she was indeed orphaned in the world. She had attended the meetings without feeling her position, but on the previous day, while .

following her domestic duties, the Spirit had come upon her bidding her to speak. And she did speak!—her address being remarkable for one who had never spoken before in public. Yet another woman made public confession that she had come to the meeting in a spirit of idle curiosity, but that the influence of the Holy Ghost worked within her, causing her to go down on her knees in penitence . . .

At 2.30 o'clock I took a rough note of what was then proceeding. In the gallery a woman was praying, and she fainted. Water was offered her, but she refused this, saying, that the only thing she wanted was God's forgiveness. A well-known resident then rose and said that salvation had come to him. Immediately following a thanksgiving hymn was sung, while an English prayer from a new convert broke in upon the singing. The whole congregation then fell upon their knees, prayers ascending from every part of the edifice, while Mr. Roberts gave way to tears at the sight. This state of fervency lasted for about ten minutes. It was followed by an even more impressive five minutes of silence, broken only by the sobs of strong men. A hymn was then started by a woman with a beautiful soprano voice. Finally, Mr. Roberts announced the holding of future meetings, and at 4.25 o'clock the gathering dispersed. But even at this hour the people did not make their way home. When I left to walk back to Llanelly I left dozens of them about the road still discussing what is now the chief subject in their lives. They had come prepared with lamps and lanterns, the lights of which in the early hours of the morning were weird and picturesque.[16]

It is rather wonderful that we have the personal testimony of one of the farmworkers who had hastened down to that Friday night meeting. Seated by his cottage fireside in Brynaman in the spring of 1961, John Lewis, then eighty years of age, told us of an experience which was engraved for ever on his heart. His first visit to a revival meeting occurred almost a week before the call to repentance, cleansing and confession changed his entire life. At first John would only ask other people to pray for him, but by Tuesday night he found himself praying with urgency, 'God be merciful to me a sinner.'

The meeting in Moriah on Friday night, 11 November, will never be forgotten by me. Evan [Roberts] called every one who was under conviction into the 'big seat' so that he could see them and go to help them. In that meeting I came out of the 'slough of despond'. I believed with all my heart . . . that Jesus and His Atonement was sufficient even for such as I. My heart was filled with joy and thanksgiving to God for His mercy and grace.

37

To me, this was the secret of the success of the revival: conviction, repentance and consecration.[17]

Such vivid reports and remarkable testimonies confirm the wider picture of revival events given by a Christian journalist, to which we turn in the next chapter. Together they help us to understand the main theme of this story, which can be summed up in one verse: 'Not by might, nor by power, but by my spirit, saith the Lord'.

2
The Voice of a
Christian Journalist

'My tongue is the pen of a ready writer'
(Psalm 45:1)

There was one official eyewitness of most of Evan Roberts's revival meetings in the old county of Glamorganshire who cannot be dismissed as a one-visit commentator like some of the more celebrated journalists. His pen-name was Awstin, the Welsh form of the name Augustine. He was a Baptist minister's son from Pontypridd who at one time owned the local newspaper but later became *Western Mail* representative there and in the Ammanford district. In later life he was an *eisteddfod* enthusiast and a mining correspondent, but at this stage of his career he was deeply influenced by his meetings with Evan Roberts, who confided in him more than in any other journalist.[1]

Like W. S. Jones of the *Rhos Herald* in Clwyd, Awstin stayed simple and sincere as he set down what he witnessed. Somehow he is so attuned to the mighty workings of the Holy Spirit in those five months of revival that we can trust him to discern that which is of lasting worth. The selected extracts thus show how the Holy Spirit fulfilled exactly what the Lord Jesus Christ had promised in the solemn hush of the Upper Room; inspiring praise, teaching truth, glorifying the Saviour and Lord, reaching into the heart of society with convicting power (John 15–16). Sidney Evans summarized some of the visible effects in that excellent memorial volume *Cyfrol Goffa Diwygiad 1904–1905*. The results, he said, were freedom through obedience to the Spirit; specific answers to prayers; family reconciliations; healings from sickness of spirit; confession of faults and sins, and cries for forgiveness; testimonies; inspired, joyous praises; then a strong desire to save souls.[2]

When he comes, he will convict, says the Word of God of the Holy Spirit. Evan Roberts convinced his listeners that cleansing by the Spirit was essential because 'nothing dirty and foul can ever enter heaven'.

The Spirit of conviction came down at Loughor on 6 and 7 November 1904, as he spoke about confessing all sin; there was similar heart-broken weeping and lamenting at Aberdare.[3] Many observers noticed the sudden change of mood at a Temperance Association meeting in Pontycymer: sighings, prayers, ecstasies; some shouting; others in anguish, weeping tears of repentance.[4] Awstin came over to the Wednesday evening meeting at Pontycymer and noticed the signs of deep conviction. Even more stirring was the Thursday evening service. Accounts of both meetings appeared in the first *Western Mail* Revival Supplement:

Wednesday, 16 November.

Without any invitation, a young woman came forward to the 'set fawr' [the big seat, i.e. the deacons' seat], and, going on her knees, made a piteous appeal for forgiveness. The impression produced was intense, and her voice was drowned in a sudden chorus of 'Amens'.

Then an elderly woman stood up in her pew. She also prayed, and was remarkably eloquent. Strong, rough-looking men, who had hitherto betrayed no signs of emotion, now took up their handkerchiefs, and wept bitterly. One of these shrieked 'Amen' again and again in a shrill voice, which was weird and piercing . . .

One man rose from his seat and made gesticulations, but could not make himself heard. His voice was choked with weeping, and he had to sit down without having spoken a single word. Then every man and woman joined simultaneously, some praying, others singing, and others, again, endeavouring to speak. All this while Evan Roberts sat in the 'set fawr', clapping his hands and exhorting the people to go on.

The following night.

Mr Roberts then resumed the conduct of the meeting, smilingly inviting all to receive the great and eternal fortune offered them. From all parts of the building cries could be heard from penitents. With tears coursing down their cheeks, they declared their acceptance of the offer. Prayers were invited, and a middle-aged man under the gallery immediately responded. There was no half-heartedness about the prayer. The man's eyes were closed, his fists clenched, higher and higher rose the voice, supplicating, entreating, bursting now into agony, now into overwhelming grief . . . A middle-aged woman sitting in the aisle declared, 'I have fallen as low as it is possible for anyone to fall, and He has received me. Come unto Him all of you.' A chorus of 'Amens' followed, and the majority of the congregation burst into tears. A large number now announced their conversion, some shouting, 'O Arglwydd, cymer fi!' ('O God, take me!'). At eleven o'clock the meeting had not lost any of its fervour.[5]

What Awstin saw as a tumult of praise, many others saw as chaos. The total lack of form never ceased to fascinate and worry observers from the churches and the press, but Awstin accepted it as quite natural. On one occasion in the Rhondda Valley about a hundred men, mainly rough and rugged miners, sat behind the team. Following the stirring rendering of a hymn, three of these stood at the same time, two praying in Welsh and one in English, each 'so wrapped up in the intensity of his own feelings that he seemed oblivious of the utterances of the other'. Now the meeting went along strange ways:

> Men clapped their hands and gesticulated with joy. A collier, . . . who carried his arm in a sling, sprang to his feet. He was pale with excitement, and, roughly attired as he was, with a muffler round his neck, he presented a strange figure, indeed. He prayed fervently, and another man who sat near him was so moved that he, too, rose to his feet. In a voice quivering with emotion he cried aloud, 'Ring the bells of Heaven and frighten the devil to fly away from these valleys.' 'Amen' and 'Diolch iddo' ['Thanks be to Him'] made the building vibrate. A dozen men jumped to their feet simultaneously. There was a perfect Babel of Welsh and English prayer . . . Some of the ministers present essayed to speak, but their efforts were swept away by the torrent of song and prayer.[6]

A pre-Christmas revival service in the Rhondda is worthy of mention. It was a mass meeting at Gosen Chapel in Clydach Vale, a typical mining village. So many wonderful things happened there that one can only afford a bare summary of the proceedings. A man prays for swift-spreading revival; a working man tries to persuade his hostile friends; a professional soldier announces that he has now become a recruiting sergeant for the army of Jesus; a woman crushed by her sins has to be dealt with by the missioner. The evening meeting was held at Libanus Chapel where the fervour of the afternoon was once more evident. A number of testimonies were given even before Evan Roberts appeared. We take up Awstin's story at about eight in the evening:

> When Mr. Roberts had somewhat recovered his composure he went on to refer to the lonely Saviour in the garden.

'The disciples were sleeping,' he said, 'and they are sleeping now—hundreds and thousands of them'—a point which elicited an immense volume of 'Amen,' and while this pathetic picture was being drawn, Mrs. Howell, Clydach Vale, sang, 'O na bawn i fel Efe' ['O that I might be like Him'], and no sooner had the last note died away than Miss Lewis, quite a little girl, struck up another sweetly pathetic hymn which deeply stirred the congregation, [which] . . . burst forth into the strains of 'Dyma gariad fel y moroedd' ['Here is love, vast as the ocean']. Then, while the tide of music and fervour was in full flood, a young woman stood up in the midst of the congregation and prayed in English, and when the music ceased there was heard the voice of a little boy (who has only just started work underground) praying (with his head leaning on his arms on the front of the gallery) for 'showers of blessings' and the 'descent of the Pentecostal fire upon the meeting.' An Englishman standing in the aisle promptly followed with a fervent petition to God to spread the revival throughout the land . . . and another Englishman prayed God 'to melt or smash hard hearts in that meeting.' 'Come to Jesus, come to Jesus, now,' sang Mr. Tom James the Clydach Vale miners' agent, and the people joined in subsequent lines and verses in Welsh and English.

> 'Mae E'n maddeu, Mae E'n maddeu, 'Rawr hon'
> ['He forgives, He forgives, now'],

sang one; 'Mae E'n eiriol' ['He is pleading'], struck up another; 'I believe it now,' cried another. 'Mae E'n derbyn, 'rawr hon' ['He receives now'], said another; and so the singing went on, while one of the converts . . . shouted at the top of his voice, now exhorting, now warning, and then praying, 'Llanw'r lle yma a Dy gariad' ['Fill this place with Your love'].[7]

Awstin was not the only observer who witnessed the working of the Spirit in the midst of giant mass meetings, but he had a keen eye for the signs of true repentance as well as the moments of ardent praise. Some weeks later, when Evan Roberts was in the little townships around Swansea, the journalist was present at a fervent prayer meeting in Siloam Chapel, Pentre Estyll, just north of Swansea. There the pastor, Penar Griffiths, was aflame himself:

An impressive scene was witnessed when the Rev. Penar Griffiths engaged in fervent prayer, the whole congregation meanwhile standing with their heads bowed low. A noticeable feature was the amount of Scripture which was read. A man in the gallery read Acts iv . . . Another man read a chapter from St. Luke, whilst another engaged in prayer, which was a simple, but very impressive, recitation of Psalm liii. Quite a refined tone was given to the meeting by a young lady in the gallery, who offered eloquent prayer, her petitions including one that the Church should awake to her responsibilities.

The afternoon meeting was no less remarkable than the morning meeting, and in many respects was almost identical to it . . . The evangelist was not quite satisfied with matters at first and he adjured the people not to play with holy things. 'Don't rise to show yourselves, or God may strike you down,' was his warning. Touching upon emotionalism, Mr. Roberts observed, 'If there is to be no feeling this side, I am afraid you will have to feel in the next world.' While making some further remarks he completely broke down. The Rev. Penar Griffiths then essayed to pray, but he, too, broke down, when an old lady in the gallery prayed.

So impressive was the meeting that Mr. Roberts made the remark, 'This is a terrible place. I have never felt the terrible so much as to-night before.'[8]

Both Awstin and D. M. Phillips were present at Tonna, Neath, on 12 January 1905 when a number of visitors asked for prayer for revival in their lands. Before Evan Roberts had come on the scene with Annie Davies and Mary Davies as his helpers, the large congregation had been praying and singing. What Phillips called the 'Great Hymn of the Revival'—*Dyma gariad fel y moroedd'* ['Here is love, vast as the ocean']—had been sung with magnificent effect, and an aged minister had read the account of the vision of Isaiah with great spiritual energy. The Awstin report continues:

Mr. Roberts could not speak much, but when he was given an opportunity he spoke of the necessity of prayer, and then the people sang softly, tenderly, 'Gad im' deimlo, awel o Galfaria fryn' ('Oh for the soft breezes from Calvary'), and this led the missioner to remark that they should sing these words prayerfully and tenderly. For it was a prayer, and they should not sing it too strongly, for a breeze from Calvary was all that frail humanity could stand; they could never stand a hurricane from Calvary.

The service was by this time most impressive, remarkably so, for pretty well the whole congregation were praying. It was in very truth a season of wrestling in prayer. There was a Babel of voices—a beautifully harmonious Babel, though—breaking forth simultaneously in prayer and song. Often, indeed, the prayer would imperceptibly glide into the singing of a stanza or two of Miss Crosby's hymn, 'Pass me not, O gentle Saviour.' But such singing—singing in which there was a soul full of prayer. Several of those who sang did so in the attitude of prayer. The burdens of the prayers were responded to on the part of the congregation in song. 'Bend us' was the burden of many a prayer, and then the people sang:–

'Bend us, Lord:
Jesus only would I see.'[9]

Later in January, only four days before he was so bitterly attacked by a minister from Dowlais, Evan Roberts had been there for three days of meetings, which reached their climax in a revival service at Hebron Baptist Chapel on the evening of 24 January. There was special warmth at Hebron, whose minister was in full sympathy. Every traditional and much-loved revival hymn was sung over and over and then came the dozens of prayers for the salvation of named people. Eventually the meeting reached fever pitch:

Prayers were . . . offered for the spreading of the 'flame' throughout the world, and while this was at its height the majority of those present sang softly in English and Welsh alternately, 'For you I am praying.' Then, when the 'test' for converts was made, and people rose to signify their surrender, the singing of 'Diolch iddo' ['Thanks be to Him'] became literally triumphant, and when the enthusiasm grew, the singers, hundreds of them, actually clapped their hands with joy, keeping time with the music by the hand-clapping. Handkerchiefs were waved, and the scene formed another feature of this truly wonderful meeting . . .

The enthusiastic pastor publicly thanked God for the meeting and for raising Evan Roberts to arouse the young men of Wales to lead the way in the salvation of the world. The hymn, 'Marchog Iesu yn llwyddianus,' was sung and when this crowning gathering of the Dowlais series was dispersing the people sang in the open air, and sang in the streets, and sang in the trains that victorious Welsh march, 'Marchog Iesu,' translated . . . :

'Blessed Jesus, march victorious,
With Thy sword fixed at Thy side;
Neither earth nor hell can hinder
The God-Warrior in His ride'.[10]

Our last examples come from the February week in which Evan Roberts was at ease for the last time in the South Wales revival meetings.

44

He had been invited to the three little valleys to the north of Bridgend—the Llynfi, the Garw and the Ogmore—and the Spirit came down upon them. With days of trouble and tension about to dawn and signs of lessened interest even in Awstin's reports of services, it is good to read of how the blessing came to two centres.

1. *Nant-y-moel*

The night meeting in Saron Chapel (where the revival fire has for weeks been burning brightly) was from the outset unique in its spiritual temperature. The crush was in itself an indication of the intense expectation prevailing, for, notwithstanding the 'strangeness' of the previous night's meeting, this was a Pentecostal gathering. The prayers and hymn-singing . . . culminated in high tension from the time of the opening of the night service. Very tenderly Mr. Evan Roberts soon after entering the building asked those who had not received Christ to abstain from singing, for they could not possibly sing from their hearts—an appeal which silenced some, but which elicited a literally tremendous outburst of hymn-singing and simultaneous prayers.

Mr. Roberts remarked that the service was a powerful illustration of the fulfilment of the promises of God. The promise of the previous night—that He would give His presence at this meeting—was amply fulfilled already. Another outburst of prayer and song followed, the repeat of several of the hymns being extraordinary in frequency and fervour . . .

Miss Annie Davies (Maesteg) delivered a telling and pithy English address, and concluded it with the recital of the Welsh hymn, 'O gariad, O gariad, anfeidrol ei faint' ('O wonderful love, how immense is its scope!') and 'What will you do with Jesus?' was sung, and, with not a chance for a pause, testimonies and prayers were launched forth as if the 'Love like mighty torrents' which had been sung of earlier in the proceedings had filled all hearts to overflowing. So mighty was the flow that there were frequently prayers, praise, and testimony given at the same time, astonishing some visitors, who cried, 'Hush!'

Awstin noted the many responses to the revivalist's appeals to Christians to show more concern in praying for those sitting near them. Troubled by the indifference of the unconverted, Evan Roberts was heard saying passionately, 'The devil laughs with glee at the very thought of Welshmen refusing to accept Christ in a land so greatly blessed by the Gospel as Wales!'[11]

2. *Maesteg*

Mr. Evan Roberts, Miss Annie Davies, and Miss Mary Davies arrived [at Bethania Chapel] before seven o'clock, but the evangelist did not rise to speak for some time. A wonderful scene was witnessed when 'Dyma gariad fel y moroedd' ('Here's a Love like mighty torrents') was struck up by the congregation. The people rose and sang with extraordinary spirit and power the great lovesong of the revival, repeating three times in every rendering the line, 'Dyma gariad na'd a'n anghof' ('Love that will not be forgotten'). Then when the singing ceased Miss Annie Davies . . . delivered a brief address, urging all there that night to accept salvation, and the pertinent speech, delivered with the simplicity which marks the sayings of this young lady, so aroused the congregation that a scene which beggars description followed. Scores were speaking, shouting, gesticulating, praying, and testifying, and then all the voices were merged in a triumphant rendering of 'Ar Ei ben bo'r goron' ('Crown the Lord, my Saviour'). A new verse, interpolated by the pastor of Bethania—

> 'Rho dy galon iddo,
> Byth am gofio llwch y llawr'

> ('Give him thy heart, thy self,
> He hath loved man who is but dust')—

was sung with fervour.[12]

During his extensive travels with the revivalist, Awstin's discerning eye noted a few factors which seemed to work against the atmosphere of vitality and freedom and enthusiasm of many revival meetings. One of these was overcrowding; the second was the attempt to control meetings by catechizing the people; the third was the permitted activities of 'Christian workers' while the meetings were in progress. All these can be illustrated from his eyewitness reports at this point.

a) Intolerable Overcrowding

Caerphilly: Monday, 5 December 1904

To see the Market-square of Caerphilly thronged, while two or three chapels were crowded to overflowing, under such circumstances, was a sight in itself worth seeing, for it indicates the hold which the religious revival has taken of the people in the town . . . Farmers on horseback, tradesmen in traps, hundreds by motor-cars, hundreds more by train, colliers and other workmen trudging on foot: there was a variety presented . . . Nowhere else have I seen anything like the rush of people in the street just to catch a glimpse of Mr. Evan Roberts when he merely passed from the chapel to the chapel-keeper's house at the close of the afternoon service.

The afternoon service was held in the Calvinistic Methodist Chapel, and the congregation was so closely packed that the people actually trod on the gaspipes, jambing them to such an extent as to make it impossible to get light to hold the evening meeting there.[13]

Merthyr Vale in the Taff Valley: Wednesday, 14 December 1904

Accompanied by his host, Mr. Edwin Morgan, and by Miss Annie Davies he [Evan Roberts] walked across through the dark and muddy streets to Merthyr Vale. A surging, singing crowd followed him all the way, and outside Calfaria he found another huge throng besieging the doors . . . The people were wedged together in one solid phalanx. But somehow the revivalist and his party made their way through, and set foot inside Calfaria in a state of exhaustion.

The heated atmosphere was overpowering. Women were fainting here and there, but could not be carried out. The aisles were packed, and the people crowded on the window-ledges. Evan Roberts appealed for the windows to be opened, but back came the response that all the windows except one at the rear of the building, could not be opened.

'It is unhealthy here,' he said, 'and some of us will feel the effects again.'

There being no possibility of more air, Mr. Roberts pleaded earnestly for silence. Those who were jammed in at the doors and vestibule made spasmodic efforts to keep quiet, but those who were outside clamoured to get in, and the noise was incessant. Worse than all some fervent spirits grouped themselves together and sang hymns. Their singing could be heard only too distinctly inside the chapel, and people wriggled with uneasiness.

Stentorian shouts for order were of no avail, and the revivalist, after exhausting all his persuasive powers to get the people to leave and to go to other chapels where there was more room, threw up his arms and said he would have to leave. The scene bordered on panic . . .

[Then] for some minutes there was a semblance of silence, and Evan Roberts, seizing the opportunity, said that they had evidently been attracted there by the man, and not by the Spirit. There was a time, and not so long ago, when the difficulty was to get people to come to chapel, but now they could not get them to leave . . . Passing on to another subject in his peculiar, disjointed style, he said that formality had been chilling and destroying the spiritual life of the Churches for many years . . .

Another outbreak of noise now disturbed the service, and Evan Roberts, throwing up his hands in despair, sank back into his chair. Miss Annie Davies promptly came to the rescue with 'Lead, kindly Light,' which she sang with delightful tenderness . . .

One feature of the gathering was the presence of so many women with tiny babies in their arms. Long before the service closed many of these mothers struggled to get out, and the wonder is that the little ones were not seriously crushed.[14]

At Maesteg, Bridgend, Pontypridd, and Anfield Road, Liverpool, it became necessary for the police to control the crowds, and the din was tremendous. If one adds the constant interruptions to the speakers caused by excited men and women wanting to pray, testify, sing, ask questions, recite verses, etc., then one has to concede that not only was formal preaching an impossibility but sometimes the work of the Holy Spirit could be greatly hindered. Evan Roberts was heard saying, 'There can be no blessing in this meeting until some of you are willing to go elsewhere.'

b) Catechizing

There were two ways to restore order, but both of these would raise doubts about interfering with the direct control of the Holy Spirit. One way was to appoint gospel singers, who would be listened to at once. This practice is considered in another chapter. Another way took several forms. Evan Roberts would catechize the congregation and demand a repeated group response to questions. In the original meetings, he had adopted the course of putting four points to the congregation. Towards the end of his messages he would ask everyone to confess every known sin, remove all doubtful things in their lives, give themselves in full obedience to the Holy Spirit, and confess Christ publicly.[15] Later he began to use appeal questions to bring people to a decision, and challenge questions to call Christians to obedience. A major change was noticed during one of the missions. At the close of the meeting a new catechism was used which included the following tests:

(1) 'All church members to stand.'
(2) 'All who love Jesus to stand.'
(3) 'All who love Christ more than anything else stand.'
(4) 'All who wish to love Him more than anything else stand.'[16]

Awstin was acute enough to see one of the purposes of this method:

> The audience realise that they have not come to an entertainment, but to 'show their side'.[17]

This was of great value when dealing with non-members. It made Christians far more thoughtful and quiet.

In the New Year services in and around Swansea, Evan Roberts adapted this same method in order to test churches as to whether there was malice or curiosity or hypocrisy or impurity in them. Reactions to this ranged from angry rebuke to honest discomfort, as the following incident at Llansamlet shows. There he told the congregation that there were three spirits in that meeting—the Spirit of God, the spirit of man, and the evil spirit—and asked them quite suddenly whether they had done their best for Jesus. If they had, they were to stand. The crowd stayed seated and so did the ministers and deacons. Then Penar Griffiths had to protest. Though he had done his best, not everything he had done was as pure as it might have been.[18] Accounts of West Wales meetings represent these questions as more like accusations, which were bitterly resented. Even some revival children began to murmur that this would quench the Spirit.

c) Volunteer Counsellors

In the hurly-burly of such crowds, Evan Roberts and the others had to give up their earlier habit of coming down among the people to speak to distressed sinners or to debate with disobedient Christians. For some months he experimented with using the kind of network of Christian counsellors that Seth Joshua and R. A. Torrey had also used. Evan Roberts's instructions to these were:

> Put one hand on their shoulder, and the other hand in their hand. Ask them to pray God to forgive their sins for Jesus Christ's sake. Then ask them, do they believe in God; and if they will say they do, ask them to thank God for that.[19]

Soon it became quite normal to see chosen workers going across the seats behind the singing congregation and planting themselves alongside a weeping person. At a later stage in the revival they were also sent to sit alongside anyone who refused to stand up when the meeting was being tested. One report says that when some drunkards stayed behind, the workers went to them and took their names. These were read out to the congregation which was waiting anxiously. But this is the very thing men like the experienced Awstin saw and worried about.

In December 1904 the Congregational newspaper, *Y Tyst* ('The Witness'), said that the revival was 'more a matter of spirit than of plan . . . but that there is a plan which is followed in the majority of meetings'. It then went on to print a report of meetings at Pentre Esyllt, Swansea, which 'illustrate that plan better than anything seen to date', but added one thing to the report, 'something which is an essential part of the plan':

> When the meetings reach a certain point, a number of brothers and sisters undertake to go through the congregation seeking those who are inclined to come to the SAVIOUR. They go from seat to seat, and when they succeed in getting someone to make a public confession of Christ, the news is received by –
>
> *'Diolch iddo, diolch iddo*
> *Byth am gofio llwch y llawr'*
>
> [Thanks be to Him, thanks be to Him,
> For ever remembering the dust of earth]
>
> being sung with great passion. Many a hard battle is fought by these brave messengers, and 'gathering the harvest' depends very much on their skill and faithfulness.[20]

There was obviously a great danger here, for out of dependence on human zeal comes the temptation to press hard for an on-the-spot decision and to shout the name too soon. The wise minister Keri Evans was to warn later that conviction is not conversion, neither does awakening mean conviction:

> The Holy Spirit must pass through the imagination and the emotion to the conscience to produce conviction, and through the conscience to the will to lead to conversion.[21]

Towards the end of the revival, Evan Roberts was not using a chosen few but asking and commanding all members to obey the Spirit by turning round to 'throw the lifeline' to any nearby person who was in deep distress. The bands of Christian workers were a practical answer to the problem of overfull rooms with crowded aisles and no place for counselling. But they may have seemed to some a hindrance to the Spirit's work, just as the overcrowding, the tumult and the interruptions would become a hindrance to the real 'liberty of the Spirit'. It was another and very different journalist, W. T. Stead, who realized that despite these fleshly obstacles the Spirit of God was still exerting a mighty power which moulded thousands of people into a wonderful fellowship of praise and testimony: 'You can watch what they call the influence of the power of the Spirit playing over the crowded congregation as an eddying wind plays over the surface of a pond.'[22]

It says a great deal for Awstin's insight and passion for truth that this feeling of the overwhelming presence and direction of the Holy Spirit comes through clearly in his many reports. He seems also to have been very interested in the kinds of psalms, hymns and spiritual songs in which revivalists and converts delighted. He perceived the vital role of solo singers in many of the meetings, as well as the impact of the congregational singing. It is important to use direct testimony in order to fill out his impressions of how the singers contributed to the awakening. This was true mainly, but not exclusively, in the South Wales valleys.

3
The Singers of the Dawn

'My heart greatly rejoiceth; and with my song
will I praise him'
(Psalm 28:7)

Although Evan Roberts had encouraged members of the West Wales team to witness in song, he had no set plan to use singers. It was during one of the Gorseinon meetings that five young ladies came forward to offer their talents to the Lord.[1] The *Llanelly Mercury* described Priscilla Watkins as a minister's sister-in-law, Sunday school teacher, choir member and chapel organist. She was a local schoolteacher, and her decision to go on a mission caused a minor tremor.

At the meeting of the managers of the Gowerton group of schools on Wednesday it was reported that one of the teachers at Penyrheol Schools [*sic*], Gorseinon, had departed with the revivalists without tendering notice. The Chairman (Mr Rees Harries), Rev. John Stephens, and Mr Thomas Davies, Pontardulais, expressed the opinion that the action of the teacher in question (Miss S. P. Watkins) was excusable, that no legal steps be taken against her, and that she be paid her salary in full up to the time of leaving. A motion to this effect was unanimously carried.[2]

Lavinia Looker was a 21-year-old dressmaker and Sunday school teacher. She was a choir member but 'until lately had been too retiring to sing a solo in the chapel'. Mary Davies was from the Post Office in Lower Gorseinon, the daughter of a prominent Anglican, a Sunday school teacher and a Board teacher for a while. Not very strong, she soon returned from the tour and is said to have devoted much time to religious painting, living at home very quietly until God called her out to minister to a second, smaller revival in the late 1920s. Also heavily involved were another Mary Davies who was a mason's daughter, and Annie May Rees, the daughter of a phrenologist, 'Professor' Rees, trained in elocution and poetry readings as well as in singing.

Although these girls always lodged in homes in the valleys and were under the eye of local church leaders and their wives, there was still some ill-natured gossip about them. Even to go on a gospel trek would raise many an eyebrow in an age when people were such sticklers for social conventions. It is no surprise that one father went over to the Rhondda to persuade his daughter to come home. She responded very dutifully, 'Are you demanding and compelling me to come home? If not, I am going to proclaim the gospel.' She was allowed to remain and with her beautiful voice and earnest manner was often engaged in reciting hymns or narrating some Bible story.

The most colourful of these young ladies was Annie May Rees. A gifted speaker before the revival, in the new-style meetings Annie was in her element. She accompanied Evan Roberts and the other four to Trecynon, Aberdare, and worked with them in the Rhondda meetings, but then became a missioner in her own right. More will be said about this remarkable young lady when we describe the revival missions in Cardiff.

After Christmas some of the group turned back to local meetings, while Mary Davies went further afield. The team was quite flexible and could take on other volunteers from time to time. Awstin saw two of them arriving with Sidney Evans in the middle of an Evan Roberts address on the theme of obeying the Spirit—'You must do anything and everything, anywhere and everywhere':

> There was a stir in the aisle, and three young people marched up towards the 'big pew.' Down from the pulpit came the evangelist, and, extending his hand to welcome the newcomers, he said, 'This is Sidney Evans and two other workers,' and within a few minutes the newcomers were at work.
>
> Mr. Sidney Evans ascended the pulpit, and with the familiarity of a brother Mr. Roberts turned to him and said, 'A oes genyt ti air i'w ddweyd wrth y bobl?' ('Hast thou a word to say to the people?') . . . In a few pithy sentences he [Mr Evans] dwelt upon the fulness with which God could endow people who came ready to receive.[3]

In addition to these five, who formed the main team in the early days of the revival, many meetings were assisted by other singers. At various points in the Rhondda meetings one hears of a young lady from Treherbert who led such choruses as 'I do believe' and 'Count your blessings'; a Miss Hopkins who came over from Loughor; and a Miss

May John of Tonpentre. Madame Kate Morgan Llewellyn had the gift of improvising new tunes. Lastly there was the 'little girl'—Miss S. A. Jones of Nant-y-moel—who described herself as 'formerly a frivolous and worldly girl' but who grew in spiritual stature as the Spirit made her preach boldly.[4]

All these were overshadowed by the young woman who became celebrated as the 'nightingale' of the revival. Annie Davies and her sister Maggie came from a very musical family in the Maesteg area and each sister was loved and honoured for her gifts. Maggie Davies took part in the Swansea meetings where she first stirred up both solemn and joyous feelings. Annie Davies had been trained professionally by Madame Clara Novello Davies and Harry Evans of Dowlais and used such techniques as whispered singing ('Flee as a Bird'), dramatic renderings ('The Dear Little Bible'), and sad, appealing songs which ended in floods of tears. A correspondent said that her songs fitted into the prayers and praises of the congregations 'as if she were playing a touching accompaniment'.[5] Perhaps he had not noticed that she had been down from the platform to mingle with those people and to sit alongside troubled souls, and could thus put their longings into song. Evan Roberts would smile gently as she punctuated his exhortations with quiet background singing. He also accepted those stressful moments when Annie's powerful emotions overcame her. At one Rhondda meeting, for example, she broke into song while Evan Roberts was speaking:

> When she had concluded Mr. Roberts proceeded, but had not gone far before she again, evidently under very deep emotion, began singing,
>
> 'Dim ond Iesu'
>
> ('Jesus only'), when she utterly broke down, and, sobbing aloud, exclaimed, 'O! Iesu, Iesu, drosof fi' ('O! Jesus, Jesus, for me!') She wept bitterly, and caused hundreds to sob, raising her voice in loud lamentation. The tension became painful, overcoming the revivalist himself.[6]

Not only would she break across Evan Roberts, but other team members also. While Mary Davies was speaking, for example, or Annie Rees testifying, she would break in, sing her favourite lines and then break down, and the crowd with her. One might be forgiven for thinking that Annie was stealing the show at times.

The team were together at meetings in Pontypridd at the beginning of March 1905,[7] but there were rumours of strained relationships after this. The singers eventually attached themselves to different revival speakers, Annie Davies and Mary Roberts (Evan's sister) accompanying Evan Roberts to Liverpool and North Wales.

What caused Annie Davies, her sister Maggie, and her friend S.A. Jones, to enter into revival missions? The answer lies in a letter Annie wrote to D. M. Phillips in January 1906:

DEAR DR. PHILLIPS,

I shall now endeavour, in the best way I can, to tell you how I started with the work.

Hearing and having read that Mr. Evan Roberts was at Pontycymmer holding a Mission, I decided to go there and see what the meetings were like. That was November 17th.

When preparing to go to catch the train, the tune called 'Britain's Lament' came to my mind; also the words of the hymn 'Here is love vast as the ocean' flashed across my mind, and I could not resist singing it in the house. I reached Pontycymmer a little after 7 o'clock. I got to the entrance of the chapel where Mr. Roberts conducted a meeting, and I found great difficulty in getting in, as the place was crowded. However, two hours passed before I could get in, and when I did the first I saw was my sister Maggie, and her face showing that her soul was in great agony. It was evident that the Spirit of God was working within her.

I did not enter the meeting in the right spirit, the consequence being that I felt very indifferent and full of curiosity. I continued so until nearly the end of the meeting, when, just before closing, Mr. Roberts asked all those who could stand up and say in their own hearts that they loved Jesus above everything else to do so. My sister and I sat together, and our first impulse was to get up and show that we were of those who could stand up and say so, but we were checked from doing. An irresistible power kept us to our seats. Soon after the meeting closed, but I felt very unhappy; conscience spoke very loudly to me. It told me that I had betrayed my Saviour. I had been a member for years before, but had not done anything for the glory of God. I felt God could never forgive my countless sins. I tried to sleep and forget all about the meeting, but found it quite impossible to do so. I knew things would have to get different from what they were then, as everything seemed quite empty to me. I felt I had to find peace or die.

I was counting every hour before the time arrived for the second meeting. At last the time came. When entering the chapel I knew there was a great power working there. My soul was moved to its depths. My tears flowed freely when the Rev. David Hughes asked me and said, *'Cana rywbeth,* Annie' ('Sing something, Annie'). With an irresistible force I leapt from my seat, and sang 'Here is love vast as the ocean' to the tune 'Britain's Lament'. I could not finish it, as I was sobbing too much. I could not refrain from weeping throughout the meeting.

After coming out, Miss S. A. Jones, Nantymoel, met us. We had never met before, but she felt compelled to speak to us, and in a short time she told my sister and me how she felt. It happened that she felt very similar to what we did. We three felt drawn to each other immediately. We felt a great desire to consecrate our voices to the Master. We met Mr. Roberts and told him of our desire. He told us to pray about it, and ask to be led in the right path. We went again to the afternoon meeting. I felt a wonderful peace filling my soul, and could not refrain from taking part. I felt convinced that God had called me to the work.

I remain,

Yours, in the service,

ANNIE DAVIES[8]

This corrects certain stories which represent Evan Roberts as prompted by the Spirit to discover their gifts. Annie was certain that they had made the first approach. Fifty years later, sitting in her Bridgend cottage, she told the 'man from the BBC', Aneirin Talfan Davies, about the letter from her sister which persuaded her to queue up for that meeting in Bethel Chapel, Pontycymer, and about the moment at that meeting when she first sang 'Here is love, vast as the ocean'. This is her simple story of an important call:

After the meeting Evan Roberts spoke to me saying, 'You must come with me.' I went with him, and I was with him all the time that he was journeying to and fro.[9]

Very few men felt the call to leave their secular employment to travel through Wales singing in the chapels, but there were a few. Tom Roberts of Towyn was singing in the valleys of South Wales during the Christmas season, whereas Emlyn Davies of Cefn, near Ruabon in North Wales, was heard mostly in the predominantly Welsh-speaking regions. He had started studying at the Royal College of Music in London with a view to becoming an opera singer, but after he had sung during the special services conducted by R. B. Jones, he felt constrained to devote himself to God's work. He told friends that it was not until January 1905 that he had really obeyed the Spirit by consecrating all his gifts to revival missions instead of the concert circuit. He was still using a semi-classical repertoire at a conference at Calfaria Chapel, Hendy, near Pont-arddulais, where Mrs J. M. Saunders and Evan Lloyd Jones were proclaiming Christ,[10] but he sang gospel songs in subsequent meetings held in the Ceiriog and Dee valleys. R. B. Jones had a four-day mission at Corwen in Clwyd, where 'Mr Emlyn Davies sang several verses with much effect, and he also gave a personal testimony . . . the meetings were characterised by great fervour.'[11] His brother Arthur was a willing helper at campaigns during and after the revival, and he often sang for John McNeill, the Scottish evangelist. In later years, when he became minister of Gilgal Chapel, Porth-cawl, he would still break into a gospel solo or testimony in the middle of his Sunday sermons, often with remarkable effect.

One of the most interesting local singers was Richard Looker who worked as a collier in both the Loughor area and the Rhondda Valley. He had a strong reason to respect Evan Roberts who had helped rescue him down the mine, but he testified that it was in a Rhondda meeting that he was made to realize that he owed even more to the Lord Jesus Christ:

> After the prayer-meeting we went out into the main service. He preached, and the verse that went like an arrow to me was, 'Believe on the Lord Jesus Christ, and thou shalt be saved' . . . I was never the same man again. I went back to work for a day, but I just couldn't work . . . You see, I felt I had to do the same as that woman by the well in Samaria . . . Just as she left her pots, I felt I should leave my mandrel and my axe and shovel. I went about for a fortnight following Evan. I was swimming in love.[12]

He used to sing the following lines in the style of the old Welsh folk ballads. An approximate English translation is printed after the Welsh original:[13]

Rwy'n cofio, rwy'n cofio'r hen hanes
Yn llonni saint Cymru yn llu;
Y bennod a'r emyn yn gynnes
Fel neges o'r oesau a fu.

Rwy'n cofio am ddyddiau'r Diwygiad,
Ysgubo'r eglwysi yn lân,
Y brodyr dan ddwyfol gymhelliad
Yn taflu'r hen bibell i'r tân.

Rwy'n cofio'r hen ddiod sy'n feddwol
Bron colli ei chaethion yn llwyr;
Hen feddwon 'rôl sobri yn wyrthiol
Yn diolch o fore hyd hwyr.

Rwy'n cofio angerddol weddïau,
Gweddïau difrifol a dwys;
Cael teimlo maddeuant pechodau
Bryd hynny oedd fwyaf ei bwys.

Rwy'n cofio rhyw felys oedfaon,
Llond capel mor siriol eu gwên,
A'r nefoedd yn tywallt bendithion
I galon yr ifanc a'r hen.

Y meibion a'r merched afradlon
Dônt adref o hudol wlad bell;
A chafwyd gorfoledd yn Seion
O'u gweled ar lwybrau gwlad well.

Rwy'n cofio'r sancteiddiol dystiolaeth
Feunyddiol o'r gwyrthiol a gaed;
Ni allai neb wadu achubai'r
Dihirod drwy gymod y gwaed.

Ymledai goleuni'r Diwygiad
Drwy'r lofa a'r farchnad a'r ffair;
Deffrowyd cymdeithas i brofiad
O ysbryd a bywyd y Gair.

Rwy'n cofio aelodau newyddion
Yn dyblu a threblu y gân,
Fel rhoddent ar lethrau Bryn Seion
Fel debyg i goedwig ar dân.

Wrth gofio'r llawenydd a'u dagrau
Tra'n moli Gwaredwr yn wir,
Saint annwyl, gweddïo wnawn ninnau
Am arall ddiwygiad cyn hir.

[I remember the old, old story rejoicing the saints of Wales;
chapter and hymn, warm echoes of past times.

I remember the Revival days, churches swept clean,
men moved by divinity casting their pipes in the fire.

58

I remember old man drink, his slaves slipping his grasp;
  drunkards miraculously sobered praising from dawn till dusk.

I remember the prayers ascending, solemn and intense to God;
  the great experience of a felt forgiveness of sins.

I remember sweet gatherings, chapels full to the brim,
  heaven pouring its blessings on young and old.

Prodigal sons and daughters coming home from a far country;
  joy in Zion to see them on the paths to a fairer land.

I remember the testimonies given daily to miracles of grace;
  no one doubting old rebels could be saved through the blood.

The light of the Revival spread through coal-face, market and fair;
  people awakened to feel the spirit and life of the Word.

I remember new converts repeating songs of praise,
  aflame with worship on Zion's hill, like a forest on fire.

As we think of the old joys and tears of true praise to a Saviour,
  dear saints, may we be found in prayer for another reviving.]

There was one male singer who received a great deal of publicity from the journalists because of the songs associated with him. Sam Jenkins was a 25-year-old workman at Burry Tinplate Works in Llanelli when the winds of revival took him up and carried him singing from town to town. He was soon called 'the Sankey of Wales'.[14] During the winter months of 1904–5, he accompanied Sidney Evans on a series of meetings in the Gwent valleys, where he would sing songs of appeal, such as *'Y Ddafad Golledig'* ('The Lost Sheep'), *'A glywaist ti sôn am Iachawdwr y byd?'* ('Have you heard of the Saviour of the world?'), or 'I shall see Him face to face'; then he would give a testimony.

Sam Jenkins explained in one article how he came across the 'Song of the Rebel', which caught the mood of the revival meetings. He had seen the words in an old copy of Sankey's *Sacred Songs and Solos* and had sung them on many occasions in meetings at the Llanelli YMCA. While holding revival meetings at Beaufort in the Gwent valleys, he stayed in the home of Llynfi Davies, a minister and bard, who stayed up all night translating the song into Welsh. The singer asked him to change the word 'sinner' to 'rebel' because he had seen its impact on various congregations. Wherever he went, he sang about the 'old rebel':

These verses were of priceless value to me, because wherever they were sung, they were followed by blessing.

Once, when I was singing the hymn in Calfaria, Porth, Rhondda, as I was drawing to a close, those words 'Mi ganaf ei glod' ['I will sing his praise'] caught hold of me, and when I was singing them for the third time the chief deacon sprang to his feet and shouted a number of times at the top of his voice, 'I will sing also,' until the meeting was at white heat . . .

The late Rev. W. Llywelyn Lloyd recounted the story of one who was mending his nets in Anglesey while I was singing the song in a field meeting in Bryn-du. He would not come to the service, but he was caught by the voice which the wind carried from the field, and he heard on the breeze the words, 'Am achub hen rebel fel fi' ['For saving an old rebel like me']. As a result he left his nets and set sail for the Chapel and gave himself to Christ.

Only eternity can tell how many barriers fell or how many mists of doubt were swept away as these young men and women sang. This is what happened when Sam Jenkins was at a Calvinistic Methodist Association meeting in Llan Ffestiniog in North Wales:

I heard that the two preachers invited to speak at the young people's meeting were unable to be present; and instead of Dr Cynddylan Jones and the Rev. Joseph Jenkins, Mr Sydney Evans and I were asked to take part in the meeting. We agreed on condition that Dr John Williams, Brynsiencyn, presided. When Dr John Williams announced that both of the preachers expected had failed to come, signs of disappointment were seen on almost every face. 'But there are two lads here,' said the Doctor, and everyone laughed, 'and you shall have whatever they have with them.' During that service, I sang 'Am achub hen rebel fel fi' ['For saving an old rebel like me'], and the message was carried by the Spirit of Truth into a host of hearts . . .

After the meeting in the Chapel I was privileged to sing the same song on the Association field, and I remember Dr John Williams rising to his feet at the close and saying, 'I am going to do what was never done in an Association before—I will test the Association,' and there were many who enrolled under Christ's banner for the first time.

As the meeting was being tested and we were singing . . . someone cut across the singing and said, 'There are two here who are resisting.' 'Why, I wonder?' said the Dr, and I rose quietly beside him and sang three verses to the tune 'Bryniau Cassia' . . . and the whole congregation joined in singing [the words exhorting people to press through the crowd to come to the Saviour]. At the end of the singing someone called out—'The two here are coming.' 'Thank God, and may the crown rest on His head.' And Dr John Williams said, 'As long as Sam continues to sing, I will continue to test [the meeting].'[15]

Dr Cynolwyn Pugh spoke for all who owed their membership of the true church to the revival when he wrote:

It is scarcely possible for us to give the present age any idea of the stirring effects of this singing and the saving influences that went with it. The explanation, it seems, is the fact that the Holy Spirit had taken hold not only of the singers but also the listeners: the atmosphere was such that the inspired words of the speakers and the words of the singers alike were winning their place in the minds and hearts of the people without too much effort.[16]

II. PROPAGATION

Come, old and young, now come
  To Jesus, why delay?
For you the Son of God
  Has waited till this day.
'Tis growing late, you treat Him ill,
Yet mercy's door is open still.

Morgan Rhys (1716-79);
tr. by William Edwards (1848-1929)

4

Holy Spirit Revival
in South Wales

'The wind bloweth where it listeth . . . so is
every one that is born of the Spirit'
(John 3:8)

Ministers, reporters, curious visitors, thoughtful commentators, poets and hymn-writers all came away from revival meetings with two over-whelming and permanent impressions—that everything that took place was undirected and unprogrammed by man, and that all was under the direct control of the Holy Spirit alone. J. W. Ewing told his readers how he had discovered a crowded chapel in which stood an empty pulpit which 'seemed to say—"The preacher to-night is the Holy Ghost."' Thomas Phillips of Norwich referred to the wonders of a revival which was 'like the rain and the dew, direct from the finger-tips of God'.[1]

Evan Roberts himself asserted that neither he nor any revival instru-ment could move one step without clear commands from the Holy Spirit. Waves of blessing and power ran through villages and towns far from his track. People were being transformed by the hundred as they felt, not the magnetism of a man nor the emotional pressures of team witness, but the power and presence of the Holy Spirit. Everything seemed to happen simultaneously. Speaking at the autumn meetings of the Baptist Union of Great Britain and Ireland at Northampton, James Owen, a minister from Swansea, showed how even the first flames of the revival had broken out 'in some three or four places about the same time, in an unexpected way'.[2]

The present age has conditioned us to find a single, charismatic per-sonality behind each revival, but in 1904 that model would not pass the most elementary statistical test. From late December 1904 to May 1905, the period which spans the revival, a minimum of six meetings was held each day in many large industrial villages and even more in big towns, not counting overflow meetings and all-night meetings. A conservative estimate would suggest a hundred such communities in all Wales holding five hundred *seiadau* (meetings for sharing fellowship and experiences), prayer meetings and open-air services per day for one hundred days. It is worth recording that about one in twenty of the population yielded to Christ at this time. Evan Roberts and all his associates could not have been present or even nearby in more than 10% of these instances, with perhaps another 10% sparked off by a homecomer's testimony or by someone reciting stories of Roberts from a letter or newspaper. Yet the remaining 80% all witnessed and experienced the same spiritual phenomena. In every town rose sounds of ecstatic praise, weeping confession and earnest vows; everywhere hardened sinners were struck down.

It is also sometimes forgotten that there had been signs of awakening long before Evan Roberts received his call. A year previously there were times of marked blessing at Caerau and Pen-coed, near Bridgend.[3] In January and February 1904, revival meetings held at Cwm-bach, Aberdare, began with a young people's meeting and turned into a general awakening.[4] A series of special services at Calfaria Chapel, Gilfach-goch in July was:

> tempered by the divine influences of the Holy Spirit . . . The vestry was too small to hold the congregation so they moved to the chapel and this was filled in every service held. Men left their work to come to prayer meetings.[5]

The mini-revival at Ponciau near Rhosllannerchrugog in north-east Wales in June 1904, when 'strong men were seen weeping bitterly and the Spirit of God working mightily', is described later. A week later another congregation was prostrated by the Spirit of God until even the cries of 'Amen' and 'Hosanna' were 'drowned in a weeping of praise'. However, in each of these cases the first faint stirrings of the winds of revival had died down by August 1904 and many churches seemed to go to sleep again.[6] But enough had happened to show that the Spirit of God was beginning to move.

In this chapter we will focus on meetings where the presence of Evan Roberts was not a factor. This is not to disdain God's messenger but rather to show how a Sovereign God used other young men and women as instruments in revival meetings which took place from Ammanford in Dyfed to Newport in Gwent. The starting-point is Ammanford, in the chapel served by Nantlais Williams, whose own surrender to the Holy Spirit is described later. The story is presented just as he wrote it:

On the first Sunday of November, 1904, we held our preaching services in Bethany, Ammanford, with Joseph Jenkins preaching—as arranged some years before. But now a few months before the meetings the news had reached us that something wonderful had happened at New Quay. Indeed, I remember one *seiat* ['fellowship meeting'] held in Bethany in August, 1904, with Mr David Thomas the schoolmaster of Penmorfa, a place not far from New Quay . . . venturing to tell us the story of what was going on in New Quay until we were astounded and our hearts glowed. That was the firstfruit of the Revival for us in Ammanford, the luggage we received in advance.

The last Sunday in October I was preaching at home. Fully aware that Joseph Jenkins would be there the following Sabbath, I took as my text 'Repent . . . and ye shall receive the gift of the Holy Ghost.' My purpose was to prepare the way for the famous preacher. But even better was the work of the officers in agreeing to hold a week of prayer meetings to prepare the way for Mr Jenkins, though it was a very new thing in those days to hold such a series in the churches. The following Sunday morning Mr Jenkins preached on Zacchaeus, and he urged us to get down quickly from the branches of our self-righteousness. 'Take your fall tidily now,' he said. There was a heavenly electricity in the meeting. At the end I got up without consulting anyone and announced, 'There will be a prayer-meeting here in the vestry at five o'clock before the evening service.' As we went home from the meeting Mr Jenkins said to me, 'Man, the Holy Spirit is fully among you here.' I did not know that because I was not instructed in the ways of the Spirit as was the preacher.

The afternoon meeting was set apart for relating the story of the Revival in New Quay. The chapel was full to overflowing and a stillness and intensity of a formidable kind possessed us all as we listened to the stirring story. In the middle of his address Mr Jenkins referred to a meeting where the congregation had broken into singing:

> *Dowch hen ac ieuanc, dewch*
> *At Iesu, mae'n llawn bryd—*

> [Come old and young, come
> To Jesus, it's high time].

With that, David Thomas, one of our quietest deacons, cut across Jenkins, turned his face to the congregation and said, 'Let's sing that hymn now, shall we?' What liberty! The crowd broke out into song with a passion and rejoicing beyond description.

My anxiety now was for the 5 p.m. prayer-meeting. Would anyone come? Well, when I reached the vestry, to my astonishment it was packed full. The first light of dawn had come. The hilltops were rejoicing and the sun was quickly drawing nigh.

There followed a week of meetings, of which the Tuesday night prayer meeting proved to be the most remarkable:

The Tuesday night after Mr Jenkins left, the sun rose in its power at Ammanford . . . [At a packed prayer-meeting that evening], there was no need for anyone to lead because the infallible Leader had taken the helm. About ten o'clock a young girl in the corner to the right of the big seat rose to her feet and prayed with an explosive passion until a Pentecostal cloud broke over her. It poured out its contents everywhere, until everyone lost control and turned to praying, yes, and shouting, some asking forgiveness, some giving thanks, and some praising—everyone in a confusion doing something. Never before had we seen such a holy disorder in a religious meeting. But, despite all the disorder of the meeting, no clash of spirit was felt there. A beautiful harmony was sensed in the confessing, praying and praising. The quiet thanksgiving heard here and the broken-hearted cry sounding over there were in the same sweet counterpoint as are the tender tinkle of the harp and the trombone's strident notes in an orchestra. The harsh sounds of self were nowhere to be heard. The meeting continued till half past two in the morning.[7]

An important eyewitness of this awakening at Ammanford was Seth Joshua who arrived on 19 November for a Forward Movement mission. His personal impressions are recorded in his diary and speak of the wonderful fire burning, the prepared ground, the divine life springing up and the 'doctrine of assurance . . . getting a deeper hold upon the people'. He recognized that the planned missions had been merged into revival because 'the Holy Spirit was indeed among the people'.[8]

Meanwhile, through the new converts at Ammanford, revival influences reached from Llandeilo to the north and Cwm-twrch to the east as far as Pontarddulais and Pontardawe to the south. Gors-las and Cross Hands to the west of Ammanford were likewise affected, but the main push was along the Amman Valley.

At the same time the main streams of revival were flowing onward in Gorseinon, Llanelli and Morriston, from which come detailed eyewitness accounts. The new leader to emerge here was Sidney Evans. Although not a charismatic or prophetic figure, nevertheless he had been close to Evan Roberts when the Holy Spirit began his special work. Biographical notes on him, by D. M. Phillips and T. Francis, create the picture of a quiet, studious, shy, former shop apprentice who had been recommended for the ministry because his church recognized his qualities. He was a model student even when he was excited by his friend's messages and first missions. Beneath the quiet, cool personality lay powers and gifts known only to the One who said, 'Man looketh on the outward appearance, but the Lord looketh on the heart.'[9]

He was first struck by the dynamic words of Seth Joshua, whose missions in Newcastle Emlyn and Cardigan were visited by student groups. In their lodgings Evan and Sidney discussed each other's spiritual longings. Sidney witnessed some of Evan's visions and shared his agonies and joys, which became precious memories.[10] It was at the third of the conventions for deepening spiritual life, organized by Joseph Jenkins in September 1904, that he accepted the challenge of W. W. Lewis to 'give full obedience to God and to become a witness'. He joined in plans for local evangelistic ministries, working alongside the New Quay girls. Three letters reveal his journey into a new kind of life:

I do not feel altogether unperplexed; yet I possess a true joy which I have never experienced before. I have been seized by an infinite desire to save souls, and I do not exactly know what to do, but I am putting myself completely in God's hands. Mr Seth Joshua, together with some of the New Quay reformers, held revival meetings here last week, and I felt the heavenly influences very strongly. I felt constrained to rise up before the congregation and to profess the name of Christ . . . I attended a conference at Blaenanerch last week. We had glorious meetings . . . The name of Christ was exalted there. Public confession was made by several in the meetings, and others completely lost control over themselves.[11]

A brief letter to Evan Roberts, dated 1 November 1904, opens thus:

I had thought that possibly I would get a word from you this morning. They are rather anxious concerning you here. It was with tears that Ann spoke of you last night. We had a glorious meeting on Monday evening. Heaven smiled upon us. The first meeting was closed in the usual way, but none were prepared to leave.

I said that I would like to get another meeting, and we had a meeting! There was some intensity in it that is seldom experienced . . . I am going to Blaenanerch on Sunday. Pray for me. I do not want to go alone. God be with you.[12]

And another letter to Roberts, dated 9 November 1904, contains the following:

> I had a never-to-be-forgotten service at Blaenanerch on Sunday night. The Spirit was powerful upon me and upon the congregation. I nearly lost myself completely throughout the sermon, but at the close, I lost myself while trying to bring home to the people the importance and consequence of venturing into eternity without Jesus. After the sermon, we had a prayer meeting, and it was a wonderful meeting. There were young girls there praying and clinging fast to the Throne. One old man there (about seventy) had quite lost himself by repeating the words—
>
> > 'Here's a Saviour for the fallen,
> > Healer for those bruised by sin,'
>
> and praying. Praise God. Blessed be His Name . . .
> I intend coming home on Monday. I can't get peace with the idea, and after reading your note in the corner of the letter regarding Mr. Francis's request, I am still fuller of the idea.[13]

He felt restless in his studies, but two days later, on 11 November, the battle was over and he was packed ready for his homeward journey. Within a few days, Florrie Evans and Maud Davies followed him and plunged into the work at Gorseinon. Meetings at Libanus Chapel, Gorseinon had been arranged for him by the minister, and were thought at first to be a continuation of the work of Evan Roberts, who had by then moved his base. But differences in style soon appeared and his became more personal at Morriston and Llanelli, and even more so in Gwent. Of the many accounts available, the following show that the correspondent is setting down what he himself had seen and heard. We can sometimes sense his discomfort and puzzlement, even when he is deeply touched:

> Carmel and Bethania were two of the Morriston chapels altogether given over on Sunday [27.11.1904] to the strange influence stealing over Wales. At Bethania, late in the evening, the friend of the leader of the revival, Mr. Sidney Evans, came to the service, but long before his arrival, indeed, from six o'clock until half-past eight, people had been praying with passion and singing the old hymns with an abandon foreign even to Wales. Young men, nerved by the sympathetic atmosphere, had been rising, from floor and gallery, and, without any invitation or pressure, had followed the formula set by the first, 'I get up to confess Christ.' When Mr. Evans slowly made his way up the aisle of the densely-crowded chapel, the air was electrical.

Some of the methods adopted it would be well to place on record were objectionable. There may be a division of opinion as to the advisability of requesting a whole congregation to stand and attest their surety of Salvation . . . but none who were at Bethania, that is, none but the wilfully blind, could have any doubt as to its utter ineffectiveness then. There was no need of a 'quickening' at that chapel, if all who stood up were in real earnest, for the exceptions were few. But it was apparent to anyone with eyes to see, it was plain enough to the writer, sitting in the gallery, close to a group of young men, who had taken the service as some sort of queer entertainment, that there were a great many who were not . . . [The few honest ones] had to sit it out for nearly a quarter of an hour while those on their feet sang hymn after hymn.

But there were moments so intense as to be painful. A deep hush fell over the people when a beautiful girl of fifteen or sixteen years rose from the front of the gallery and prayed. Trembling like an aspen, the petitions came at first halting and broken, but her voice gathering strength, she became passionate in her pleading. She asked that Treforis [Morriston] should be captured for Christ, that the town should have a sight of the Devil in all his hideousness, that it should also see the Saviour in His glory. The silence was unbroken for minutes after the 'Amen,' then the 'Diolch's' and 'Hallelujahs' burst out . . .

Yet another incident which fired the people. From the back of the gallery there got up a man with listless face and lustreless eyes. He spoke for a while in a low monotone, but suddenly his voice rose, and with his eyes closed, he held everyone spell-bound by ferocity—no other word will adequately describe it—of his appeal to the 'Yspryd Glan' [Holy Spirit] to descend like a consuming fire on Morriston. He heard the sound . . . of the music of souls saved for the Saviour; half the congregation involuntarily turned to the direction he was facing, expecting to hear the strains. He sang in triumphant notes the joy of the Redeemer, he thundered out the fate of the damned, he tenderly pointed the way to salvation, he sobbed over the agony of Christ. As a piece of oratory alone, and no thought of his eloquence surely was in this man's mind, it was the finest Morriston has heard for years.

* * * * *

There was a hush at first over the congregation which filled Bethania Chapel, Morriston, on Monday afternoon [28.11.1904] . . . Gone was the feverish emotionalism which moved the people on the previous evening . . . Gone were the passionate gusts of singing which on Sunday swept them off their feet. In their place was a calm too deep for sound.

71

The hymns which were sung were given with a slow impressiveness in keeping with the new characteristic of the Morriston revival.

Mr. Sidney Evans, looking brighter than on the Sunday, spoke to the audience in a quiet, conversational tone. Swinging his right hand down from the shoulder to emphasise his sentences, he strove to make the Power of Darkness a very real personage, 'seeking whom he might devour' . . .

Still the hush continued, and, although the hymns that were sung were repeated over and over again, there were few signs of over-mastering emotion . . .

The testimonies given under such conditions gained in solemnity. One man in the gallery said that since Saturday he had been striving with the Devil, but now he had placed the Evil One under foot, and gladly stood to confess for Christ . . .

It was an elderly woman, speaking with such fervour and intensity that at last she broke down, who swept away at last the barriers of reserve. A stream of fierce eloquence poured from her lips, and before she sat down exhausted, many of the congregation were in tears. 'It's the spirit of God,' she said in English, 'it's His Spirit which for once is speaking in me . . . I want, and I mean, to spend the last few days of my life in trying to raise poor fallen sinners.'

'It's not the doctor that has brought her husband around; it has been the power of prayer,' confessed another woman in the body of the chapel. Then the flood gates were opened, snatches of hymns were started here and there, they were taken up with passion, and people became so eager to speak that often two or three were on their feet about the same time.

The service, which opened in quietness, ended with 'fire.'[14]

Some people began to notice the dark rings round Sidney Evans's eyes, and it was realized that he had no one to relieve him except the girl singers, and also Sam Jenkins when his work permitted. After a brief spell in the Rhondda he was called to Llanelli, where again a writer has left us a fair-minded eyewitness account:

When Mr Sidney Evans visited the town and asked 'Shall these bones live?' the response was unmistakeable in its significance. Mr Evans was the central figure at a wonderful meeting held at Trinity Chapel. The building was packed at seven o'clock, and the proceedings were pro-tracted until two o'clock on Sunday morning . . . 'I can see,' he said, 'that a great work is to be done at Llanelly, and before many days are past the town will be on fire.' . . . he told his hearers, however, that he had nothing new to tell them. He had his faith rested on the 'old, old story', and he told it again with a beautiful simplicity . . . His address was followed by the singing of 'Arglwydd, dyma fi,' ['I am coming Lord'] after which Miss Roberts, a sister of Evan Roberts, rose and asked the meeting if they fully appreciated what they had been singing. Then came the famous hymn, 'Pen Calfaria'. By this time the tide of feeling was running high, and when a young man rose in the gallery and asked the congregation to join him in prayer on behalf of his wayward brother there was a remarkable outburst. This was accentuated when a well-known working man walked on to the 'set fawr' [big seat], fell on his face in a paroxysm of weeping, and sobbed a broken prayer for forgiveness . . . there was not a dry eye in the chapel . . . Meanwhile the Rev. Mr Rowlands, himself deeply affected, cried out, 'Let him go on. He is fighting for his life now.' Sidney Evans then went to the penitent and administered consolation, and the Rev. Elias Davies . . . prayed that the convert might have Divine strength in the days that were to come.[15]

Sidney Evans did not have the same impact when he came back to Llanelli the following February, and there was very strong criticism of the testing of meetings.

For reasons of time and space we must leave reports on the W. S. Jones/O. M. Owen services at Cwmsyfïog near Rhymni, the work of Trevor Jones in the Llanelli Docks, the Nantlais Williams missions, and the Keri Evans mission to Carmarthen, in order to concentrate on Sidney Evans's activity in Gwent, where the Spirit was now leading him.

Gwent had been relatively untouched by revival fires. Most early revival meetings were within the Welsh-speaking constituency and culture, whereas Gwent was already well on its way to being Anglicized. Sidney Evans had been commanded by the Holy Spirit to begin at Newport, where not long before he had been a grocer's assistant. The earliest *South Wales Argus* reports call him shy and nervous in front of scoffers and suggest there was little enthusiasm for his message. He spoke mostly to church-goers, and a reporter wrote, 'He does not look like a born leader of men and he attempted no flights of eloquence.'[16]

Excitement grew rapidly once the converts flocked in from Cardiff and Caerphilly and even the Rhondda and Taff Valleys to give their joyful testimonies. Mary Roberts (Evan's sister) warned the people of Newport not to be so lukewarm when the Lord was doing such wonders for them.[17] At the meetings in Mount Zion Chapel there were outbreaks of tears and passionate prayers and repeated songs for the first time. Sidney

Evans spoke in Welsh about the need to prepare themselves for the coming of the Holy Spirit, but there was hardly any response until he switched to the English tongue.

The long-awaited rising of a mighty wind occurred during a service at Stow Hill Methodist Church. Songs such as 'O happy day' and 'When all my labours and trials are o'er' mingled with choruses such as 'Everybody should know' and the favourite 'Tell mother I'll be there', which sparked off many prayers and testimonies. A local man, Mr Lennard, joined with student Christie Davies and Pastor Thomas to give evangelistic messages, while the songs of Sam Jenkins brought many more to their knees. In the midst of all this Sidney Evans was calmly, patiently testing each congregation, counselling the seekers and warning off the many mere spectators, whose rude manners were a stumbling-block to the townsfolk.[18]

Next day it was Mary Roberts who had a dynamic effect. From a kneeling position she was heard pouring out very fervent prayers for a 'baptism of the Holy Spirit with fire'. Following her example other women began to play a more and more vital role during the afternoon meetings. Inevitably the evening meetings began to carry on very late, even after the usual dismissal hymn at midnight.

In the meetings at Ebenezer Chapel, Cwmbrân, there were volunteer soloists and testifiers, who released a flood of emotion. Again Sidney Evans insisted on the usual 'four points' until his voice was drowned by bitter weeping and confession. At Beaufort there was almost a queue of singers. When he arrived the congregation were singing, 'O Lord, send the power.' 'Don't sing "Send the power," ' he said: 'The Power is here. Sing "O, Lord, let me feel the Power."'[19]

The most vivid and personal picture of the type of meeting conducted by Sidney Evans was penned by Ilsley Charlton, a Church Missionary Society missionary from Bengal who visited one of his meetings at Ebbw Vale:

A cold, frosty day in a rather unattractive mining village (or town). I arrived at about 2 p.m. and at once inquired where the meetings were held. It was hardly necessary, as everyone seemed to be going the same way; and near the chapel, in which the gathering was to be, was a crowd holding a kind of moving open-air service. I found my way into a chapel seated for about 600 people, as far as I could judge, and was kindly shown up to the 'big seat' (a kind of circular seat for church officials, which half encircles the pulpit in Welsh chapels). The chapel was fairly full, and became quite crowded when the singing party came in.

There was no special leader, no musical instrument, no hymn books, and no announcing of hymns. Everyone was at liberty to speak, or sing, or pray if they felt led to do so—with the result that solos, choruses, hymns, prayers, praises, testimonies, or exhortations, etc. all followed one another (and sometimes went on together) without confusion or manifest disorder—perfect liberty and yet wonderful unity. Now and then, if in the intensity of the moment, two or three prayed at the same time, seemingly unconscious of each other, the congregation would softly sing, 'I need Thee every hour,' forming a sweet accompaniment to the fervent supplications.

Now and then a short address was given by anyone from anywhere, until the speaker was obliged to give way to some outburst of song, which seemed to cause not the slightest irritation or annoyance. Even when two different hymns were started from different parts of the church, one gave way to the other without discord or confusion.

If anyone signified his intention of yielding to the claims of Christ, everything else had to give way to 'Songs of Praises,' a little chorus invariably sung when anyone was converted.

After a time, during which the meeting had been taking itself as above described, Mr. Sidney Evans and a lady soloist arrived. The former, quite young, and, humanly speaking, nothing special; with none of the eloquence or attracting power, and very little of the methods, of an ordinary Evangelist or 'Revivalist;' the latter, quiet and unobtrusive, with a sweet but not a very extraordinary voice.

The 'Missioner' can hardly be said to have taken the meeting in hand; he spoke a little now and then—words of encouragement, or warning, or advice—now and then went to speak to someone in the congregation—sometimes invited sinners to come to the Lord. Several seemed to respond, and much good work seemed to be done.

The evening meeting in another chapel, to which I went later on, was much like the one just described, but was still more crowded—in fact, there were, I believe, two overflow meetings, besides a side-meeting in the schoolroom, and still there were too many people in the original place to admit of any personal work being done, and so 'members' were still asked to make room for outsiders. Great crowds of people, eager, enthusiastic, earnest and intense. Why were they there till past 12 o'clock at night? What is the explanation of the fact?

Certainly not a great speaker; for no one would pretend that the 'Missioner' could be so called. He spoke in English, with which, I believe, he was not quite familiar. He did not attempt a set address. He is quite young, and presumably inexperienced, and with no specially strong personality.

Certainly not the solos; for there were only one or two, and although sweet and attractive, not remarkable enough to musical Welshmen to account for such enthusiasm.

Certainly not the congregational singing; for, although some of the hymns were magnificently sung, the Welsh are as much accustomed to fine congregational singing as they are to mountains. Besides which they used only a small selection of quite ordinary hymns . . .

Famous oratory, an amusing entertainment, or a good concert, will, of course, bring crowds together in one particular place; but here are crowds, not in one place but in scores, not on one particular night but for many weeks, gathering together with the greatest enthusiasm and interest without any of the usual attractions!

If we acknowledge that they are moved by a specially God-sent hunger after spiritual things, it is quite easy to understand.[20]

'Moved by . . . God-sent hunger' surely means that the Holy Spirit was mightily at work in that valley, creating such longings. Long after Sidney Evans and his helpers had moved on, the Spirit continued to break, melt, mould and fill those whose hearts the Lord had opened.

So far we have visited little townships where the lives of people were bound to each other and to their chapels. What would happen when the wind and the flame reached some big city where people made their fortunes not their homes; where the old Welsh way of life was half forgotten? Would not this changed climate quench the Spirit?

There are fewer first-hand reports of Cardiff meetings, perhaps because Evan Roberts refused to visit it since he had 'no leading of the Holy Spirit'. The singers and Sidney Evans also stayed away from the city, but one team member, Annie May Rees the elocutionist, created a sensation in the new-style meetings. She had a natural flair for doing unusual things, such as bringing two converted gipsies into the pulpit at Aberdare. She served her apprenticeship in the Rhondda meetings, and when Evan Roberts fell ill, she filled up the time with the singing of hymns such as 'O Happy Day' and 'I need Thee'. From making just a few remarks on the hymns, she progressed to dramatic invitations to 'Throw out the Lifeline' after telling a story. On 2 December at Moriah Chapel, Pentre, with the main team miles away, Annie 'took her seat, alone, in the "big pew," and presently began to sing some of the beautifully touching hymns of the revival. After the congregation had joined

76

her she opened the meeting with prayer, and afterwards spoke alternately in Welsh and English, taking practically charge of the proceedings.'[21]

At Christmas she made a triumphant return to Gorseinon and was at once invited to give an address at Bethel Chapel. An observer wrote:

> The people were very much impressed by what she said, as she is only a young girl of fifteen summers, and a native of the place . . . Miss Rees said, 'My heart is in the work, and I am eagerly looking forward to the time when I shall return to Cardiff to continue the meetings . . . She mentioned the name of the Rev. Charles Davies, the respected pastor of Tabernacle Baptist Chapel, Cardiff, as one who was giving her great assistance.'[22]

The word 'return' may well refer to her first mission in Canton and Llandaff Road, before she appeared in Tabernacle Baptist Chapel in The Hayes in the centre of Cardiff.

Here follows an eyewitness report of a tumultuous meeting at Tabernacle Baptist Chapel in January 1905:

> I reached Cardiff shortly before seven o'clock on Saturday night, and an hour later found me at the doors of the Tabernacle, the largest Baptist Church in town . . . Already it was nearly full. A man under the gallery was praying fervently for Ireland, in response . . . to a letter from Mr. Boyd, of the Irish Baptist Mission. Almost before the speaker had finished another had begun.
>
> A phlegmatic Englishman, accustomed all his life to habits of self-repression, is so overwhelmed with surprise when plunged thus suddenly into a Celtic cauldron of emotion that it takes him some little time to recover. As soon as I began to find my bearings, I tried quietly to survey the scene. The chapel was crowded in every part, and round the doors was a throng of people unable to find seats. Scores could not even obtain an entrance and had to go into the vestry or to other chapels where similar meetings were in progress . . . There were almost as many nationalities as on the Day of Pentecost. English, Irish, Scotch, Welsh, Jews, French, Swedes, Greeks, Italians, negroes and mulattoes, soldiers in uniform, sailors, colliers, dock hands, Members of Parliament, civic dignitaries, learned professors, ministers of the Gospel, wealthy merchants, noted journalists—surely St. Peter himself hardly looked out on a stranger or more varied throng . . .
>
> The Welsh Revival was *sui generis*. It is like nothing else I have ever seen . . . The meetings begin, proceed, and end, guided by some mysterious impulse. They are chaotic without confusion, and decent

though disorderly. No-one can say what the audience will do next. There is no leader, and yet there is a fresh leader every five minutes . . .

Two or three prayers had been offered during the brief time spent in scanning my surroundings, and in the slight pause that followed, M. Cadot stepped to the front of the platform and essayed to speak. Unfortunately, a man whom I had already noticed sitting under the gallery, leaning forward with his elbows on the book ledge, and covering his eyes with his hands, started a revival chorus at that moment. He had a big voice that quite drowned M. Cadot's meeker accents and as the sentiment, 'Come to Jesus just now,' appealed to the audience at that particular moment, the French pastor had to wait. This chorus is a peculiarly fascinating one. You improvise as you sing. As fast as one couplet was finished others were started from the gallery, from the platform, from all parts of the building. 'Save the drunkard now', 'Save the gambler now' . . .

Poor Monsieur Cadot tried once more but was overcome by the uproar. Finally succeeding to speak, he asked for the prayers of the congregation for the struggling little French Protestant churches. Then it was that Annie May Rees took over and walked calmly into a vacant pulpit:

'Everybody, not one only,' said Miss Rees . . . 'but let everybody pray for France. Now then, come along!'.

M. Cadot prayed with great feeling, and towards the end of his prayer Miss Rees began to sing, 'I need Thee, O, I need Thee' in a low crooning voice as a kind of minor accompaniment, and when he had finished, it was taken up and sung again and again as I think only Welshmen can sing.

The excitement was growing, with two or three hymns being started at the same time. Towards the end of this meeting,

Miss Rees gave a brief address explaining why that meeting had been advertised as a 'farewell meeting'. Some of them, she hoped, were going to say 'farewell to the devil'.

'Don't mind me,' she went on. 'I am nothing. Do just as the spirit moves you. Don't be afraid of interrupting me. The only thing I beg you not to do is to quench the Spirit.'[23]

A much later report from Pearl Street Chapel in the same city suggests that she was not the only lady evangelist at work. Singers May John, Mattie Miles, Gwennie John and Nelly Sutton came there to take part and one of the speakers was a Mrs Evans, widow of the powerful Welsh Wesleyan preacher, John Evans (Eglwys-bach). These meetings were marked by many tearful restorations and family reconciliations. 'Some of the dear women hug their happiness in a dumb delight, and afraid that the millennium is only momentary and may be merely a mocking mirage.'

There is room for just one more report, this time from Tabernacle Chapel, Penarth, which had for two years held weekly prayer meetings for an outpouring of the Spirit:

> On November 21 the prayer-meeting and the Christian Endeavour meeting were merged into one service.
>
> It was there that the fire came down. Praying and singing, with ecstatic enthusiasm, continued until ten o'clock at night. There were five converts. On November 24 nightly meetings commenced and are continued to the present time. There was no preaching on the Sabbath for two months, the pulpit and pew being merged into mutual services of supplication and song, all ablaze with Pentecostal enthusiasm. There were baptisms for twelve consecutive Sundays when ninety-five persons put on the Lord Jesus Christ by immersion. Among the converts were those who attended Anglican, Nonconformist and Roman Catholic Churches.[24]

Annie May Rees and her like were allowed to take the lead because so many church ministers did not know what to do. J. Vyrnwy Morgan quotes a well-known and highly respected Welsh minister who, unable to enter a full chapel, was reduced to looking through the window from the garden behind. There people were praying in groups on the ground floor and in the gallery, each group having a number of unconverted to pray for:

> The pulpit was full of ministers: some of them sat with closed eyes; others knelt in silent prayer. One or two of them prayed aloud. Some of these ministers were looking down into the big seats, watching the converts coming in one by one and casting themselves on the floor in agony and remorse.[25]

The strange coldness and passiveness of the ministers, content to remain mere observers, robbed them of the blessing.

The Swansea minister, Penar Griffiths, however, was anything but cold and passive. Along with some of his members from the railwaymen's and foundrymen's chapel called Siloam, Pentre Estyll, he went over to meetings at Cilfynydd near Pontypridd in November 1904 and came back aflame with the new fire. Later on he said that from the day he described the revival to his flock the same fire had been kindled in them, though it did not at first break into full flame:

We had very large meetings here before Evan Roberts came here and after he left. The revival fire was fully kindled long before he came. He remained here for three days and three nights from January 1st 1905. With regard to our own Church it was on November 27th 1904 that the great downpouring commenced, and it continued in such strength and power that I was unable to preach for thirteen Sundays. It was one continual praise and thanksgiving and time of prayer. On November 30th we had a great night. The two aisles were full of young people coming on to pray of all ages from 16 to 20 years old. Mothers followed their children in tears. About forty to fifty, young and old, praised and prayed on their knees. It was a never to be forgotten scene. Praised be the Lord. I must confess although I had expected great things, I never expected such as this.[26]

In another account he gave, found in a Congregational newspaper entitled *Y Tyst* ['The Witness'], Penar Griffiths describes a revival meeting at Pentre Estyll on Wednesday night, 30 November 1904:

First a hymn is given out, then one of our oldest members reads from Isaiah—reading it with the sound of victory in his voice—and within four minutes his prayer is over—but its sparks are all over the meeting. Another hymn and prayer from one of our most fiery old people, and for two or three minutes it is red hot. There's another, and another, both of them similar in their experience. Then another is on his feet, saying that he is ashamed we are all so hard, and exhorting us to give ourselves more fully to the Holy Spirit. A stillness has descended on the meeting by now, after we have been there over two hours, but it is exactly like the calm before a storm—an expectant stillness. Then another stands, saying that those old words are on his mind:–

> *Wrth gofio'i riddfannau'n yr ardd*
> [Remembering his groanings in the garden
> of Gethsemane],

and saying that each one ought to have something to say for Jesus. 'I imagine Jesus here gazing at us in our dumbness, and saying, "So-and-so, have you no word to say about Me—I who was your best friend in the greatest distress you have known! So-and-so, do you have anything to say for me? I was the best friend you saw in your day of trouble!" '

At that a poor elderly widow leaps to her feet suddenly, and gives out an old hymn with victorious fervour.

'Is there anyone else?' says the minister.

'Yes, yes!' says a faithful brother, 'but I am expecting to see these young people breaking out.'

Another elderly brother is on his feet, and giving a word; but before he prays, a middle-aged brother rises to his feet—one of the most faithful servants of the devil years ago—original and very free in his public words always:–

'I'm bound to get up,' he says, 'or go to pieces . . . Oh! young people, break out. Don't listen to the devil—the old—the old—! Oh! I call him by every *wicked* name I can (by now the heat and the praise were powerful in the meeting); I know he is the one who is stopping you!' (The face of the speaker has a strange—yes strange—glow) . . .

With this, one of our most prominent and most self-composed people leaps to his feet, clapping his hands and shouting praises to Jesus. In a moment the two aisles between the seats were full of young people coming forward to pray, pray . . .

'This is the Prophet Joel,' cries another; 'it is worth being alive to see this night!' The most self-controlled people are waving their handkerchiefs, moving around the building rejoicing. By now one of the oldest members of the church is on his knees in the midst of some 30 or 40 young people and mothers—all praying.

It is a quarter to eleven! A young man, who was unyielding on Sunday night, and throughout the service, rushes forward among the people, and is on his knees with the crowd in tears.[27]

It is too easy to overlook the next person who was so signally used in many revival meetings. He was Evan Roberts's brother Dan, who had gone straight from Loughor British School to the mines. There he had developed eye trouble which had by the outbreak of revival rendered him unfit for work. He was well-liked and respectable, and faithful in his attendance at chapel, but on 10 October 1904 Evan wrote to him, challenging him to 'give yourself absolutely in the hands of the Holy Spirit'. His sight got stronger after his brother's return to Loughor and he was soon to become a revival preacher in his own right.

In the early days of the revival, he went to Trecynon, Aberdare, with letters for his brother. Evan was just leaving for Pontycymer and Dan was persuaded to stay and help with the work at Trecynon. This marked the beginning of his involvement as a revival preacher. His major work began, however, when he was invited to Kidwelly, Llanelli, and to Ynystawe and Ystalyfera in the Swansea Valley.

After the New Year, Dan spent five weeks in Gwent, three in Glamorgan, and three in the county of Brecon before returning to the miners with whom he felt most at home. Later he teamed up with Sam Jenkins on a northern counties mission but finally settled among the Pembrokeshire fellowships and gradually lost contact with his brother and the revival in general.

The *Llanelly & County Guardian* includes an account that almost certainly comes from Briton Ferry near Neath. It appears as though the author of this report was involved in a meeting that took place just after Evan Roberts passed by Briton Ferry without visiting it:

> The most prominent feature of the service is, of course, the singing, and the rendering of the old Welsh minor tunes is very fine and soul-stirring. The singing also serves another useful, and sometimes necessary, purpose—when a brother (or sister) becomes prosy or unduly lengthy, he is very promptly and effectively silenced by a sudden outburst of song. This is generally done with good judgment, but sometimes the interruption is untimely, as on one occasion a lady got up to speak (in English) after they had been singing, 'I need Thee, oh, I need Thee,' and, when speaking very well indeed, and very much to the point, on the words of this hymn, (I need thee), she was completely silenced by a sudden outburst of 'Diolch Iddo' ['Thanks be to Him']. There were a few racy and good addresses in Welsh and English—one (abounding in striking metaphors), by a horny-handed working man in the gallery, being much appreciated, and evoked a storm of enthusiastic approval. Although a lengthy utterance, it was not sung down, being in Welsh—it was the cold, unemotional Saxon that was generally silenced in song. One young girl (neatly dressed, of the working class order, innocent of grammar, but rich in grace), certainly not more than 14 or 15, sitting in the pew in front of me, prayed with wonderful fervour, and her emotion was so great at the close that it became almost painful to listen to her— it was the very real 'wrestling' in prayer, of one 'that had power with God,' and remarkable for one so young.
>
> Everything was so free and easy, and delightfully irregular, informal . . . One of the Dutch visitors spoke in broken English, another in his native tongue, which was interrupted by a third, and a lady from Switzerland took part. Then a big, burly man got up and said, 'I come from Yorkshire. I was an Atheist for 25 years. I am now rejoicing in the "truth."' This statement was followed by a grand outburst of 'Diolch

Iddo.' The Yorkshireman got up again—for Yorkshiremen are not easily silenced—'I want a message from you to take back to Yorkshire. We are dead and we want to live.' After he had spoken, from all parts of the chapel, various passages of Scripture (thoughtfully given in English, and not Welsh!) were given him as 'the message for Yorkshire.' This was followed by the singing of 'The crown belongs to Jesus,' repeated over and over again.

A Scotchman now prayed, and was followed by a Cornishman, who wanted to take a blessing to the west country. Now the great Metropolis was represented, and the speaker said he wanted their prayers for London, which was so hard to convert . . .

A handsome young Irishman quite captivated us with a charming address and a beautiful prayer. He told us he had only come over the night before from Dublin, and he said the revival had boarded some of the Irish steamers, for several of the sailors had been converted, and they were holding prayer meetings on this particular boat . . . Whilst one man was praying (sometimes there were two or three praying at the same time) in English, in very clear, sonorous tones, a woman started singing, and as she continued very sweetly and softly throughout the prayer, the effect was very fine. The man praying was not in the least disturbed, and the very soft singing, almost a whisper, several other female voices having now joined in, was like an angel accompaniment, a refrain from heaven in answer to prayer.[28]

One matter remains to be examined. Did any of the revival movements which were first inspired by Evan Roberts take on new features as they grew under the guidance of the Holy Spirit? David Hughes, minister of Tabernacle Chapel, Pontycymer, was present at many meetings, and his careful narratives bring the scenes to life, in spite of an occasional tendency to ramble. In an article written in 1906, he described how the Pontycymer revival meetings, which had such widespread effects, had started in a prayer meeting on Monday, 14 November 1904, with a group who had been burdened for revival for two or three months.[29] The following day, the half-yearly meetings of the South Wales Women's Temperance Union were held in Pontycymer and it was suggested that it would be beneficial to have a visit from Evan Roberts, the young revivalist who was holding meetings at Trecynon. An invitation was sent to him and he agreed to come. Hughes then describes the quiet, unassuming entrance of the revivalist on the Wednesday evening and his simple, direct way of announcing his message—that all churches must receive the gift of the Holy Spirit and that the condition for receiving the

Holy Spirit was confession, cleansing and full obedience. The first meeting then broke out into 'passionate singing', 'supernatural stirrings' and 'rejoicing at the throne of grace'. That was only a foretaste, he said, of the Thursday morning meeting, the high point of the revival, when the congregation was 'in a turmoil'. By the afternoon meeting, a host of strangers arrived and 'all who came near were floored'. After a brief glimpse of the remainder of the week's meetings and the town's reaction, Hughes's report ended with the words:

> [The revival] opened up a limitless possibility before the church of God when it walks in the paths of the Holy Spirit. Impure language was paralysed in work, home, street, and business place. The pomp of ungodliness in work-places was slowed down . . . Standards were raised . . . A new spiritual ambition was kindled in decrepid church members.

In his subsequent book on the revival, David Hughes included new portraits of the Pontycymer revival as it was seven months after Evan Roberts's brief visit. The section dealing with 2-4 June 1905 is of special interest because it gives one portrait of the moral effect of the revival and another of its cultural effect:

> By Sunday morning, when I went to the young people's prayer-meeting . . . I understood that the furnace had been heated up seven times hotter than usual. And it was the same in the chapel . . . A great eagerness to preach took hold of me that morning; and it is pleasant to remember that we had the privilege of losing ourselves very deeply in spiritual things, and thereby gained for ourselves a new consciousness.
>
> After finishing, the meeting went on its victorious way. Then a deacon stood up and referred to the Saturday night meeting . . . where a drunken man at the meeting had told the people of God 'to go to hell with their — nonsense.' 'I never heard,' said the deacon, his face transfigured, 'anyone ever saying "go to hell" in the house of God. People, we have much work praying for those people; and how can we be right with God and men if we, religious people, frequent public houses?' Never was there such an earthquake in a meeting. Everybody writhed; everyone raised their hands without anyone asking. The whole chapel said, 'Amen'; and there was a healthy spiritual stirring among the people for a long time. Some prayed. Some sang. Some wept! . . . A great and terrible fear fell on us all; and in that state of terror, we went home about half past twelve in order to return at two for the first meeting of the singing festival for adults. Before two o'clock the chapel was filled to overflowing—there were many outside who failed to get in. Anyone

who chose could start the meeting. It began with an old friend of Glyn-dwr Richards—a friend who had long been faithful to drunkenness for years; but is now at the feet of Jesus Christ 'weeping very sweet tears of pure love' as a result of the Revival. Everyone is weeping—the conduc-tor devastated. This augured a remarkable afternoon—and that before the programme began. So it was. The dams broke. The floods flowed. The place was swimming. The conductor's attempts to keep things from going too far was defeated—he had to sit down and let people lead the festival themselves.

The next paragraph refers to an inspired *cymanfa ganu* ('singing fes-tival') at nearby Blaengarw:

The [afternoon] meeting began in the midst of the fire. It flamed in a second. Singing—never was heard the note that was heard here this afternoon—volume, strength, tenderness, sweetness, harmony, adora-tion—and all this inspired! During the meeting the conductor did try to rein us in a little and put a check on us for the sake of the evening ser-vice—lest we should destroy ourselves. It was of no use. They would listen only to the Spirit, and that clear, plain, fiery, audible, in the heart of the people. Girls are praying sorrowfully:– some swooning, some blanching, and paling, and others being transformed as they cried out ... Some were on their feet crying and shouting to heaven; at times everyone calling out at the same time. We became so unconscious of ourselves that we did not know what happened, what was said, or what was sung ...

This meeting was adjourned from 4.30 to 6. Singing was heard everywhere . . . Everyone settled down immediately for another voyage on the sea of the spirit. When the conductor began his work reverent fear ruled over the place—and we felt the veil between us and the spiritual had been torn open—we and the spiritual were naked in each other's presence. Quietness, Expectancy, Readiness . . .[30]

The remaining pages of David Hughes's book show further signs that a fire that had flamed forth in November 1904, after just one address from the revivalist, was still exerting a powerful influence on a large community in the following June, to the astonishment and anger of many.

No one will ever know how many little chapels tucked away in the smallest of mining communities had the same story to tell. For example, a little booklet entitled *Precious Jewels* contains the personal test-imony of Pastor Rees Evans of the Pen-y-groes Apostolic Church, near

Ammanford. In the village chapel the revival began with united prayer meetings to prepare the way of the Lord, meetings at which women prayed fervently and a staid old deacon 'shouted and praised with all his might'. The moving of the Spirit had an impact on the whole community.

Thus is recorded just one more glorious example of weeks in Wales that were just like the times recorded in the book of Acts. Truly it could be said that every valley was exalted and the rough places were made plain as the King of glory came in to his own (Isaiah 40:4); or in the words of the apostle Peter: 'The spirit of glory and of God resteth upon you' (1 Peter 4:14).

5

Revival Missions in Rural Wales

'They that were scattered abroad went every where
preaching the word'
(Acts 8:4)

Dr Eifion Evans has rightly drawn attention to the less publicized mission work that was developing on the west coast of Wales throughout 1904. It began after the three local conventions already described, and after a mission led by Seth Joshua of the Forward Movement of the Presbyterian Church of Wales.[1] The young people's work in the area around Cardigan became so fruitful that, in the latter part of the revival, some writers claimed that New Quay and not Loughor was the first centre of the awakening. *Y Cymro* ('The Welshman') and *The Cardigan & Tivyside Advertiser* picked up the scent early on; then religious newspapers, such as *Y Goleuad* ('The Torch') of 18 November, wrote about the young people who were spreading the revival fire in Cardiganshire and Carmarthenshire, and about the multitudes who were attending meetings. From these and other sources[2] and the composite volume of reports entitled *Y Diwygiad a'r Diwygwyr* ('The Revival and the Revivalists') it is possible to trace the progress of the work.

Joseph Jenkins said that it was soon after the first conventions for the quickening of spiritual life in churches that groups of young people began to meet for prayer in Cardigan and other towns. Soon they felt a call to witness in scores of little moorland villages. The oft-told incident of Evan Roberts, Sidney Evans and others putting a list of questions on a Bible in the Lord's presence and then waiting for instructions, belongs to this first period. It was then also that local Christians joined forces with the students. Here are two letters which breathe their ardent spirit:

DEAR MR. ROBERTS,

. . . When I read your letter last week, a thrill of joy filled my heart. It was a great joy for me to think that God had given you such a glorious message, and, also, that He had given you knowledge of its true nature, and strength to proclaim it.

We have remembered you in all our prayer meetings, and every morning and evening since this day week; and have asked our Heavenly Father to be with you. I believe he has already answered our prayers.

Work on my friend, and you will find that each day will bring you more work to do—for that is what we all ask for, is it not? Work! work! work! I cannot help thinking how wonderful our God is! However great or small is the work which He gives us to do, He never forgets to give us the necessary strength to carry it through. Sometimes I am filled with awe when I think of His wonderful love towards us; and sometimes He is so near to me, that I almost feel this world passing away, as it were, and I am lifted into a sphere where all is rest, peace, and happiness—no strife, no sin, nothing but peace. It does not last long. Oh, no! It is just one of those glimpses of Heaven which help us so much, and make all work for Jesus such a pleasant task. All the work for Him takes us nearer to Him. Every hour takes us along with it, and we know—do we not?—where it takes us. To Jesus, to His home, which he has prepared for us.

Good-bye, now, my friend in Jesus; and may He give you work unlimited to do for Him. Pray for me, and ask Him to give me more also, that I may glorify Him on this earth and hereafter. Some of the friends from New Quay have promised to come down fortnight to-morrow. Do you think that some of you from Newcastle-Emlyn will be able to come?

Yours very sincerely,
NELLIE EVANS.

DEAR MR. ROBERTS,

Thank you very much for your most kind letters. They were the means of giving me great joy.

We have commenced a young people's meeting in our chapel; and, indeed, I believe the Spirit of God will put this little church on fire some day. A great number of our young people have gone on their knees before their Redeemer . . .

Oh, that we could do more for Him! We, poor wretched creatures, being able to do something for Him! What an honour, after what He did on our behalf!

Pray for me.

I am,
Your friend in Christ,
ELSIE PHILLIPS.[3]

Only Florrie Evans could speak of visions and messages, yet there was a 'still small voice' which turned young women like Maud Davies and Elsie and May Phillips into bold witnesses.

Florrie Evans's sudden word of testimony in New Quay in February 1904 had a great effect on her chapel. A faithful attender of her chapel's *seiat* (fellowship meeting), she often told of a time in her life when she was in need of help:

> Do you know that I would sometimes tire of life; time was a burden to me, and many times I thought, Why do people talk of eternity—time overwhelms me; but, thanks be, I now know what to do with eternity.[4]

R. R. Davies tells how a visit by Florrie Evans to Joseph Jenkins's house one Sunday evening earlier in February was to prove an important turning-point for her:

> While having supper that evening, someone knocked at the door, and the young girl, Miss Florrie Evans, . . . came into the house for the first time ever. For a long time both sat in silence, because she utterly failed to say what was on her mind. 'I was waiting for you in the lobby,' she said, 'hoping you would say something to me, but you didn't. I went out, and again I came to meet you on your way home, but you took no notice, except to say 'Goodnight'. I have been walking up and down in front of the house for half an hour, and I had to call. The matter of my soul is almost killing me. I cannot live like this. I saw the world in the sermon tonight. I am under its feet. Help me!' After some conversation Mr Jenkins asked her, 'Can you say "My Lord" to Jesus Christ?' 'No. I understand it,' she said, 'but I cannot say it. I don't know what He will ask me to do. Something very difficult perhaps.' 'Yes, oh yes', said the minister, 'He does ask difficult things—it is a narrow gate that leads to the peace and joy of the gospel.'[5]

In *Y Cylchgrawn Efengylaidd* ('The Evangelical Magazine') for September/October 1949, Robert Ellis tells how Joseph Jenkins acknowledged to him that God had used Florrie to help deliver him from self and philosophy. It seems that one evening in October 1904 she interrupted his sermon and began to sing 'Just as I am', until by the last verse he was on his knees, slain, singing 'O Lamb of God, I come.'

On the evening of her public confession of Christ in February 1904, she told her pastor that the Holy Spirit had compelled her to testify. Soon people realized that whenever she prayed or prophesied, she was truly in the Spirit. Before long she was to become a familiar figure in the churches of South Cardiganshire, and later her activities were to spread to North Cardiganshire also. Then she and Maud Davies went with her pastor on a wonderfully fruitful tour of north-west Wales. Florrie wept often, prayed fervently to the God of purity, truth and righteousness, and testified to that which God revealed to her. Maud sang gospel songs and recited portions of Scripture. One also hears of them taking services in the towns of Clwyd, sometimes on their own.

May Phillips was a gentle girl who stayed with the local groups going to tiny, rural chapels to pray, testify and plead with farmers and shepherds:

> The meeting when Miss May Phillips—a young girl sweet in person and voice—rose to her feet and addressed a crowd for the first time ever, was one to be remembered always. 'Oh!' she said again and again; 'Oh! I would love to tell. I just cannot,' then she paused. 'I've been failing to pray for months,' she said. 'O, it was hard; but since last night I am able to pray as much as I like—the door is wide open. Oh! let us sing, "Dewch hen ac ieuanc—dewch at Iesu, mae'n llawn bryd" ['Come old and young—come to Jesus, for it is high time'].' And in prayer she said, 'Oh! thanks be for mercy; mercy to a great sinner like me. Thanks! thou art, great Jesus, a great Saviour. Make me clean, make me pure. Thou canst not make a great one out of me—I am a little one. Make me pure, bright—a little pearl shining brightly in your blessed crown.' And as they went home, women and girls were to be heard saying to each other, 'What's that girl talking about sinning—what does a fine little creature like that know about sin?' An irreligious young man said, as he saw her passing by, 'Isn't she a beautiful girl? She always was beautiful; but she is finding something in that chapel lately that has made her like an angel.' In New Quay there was an excellent craftsman with a large family, but who was a hopeless drunkard. He was taken in hand by May Phillips, and his story is almost miraculous.[6]

Leaving New Quay, a cradle of revival, we can see how the missions spread. The two Cardiganshire newspapers traced the activity towards the end of 1904 when they were moving further afield. The first report comes from Llangrannog:

> The revival movement is expanding in the [Llangrannog] neighbourhood. During the past week, the number of special revival meetings increased in number. On Monday night, there was a crowded meeting at Capel Ffynon, where, accompanied by two brakefulls of young men and

women from Capel Drindod, had come the Rev. R. Rhystyd Davies. The meeting was conducted on the lines of the 'Evan Roberts' meetings. On Tuesday, both Llangranog and Capel Granog had their own revival meetings. On Thursday, another crowded meeting was held at Penmorfa and on Wednesday night, the Baptist Chapel, 'Capel Gwndwn,' was full, co-religionists from Llwyndafydd and New Quay having come to their assistance. The meeting was characterised with much fervour.[7]

The journalist in the *Cardigan & Tivyside Advertiser* mentions processions and open-air witness and expressed his own belief that 'new times are dawning on our Saviour's church'. Joint services became common at Cardigan and other towns, but the idea also took root in some villages further south.

News came in from Nevern in North Pembrokeshire that the Anglican church's preparatory services for Holy Communion had been marked by unction and fervour, and by the repeated singing of favourite revival hymns. Exciting news came that the leaders of a Calvinistic Methodist chapel had actually proposed joint prayer meetings with the Anglicans during Christmas week. At Cilgerran, a number of farmers and workers came down from the mountain to witness and join in the remarkable events.[8]

The hillside villages between Fishguard and Cilgerran were also much blessed. One Baptist correspondent, writing on the revival at Hermon and Star, proudly reported:

I have great pleasure in announcing that the divine and redeeming influences have visited these parts of the country. The visitation is so mighty that it has awakened the church from her sleepiness, and caused new voices to be heard in praise and prayer. It is appropriate to say of Zion in these days: 'The time of the singing of birds is come, and the voice of the turtle is heard in our land' [Song of Solomon 2:12] . . . The prayer-meetings have continued for months in their enthusiasm and popularity. The brethren and the sisters take part fervently in them. And everyone who attends them feels that it is good to be there—'That the Lord is in our midst and blessing us.' The church grows remarkably in beauty as she attends the Throne of grace; religious virtues come, lovely and attractive, into view, as flowers in the world of nature open in the warmth of a gentle spring. The old and young listeners are coming into Zion these days. Let the church persevere with her God at the throne if she is to continue to beautify, and accomplish her work among the converts. Though the great work of revival places a great responsibility on the church, the church with God is more than sufficient for the task.[9]

Of Star, the correspondent continues:

The influences of the Spirit have been felt in great measure in the church at Star. A series of successful prayer-meetings have been held in this church . . . and have received evident and unquestionable signs of Heaven's favour among them, through the building up of the church and the salvation of souls.[10]

The response of the Baptists of the area to the revival was initially very cautious. The editor of the local Baptist journal, *Y Piwritan Newydd* ('The New Puritan'), expressed the hope in January 1905 that the missions would lead to greater faithfulness, liberality, sobriety and brotherly love, although he also stated that he could not go along with the mode of activity in some meetings. An editorial in February began by saying that some did not agree with the revival meetings in the churches in the area because they felt there ought to be more fruit visible in their lives before embarking on such meetings. However, the editor argued that there was a need for sowing before reaping and that one could not expect fruit before sowing. He admitted that converts were coming together because of a desire for holiness and that there was therefore no need to fear the Holy Spirit's influences. Nevertheless, the cautious spirit had not entirely vanished. 'We cannot expect to see in rural churches the things we read about in the towns and industrial areas,' he said.

They were soon proved wrong as the revival reached those places and consumed villages and towns alike in its flames. The February issue of *Y Piwritan Newydd* contains reports by correspondents of revival in Maenclochog, Ffynnon, Llanfyrnach and Fishguard. Then we have this report from Login in the March issue:

Sometimes we were discouraged by the thought that the taste of religious people inclines to light and worthless things, the youth of our churches patronizing improper places and the reading and study of the Bible neglected. But this anxiety has been removed and the prayer-meetings given a place of honour. Is not this of God?[11]

Events on the southern slopes of the Prescelly Hills were mainly covered by the South Pembrokeshire newspapers, which were generally sympathetic. The *Haverfordwest & Milford Haven Telegraph* provides some interesting descriptions of the revival in those parts. Here were districts that Evan Roberts and other revivalists did not visit until Dan Roberts, Evan's brother, went several months after the initial outbreak. However, the Holy Spirit was there in a great flood which swept through churches, and broke down the stout stone walls of tradition, prejudice, suspicion and exclusivism.

Neyland, Sardis, Sutton and Milford Haven were among the places that came under the influence of the Spirit:

1. Neyland

There has been one topic of conversation in Neyland during the past week, and that is the revival. Every year it has been customary to hold a week of 'united prayer' in the town, but these meetings were seldom attended by more than between thirty and forty people. This year, however, people have flocked to them in their hundreds, with the result that when the services were last week conducted at some of the smaller chapels chairs had to be placed along the aisles and in every available space in the buildings. So great was the press that it has now been decided to hold the meetings in the Baptist Chapel, much the largest building in the town, which is capable of seating 600 people . . . Up to the present the converts number about 85, and at the next communion service over 40 new members will be received into the fellowship of the Baptist Chapel.

Notwithstanding these remarkable results, the Rev. B. C. Evans does not think that meetings in Neyland have yet reached 'revival point.' But Mr Evans speaks in a relative sense. He has witnessed those remarkable revival meetings which have been held in other parts of Wales, where people are more emotional and possibly more enthusiastic by temperament.

Most of the converts in Neyland are young men and maidens who have been brought up in the atmosphere of the Sunday School.

2. Sardis

Some three weeks ago the churches at Sardis and Hill Mountain joined hands to hold a series of revival meetings . . . and the great success attending them has surpassed one's keenest imagination—meetings going on until a late hour under the unction and guidance of the Holy Spirit; prayer, praise and song rolling like mighty waves heavenward; women speaking and praying; children starting choruses; young men and women, husbands and their wives standing up for Christ . . . Already there are from 25 to 30 candidates for baptism. The Lord is doing wonderful things. 'Diolch Iddo.' ['Thanks be to Him.']

3. Sutton

Special revival meetings . . . were continued throughout the whole week. The attendance was exceptionally good, the chapel being full every night, and although there was no fiery burst of enthusiasm, the meetings were pervaded with fervour, reverence, and deep religious feeling. Every one was at full liberty to worship God in the way he or she felt inclined, and doubtless it is to this we are to attribute much of the readiness and freeness with which those present took part.

4. Milford

It was again reserved for Rehoboth on Thursday to entertain the crowning meetings of the whole series. The power in the service was most marked, there was no excitement, but a holy calm seemed to pervade the sacred precincts. Christian men and women prayed earnestly for the outpouring and they did not plead in vain, for several sought the Saviour at the close.

From Haverfordwest comes the following account:

Quite a big crowd met on the Castle Square about seven o'clock, where a short and impressive service was held, during which exhortations to repentance were made with great earnestness. The procession then wandered its way to the Bethesda Chapel, where a service lasting until 10 o'clock was conducted by the Rev O. D. Campbell. Mr Campbell is not the most emotional, though he is certainly a very inspiring speaker; but on Wednesday night he seemed to have been carried away. Earnestly and passionately did he plead with those who had not yet made a public confession of Christ. He announced the unspeakable joy it would give him to see men and women he had known for so long come forward and make a declaration before the eyes of men. Old hymns which had touched many a tender chord in days gone by were sung to familiar tunes, and repeated over and over again each time with greater fervency and spirit.

One of the most remarkable and at the same time, most hopeful feature of the meeting was the part which the young men of the town took in it. Several of these got up and prayed with all the fluency of practised public speakers; others gave their experiences; and others again struck up with a melodious tune, the congregation heartily joined in the refrain. It was everybody's meeting—anyone who felt the spirit move him to rise took part in it . . .

Prayers were offered for the salvation of Haverfordwest and for those who were still unrepentant and strangers to the Divine Love.

Several speakers declared their conviction that Haverfordwest was on the eve of a big religious revival—that the heart of the town was at last being touched.[12]

Revival events in the districts north of Aberystwyth get very scant mention in the *Cambrian News* except on those occasions when student groups went out witnessing 'on trek' from Aberystwyth. One of the revival reports printed in *Y Diwygiad a'r Diwygwyr* was written by a Port Talbot minister, Moses Thomas, about Pontrhydfendigaid. He arrived one stormy evening and found the congregation praying eagerly, triumphing openly, pleading brokenheartedly for relatives and sometimes rejoicing at yet another family reconciliation.[13]

Reports by those who were present are rare and therefore it is fortunate that a lecture given by one veteran saint to his chapel society at Rehoboth Chapel, Tre Taliesin, has been preserved at the National Library of Wales. He told them what happened in the Christmas holidays of 1904 in a little village, now bypassed by the main road from Aberystwyth to Machynlleth. On the Sunday night before Christmas, someone had recounted the story of the revival in Blaenau Ffestiniog:

> Brother David Reed was there and it seems likely that the story aroused and awakened him. On the morning of Christmas Day (which was a Monday) David Reed came to our house. It was easy to gather from his discourse that he had been possessed by the spirit of the great stirring. He wanted more of the story from my brother; he was yearning for the revival to break out here also. He told us that he had been praying to God to visit this district with an outpouring of the Holy Spirit and that he had been given a very clear vision that very morning, while praying in the garden. He had seen this vestry open and the place lit up and people crowding in and the seats full, and that it was going to happen that very night. It is likely that the meeting we had on Christmas night was the fulfilment of that vision.
>
> *Tuesday evening* the young people gathered in the same place and adopted the same procedure of going through the village and singing as on the previous night, then back to the vestry by 7.00 p.m. where a great congregation was awaiting. They had an astonishing meeting; several brothers and sisters took part, some reading a portion of Scripture and then bursting out into song. We had the sensation that some mighty powers were moving to and fro through the meeting. The meeting went on late. Time was of no account. The clock was paid no attention at the time.

It was amazing how the district was changed, as if in a twinkling, into a prayerful district, and very soon we saw an inward awakening within the church. Meetings went on every night, with more coming in, and the tide reaching higher and higher each night . . . That was a fine and happy time for the church—a time when earth was raised up to the heavens and the heavens were descending. There was much traffic between heaven and earth at that period. The meetings went on for weeks. No need to announce a meeting at the beginning of the year. Everyone was keeping an eye out for every service. There was a heavenly feeling about every one of the meetings—a nuance hard to describe—yet it was easy to understand that God was in truth visiting His people.

This district was second to none. As I have told you, there were in this place about seven sisters who had begun to take part, and these persevered, and they were excellent people on their knees. There was no scarcity of people praying at that time.

Prayer was offered on behalf of many that they might receive strength to turn from the error of their ways to the Lord. (Some frequented taverns and the drink had got the upper hand over them.) It was bliss to see such prayers being answered directly and to see them coming to the meeting and then on their knees, beseeching God to forgive them and asking for His strength to follow henceforth. And from then on they were in the meetings consistently and taking part and were of great usefulness in the chapel.

We had a party from Seilo, Aberystwyth, who came here as if to water the visitation but somehow it did not work. Some were singing, praying and testifying, etc. Everyone went home for food after it was announced that there would be a meeting later. We had a very blessed meeting and everyone was in a worshipping spirit. I saw one of the children of the church who had been set aflame and was on his feet praying and, oblivious to all, was going up and down and along the aisle. Another was praying across him. That is how it was to start with, then followed the singing. There was no need to ask then, 'Ble'r aeth yr Amen?' ['Where has the Amen gone?'] That came natural. Another shouted 'Ar ei ben bo'r goron' ['The crown be on His head'] and 'Diolch Iddo' ['Thanks be to Him']. Thus the meetings went on—no calling on anyone but just as they were being prompted by the Holy Spirit . . .

A few Sundays after the revival began, the Rev. John Owen, Tai-hirion & Rhos, was preaching here. He was considered a great preacher and after he had begun to warm to his subject, there was many a 'Diolch

Iddo' and an 'Amen' to be heard. Eventually someone stood on his feet to pray, and that was the end of the sermon that morning . . . We had a prayer-meeting that afternoon instead of Sunday school and also a prayer-meeting before the Sunday evening service, for a yearning after prayer had taken possession of the land at the time . . .

A young-people's meeting was held at the time alternatively in Tre'r-ddôl; some there had also felt great things. We had a number of memorable meetings and which have surely been a strength to face life's journey. All these meetings lasted almost through the summer . . . It's true they became infrequent yet for quite a time we could still hear the echoes of revival. For example, when the time came for the Thanksgiving Services there was no shortage of people to pray there. Everyone was praising God with great zeal and the influences, the great things they had experienced during the winter, were visible in all the services—morning, afternoon, and evening at that time . . . The church didn't increase numerically but was deepened spiritually . . . Let us pray that the powers will come to work on us again as a land.[14]

From the most rural and remote areas of north-west Wales the reports of revival meetings are even more sparse. However, one does come across reports of revival meetings in places such as Dolgellau and Towyn. There is a strong probability that theological college students through their normal preaching engagements were extending the revival influence into this whole area. Sources furnish numerous examples of revival influences emanating from the various colleges in the Principality.

The students at Aberystwyth were deeply stirred after a visit to the town by the highly respected Joseph Jenkins. The experience turned some of the students into evangelists.

R. B. Jones did not identify the theological college where the students suddenly sank to their knees with their tutor during a lecture. Nor did he name the university college where, during a casual discussion of the reality of the revival, someone said, 'I should like to feel as some of those saved people feel':

After a moment's awkward pause someone started a hymn. Then came prayer, and then some more hymn-singing, the sound of which reached the other students, with the result that lectures were 'cut' right and left. The smoke-room became packed; a Revival meeting was soon in full swing. Later, a procession of hundreds, mostly students—men and women—formed and marched through the streets with very remarkable results.[15]

However this could well have been the university college at Bangor. The editor of a Calvinistic Methodist newspaper recalled vividly what happened at that college. A philosophy lecture had been disturbed by the sound of singing. At the close of the lecture he was greeted with the news, 'The Revival has broken out.' On asking where, he was told, 'In the smoke-room':

> Now I understood the explanation of the sound of singing which I had heard during the lecture in our Professor's room. Away we both went up the stairs and along the corridor to a door at its far end that opened to the smoke-room. We could go no further than the door for the room was full to overflowing. About forty or fifty people were present . . .
> When I arrived they were singing:

> > '*O! yr Oen, yr addfwyn Oen*' . . .
> > ['Oh! the Lamb, the gentle Lamb.']

> No one was leading the meeting. No one was leading the singing. But one hymn followed another and one boy followed another in prayer and petition in a completely orderly manner, and this made one remember the account of the descent of the Holy Spirit at Pentecost in Jerusalem.
> If there was a human leader at all, that was 'H. K.', and it was said that it was his starting to pray that morning in the smoke-room that caused the dam to burst . . .
> Hugh and Tom, along with others of their fellow-students, especially those who, like them, were Philosophy students, had been very critical of the Revival. Day after day they read in the newspapers about the Revival in the South and about the way it was sweeping men off their feet. 'It was all naked emotionalism!' . . .
> Suddenly [Hugh] leapt to his feet, waving his hands in the air, and pouring out an intense sort of prayer, in an almost unearthly voice. I do not remember hardly any of what he said, but I know he was confessing his coldness, his critical attitude and spirit . . .
> The meeting went on until about mid-day, if not longer. Then, about two o'clock in the afternoon, without anyone, as far as I know, arranging or announcing, a great number of the students, men and women, came to a large lecture room called the 'New Hall' . . . According to my memory almost all the seats were taken, with about 120 to 150 present.
> Again there was no one leading, but everything went on exactly as though there was a leader . . . I believe it would be impossible to

explain, without believing that some Spirit greater than that of any individual, indeed, greater than that of all this group of young people, had
possessed us . . .

I do not rightly know exactly what spiritual endowment I received
[through the powerful stirrings of 1904-6] but I know for certain that
my intellectual pride and self-confidence received such a wound that
they never recovered from it.[16]

The Welsh Baptist newspaper *Seren Cymru* ('The Star of Wales')
has a long account of the visit of W. S. Jones from Llwynypia in the
Rhondda to Bangor for a fortnight of revival meetings from 13 to 24
February 1905. He spoke powerfully about forgiveness and about divine
love which, he said, compelled everyone to give out and go out.[17] This
was certainly true of the students who began open-air work and visitation and tried to take food and clothing to the poorest districts, and
eventually ran missions at Penrallt and Kyffin Square for compassionate
purposes.

Bala Theological College was situated in the centre of rural North
Wales and overlooked what was then a thriving market town by the
lovely Bala Lake. This is what happened there on a weekend near the
end of autumn term:

It was hardly to be expected that Bala, the Jerusalem of Wales, was to
be uninfluenced by the great wave of religious feeling that has come
over Wales. There are some seventy students in Bala this year and they,
together with the most earnestly-minded men of the town, were gladdened at the news received through the newspapers of the wonderful
results in South Wales and at Rhos, in North Wales. A desire arose that
God's arm might be similarly laid bare at Bala. It was among the students, then, primarily that revival broke out at Bala. A fortnight ago
prayer meetings were held at the College and last Saturday week something unusual was felt stirring the hearts of the students. After the usual
prayer meeting on the Monday night following, when glowing accounts
were given of the work at Rhos, it was decided to hold prayer-meetings
every afternoon throughout the week. At first these meetings were dis-
appointing, but on Friday afternoon at three o'clock the heavens were
opened and it was remembered that it was on Friday afternoon at the
same hour that another victory was won, of which this Diwygiad
[Revival] is such a notable result. At the end of this meeting there was a
spontaneous wish on the part of all present to hold another meeting in
the evening to convey to others the heavenly vision vouchsafed in the

afternoon. Before the meeting the students en masse paraded the streets singing and inviting and this was one of the most wonderful things seen in the student life of Bala—to see young men who a week before would have shuddered at the very idea of marching heedless of taunts. The spacious schoolroom of Capel Mawr [Big Chapel] was soon filled to its utmost capacity. The curiosity which evidently brought most of the people together, soon gave way under the fervent singing and earnest prayers to an intense seriousness. From that evening there has hardly been any abatement of enthusiasm. Those who were present at the meeting of the young people of Capel Mawr on Sunday night will carry with them to their grave an indelible memory of the remarkable things felt there. One young man had a vision of Christ that was so powerfully real that he broke out into the most fervent soul-stirring prayers ever heard and as he exclaimed 'O! Rwyt Ti'n glws' ['Oh! how beautiful Thou art'], sobs and half-suppressed cries could be heard throughout the room. The students felt themselves being so irresistibly constrained to continue this work that their ordinary duties had to be laid aside and in the face of this the College Senate have decided to defer the usual terminal examinations which were to come on next week till next term . . . Bala is veritably in the grip of the Spirit, and stranger things are yet expected.[18]

It seems appropriate at this point, before entering into the main spheres of revival power in North Wales, to consider the vision and activities of that large and indeterminate body known as the 'Christian Workers'. This unique company included some of the converted students who had taken part in the initial activity, such as processions, but who had gone on to 'attempt great things for God'. Now they were prepared to work humbly and cheerfully alongside converts from all walks of life in order to spread the flames of revival.

6

The Young Christian Workers

'Go out into the highways and hedges, and compel them
to come in, that my house may be filled'
(Luke 14:23)

The idealism, energy and self-sacrifice of some groups of converts have never been given their proper due. Those who helped 'seekers' at the revival meetings drew attention as they knelt and struggled with desperate sinners, and naturally the press made much of those who sang or spoke from the front pew or platform, but there were others who obeyed the revivalist's call to costly obedience by going outside as prompted by the Spirit. A number of small groups went out, in their own words, 'hunting and fishing'. They were not organized or led by church officers and were not always encouraged or even liked. There is such a narrow dividing line between these improvised groups invading some street or square and the well-organized bands that they are considered together in this chapter.

Why did so many of these ardent youths plunge almost at once into the work of evangelism? Awstin told a humorous story of a young collier who stood up in the chapel gallery, took off his jacket, and threw it on a seat, declaring that he was ready for work, because Evan Roberts had 'appealed for active workers in the Churches'. Evan Roberts had declared that 'God does not want idle people. "Are you not prepared," he asked, "to take off your coats?" '[1]

The motive that bound these young men and women and made them so bold was a passion for souls. This was the dynamic which stirred the Christian Workers into action. An early example comes from Gorseinon where, according to Miss Hughes, a group of young people, including the five singers, left a Sunday afternoon meeting and went out to the gipsy encampment on Kingsbridge Common where some of the women were brought to repentance. Others chose to go out to nearby villages,

101

from Gower in the south to Llandeilo in the north. Others witnessed in the towns and were soon engaged in stern battle, as Mr Webb could testify:

> Open-air meetings were held in every street every Saturday night for years. The saved would assemble at Seion, High Street, for an hour's prayer before appearing on the steps outside. At that time there was very little traffic, so people assembled on the road to hear the gospel preached. Much blessing came from these meetings. In one case there was a drunken man in the midst of the crowd and he was always in opposition. After much prayer on his behalf he at last repented and believed and changed sides and joined the company of believers and testified . . .
>
> We were storming the force of sin and we were trying to gain an entrance to the Mardy Hotel one night when we were met by pints of beer thrown over us. After a while the drinking bars were empty and the publicans were born again.
>
> I well remember during an open-air meeting in Lower Lime Street, Gorseinon, with the Rev. M. J. Jones speaking, a certain man was standing on his doorstep. He rushed through the ring and gripped the speaker with both hands round his throat, trying to choke him. With much difficulty we released Mr Jones from his clutches.[2]

Mr Webb was himself caught by the throat and threatened with violence at work after he had named five of his workmates as being in particular need of prayer.

Penar Griffiths described his church activists when hard at work and facing some risk during late-night meetings:

> We moved out to the front of the chapel by the roadside leading from the town. Here we caught gangs of young men coming home from the dens there, and held them until 1.30 in the morning, and some of the ringleaders confessed Christ.
>
> . . . We had great meetings on the street-corner near the public-house. Once we were sent away by a policeman who said we were out too late singing hymns and disturbing people in their beds. But we surmised it was a complaint from the publican, which proved to be the case. However we yielded, and for succeeding nights we had nothing like the meetings we had previously experienced. Some one suggested that it was because we had so yielded, and that if we dared once more, the Lord would amply bless. We did, and such was the case.[3]

Freystrop, near Milford Haven, is a remote and placid village normally, but one day it was invaded:

> The young men of the church are filled with a profound passion for the salvation of souls, and the pastor, the Rev. Jenkyn James, says he has never witnessed anything like it. Not satisfied with their efforts in the chapel, a band of young men held a meeting on Sunday night on Freystrop Cross . . . two more converts—one of whom was on the verge of 70—came forward at the open-air service. On Monday night, in spite of the bitterly cold weather, there was a large gathering in the chapel, whole families being present.[4]

Out of this great pool of bold, earnest witnesses were drawn those who would form the trained bands of Christian Workers who travelled further.

Meanwhile a new society had been formed by J. Cynog Williams, a minister at Aberdare. It was called 'Diwygwyr Cristionogol' ('Christian Reformers'), and was composed of total abstainers and anti-smokers who could enter the taverns and houses of ill-fame without danger to their persons or their reputations. The activities of Cynog Williams's team at Maerdy in the Rhondda had led to no less than five hundred converts being recorded in that district before Evan Roberts's visit there on 11 December 1904.[5] Each member of this organization took this solemn vow:

> I pledge myself in the strength of the Holy Ghost by entering into a covenant with God to fully consecrate my life to Christ, my King and my God, to confess Him before the world whenever I have opportunity to do so, and to deny myself all things which tend to lessen my personal influence in His service.[6]

There were also mission bands who travelled out from Ammanford to Llandeilo and Ystalyfera. In early December it was reported that a party of revivalists from Pontarddulais near Swansea, led by a student from Llanrwst in North Wales, had visited Bethesda Chapel in nearby Llangennech. There young women sang hymns and testified fervently in the face of a cold, critical reception. Nantlais Williams took a band of young people into the Dynevor Arms at Pantyffynnon, Ammanford, and the young girls with him fell on their knees in front of the bar in fervent prayer. One man threw his beer into the fireplace; others walked out; a few joined in the prayers. They were less polite at Llanelli when a procession halted outside the New Inn and began prayers. The reporter says that the inmates came out and offered them beer and that a girl came out and danced an Irish jig, after which 'water was thrown over them from a top window'.[7]

Many of these Christian Worker groups showed enterprise as well as courage and faith. At Bridgend on 19 November, writes Awstin, when Evan Roberts, followed by prominent laymen and ministers, had gone on to Pyle:

> Shortly after two o'clock in the afternoon there stood at the side door of the [Town-]hall two young men and five young ladies singing the touching lines:–
>
> > 'Calon lan yn llawn daioni,
> > Perffaith fel y lili dlos;
> > Dim ond calon lan all ganu,
> > Canu'r dydd a chanu'r nos.'
>
> > ['A clean heart full of goodness,
> > Perfect like the lovely lily;
> > Only a clean heart can sing,
> > Sing all day and sing all night.']

> I entered, and found the Town-hall absolutely empty, but I was quickly followed by the singers, and gradually by people from the street, and to hear and see the service that was conducted by these young people, alone and unaided—except as they were, as they prayed, 'directed by the Spirit'—was a sight which I shall never forget.[8]

One evening after the chapel prayer-meetings, some young men gathered on the square near the Cynlais Stores in Ystradgynlais at 10 p.m., and began to sing hymns 'over the now quiet village'. A crowd gathered around. Instead of protesting at the noise many residents left their beds and went to join the meeting, 'which was by this time in a ferment of feeling'. No one worried about the early morning shift!

A huge procession was then formed, and the people made their way to Sardis Vestry, singing as they went their favourite hymns. The vestry was reached at about 11 o'clock.

The meeting in a few minutes was again ablaze, young men and women praying, singing and repeating their favourite hymns with indescribable intensity of feeling. Prayers were offered for brothers, husbands and friends, whose names were mentioned.[9]

The bolder spirits were prepared to sing revival hymns at the exit gates of sports grounds. Braver still were those who visited lodging-houses. These were warmly praised by David Matthews, himself a well-known evangelist:

> They flung boundless energy into the work, holding nothing back. Their youthful minds having been saturated with Holy Writ during the years of Scripture training in the Sunday school, they were enabled to express their thoughts intelligently and scripturally in prayer or testimony as they were led or impelled by the Spirit of God . . . Into the lodging houses went the groups to sing or pray, exhorting and encouraging the most abandoned to 'come to Jesus' . . . Young women, beautifully dressed, knelt with vagabonds of the road who had casually turned in for a night's lodging. They pleaded with them to 'turn from the error of their ways' to Christ, 'the new and living way' . . . As these young people knelt on dirty, dusty floors, surrounded by banana skins, orange peelings, cigarette butts, newspaper scraps, hardened toast-rinds and egg shells, praying for these callous wanderers, the unkempt room seemed to be filled with the glory of God.[10]

As the church leaders and ministers ceased to go out with the converts on such missions, people tended to form unattached teams such as that in Pontypridd—Mr John and Miss M. J. Jones, Miss Lizzie Lloyd, and Mr David Daniel.[11] Soon the denominational leaders were demanding that they be formally organized. Chapel officials in South Wales began to attack their methods. No doubt the same fate overtook the teams who evangelized the villages of Clwyd.

It was after a visit to Dr Torrey's mission in Liverpool that Clwyd converts decided they ought to have special meetings, or some means of training for outreach. Typical of the results of this preparation was the following incident, described by W. S. Jones of Rhos:

> At the invitation of a person from Bwlch-gwyn, a number of young men from Rhos went there on Tuesday afternoon. They were given access to the Congregational chapel, and a short Prayer-Meeting was held there. Subsequently those who had gathered moved out, and a procession was formed. They walked through the streets and made a halt on a suitable corner . . . Though the young men attempted to go home in time for the evening meeting in Rhos, they were not allowed to go. The largest chapel in the place was opened up, and in a short time it was crowded out. One of those lads from Rhos took charge, and though there were

many older than he there, and several church officers, he led the service himself. He delivered a fervent address, and raised his hearers to a very high pitch. He said afterwards that he did not know what he was saying, but he felt he was given unusual powers. The only thing he was conscious of was the congregation shouting 'Amen' and 'Bendigedig' ['Blessed'], 'Diolch Iddo' ['Thanks be to Him'], &c. Truly the prayer of the brother in Capel Mawr ['Big Chapel'] on Monday evening on behalf of Bwlch-gwyn had been answered and as a result the whole place has been roused, and the divine fire is burning high there.[12]

There are far fewer signs of Christian Worker teams in Gwynedd where the more conservative North Walians would do nothing more than adapt the old Easter and Whitsun processions into a vehicle of evangelism. But there is mention of a group holding open-air meetings at the Old Cross, Holyhead, and another band witnessing in Caernarfon under the aegis of a united committee of young people.[13]

Students proved to be a great asset because of their sound grasp of the Bible, and especially because of their cheerful, tireless enthusiasm. It is commonplace today to use students as counsellors, stewards, singers and open-air workers. Then it was a novelty because Town and Gown simply did not mix. This was especially true of theological students, who lived secluded lives. It is therefore interesting to be reminded of the story of the 'Bangor Eight', as told to the author by D. C. Griffiths, one of the members of the group, later a minister at Aberduar, near Lampeter:

It was during a visit of the Rev. W. S. Jones of Tonypandy that we were first challenged and disturbed as he called us to obedience and consecration. Eventually a small group—W. J. Rees, Evan Williams, Morgan Jones, Llwchwr Jones and myself—became even more concerned. Then one of our Bangor students was influenced by revival meetings in South Wales and he brought back the news, 'Something worth having is there.' Later on we heard that R. B. Jones was conducting a mission in Anglesey after coming from Rhos—and it was assumed that it would be at Holyhead.

A party of six of us took the train to Gaerwen Junction to make enquiries. Fortunately we met David Lloyd coming back from Holyhead, who told us to go with him to Llannerch-y-medd. In the compartment we decided to leave the train at Llangefni and to hold a meeting in the market-square. We had an on-the-spot meeting which was so fervent that Will Rees had to be interrupted because the next train was drawing in. In the square at Llangefni a fountain with a ledge was used as a pulpit.

As we sang, the crowds left shop and stall and listened to Evan Williams who was testifying how his father's prayers for him had been answered and how the prodigal son had come home.

We left the now silent crowd and travelled on to Llannerch-y-medd. There David Lloyd ushered us into a shop where the Rev. R. B. Jones was sitting all alone in the middle room. 'Hallelujah!' he cried, 'The Lord has answered prayer. I have been asking him to give me some helpers.' In next to no time the people of Llannerch-y-medd had found lodgings for us; two of us stayed with Mr and Mrs Sturdy, the parents of Mrs Tecwyn Evans. We found ourselves staying the week without our Principal's knowledge or consent.

The chapels were full and practically everyone surrendered to Christ in the prayer-time even though R. B. Jones insisted on preaching at every service. When he preached one Friday afternoon on the need to give up everything doubtful, even smoking, a shower of pipes and pouches fell from the gallery into the pulpit. One student also, W. J. Rees, handed them from the big seat into R. B.'s low pulpit, and at once R. B. gave him his blessing upon his entry into the ministry. One thing I cannot forget is a nineteen-year-old youth from a bad home who joined us and became an effective prayer-warrior. He had a voice like a lark; a radiant face and language most beautiful.

R. B. Jones asked to see us students by ourselves in the vestry of the Baptist chapel and he spoke to us about assurance of faith. 'Believe you are saved, then confess it.' His last act at Llannerch-y-medd was to ask all the young people whose hearts had been touched, to meet in the vestry. Three hundred turned up at this service of dedication. Mr Jones spoke of how Elijah had prepared the altar and the sacrifice so that everything was ready and waiting for the fire. Then he said, 'You have been touched; you have thought it over; you have given yourself to the Lord. Now I pray that the Holy Ghost will come.' All prayed and sang and promised total obedience.

Meanwhile our Principal had sent Tom Bassett, late of Blaen-rhondda, to bring us home—but he got infected by the excitement and he actually danced his way into a pew . . . Two or three students went on to Amlwch where R. B. Jones preached on Isaiah 6. As usual we gave prayer support and we helped those under conviction . . . After Amlwch they moved to Llangefni on Thursday, which was market day. R. B. Jones held a meeting in the Market Hall which was full even at midday. He spoke about the God who protests against the drunkenness of the Rhondda, but who also protests against the immorality of Anglesey. Principal Silas Morris was now there and he asked us students

107

to stay behind. He said, 'Come back to college now and we can make arrangements if a church wants you.'[14]

All these testimonies and first-hand reports have given some idea of what the Christian Workers hoped to achieve. It was not a long-lasting episode and may not have been as effective in the long run as direct church-based evangelism of the kind described in a later chapter.

There is a remarkable story of team witness conducted by Welsh students who were based at Spurgeon's College in London, but whose hearts were set on fire while they were home for Christmas and saw the work of the Spirit. One of the six students, Caradoc Jones, lived at Rhosllannerchrugog. According to a letter written from Brittany where he served as a missionary, it seems that in January 1905 all six students were invited by the Principal to tell of what they had seen and heard of the fire during the Christmas vacation:

> I did, and the fire burned and the Principal thereupon said he would go and see the Rev. Thomas Spurgeon of the Tabernacle to ask him if he would like to have the Welsh students to conduct Revival meetings in the Tabernacle and he placed the matter before his Deacons and Elders.
>
> On the first night the basement Hall, which held a thousand, was too crowded and the great Tabernacle had to be opened. Crowds came every night and conversions took place every night for three weeks, and midnight meetings were held, being heralded by the Revs Thomas and Charles Spurgeon, Dr McCaig, Profs Hackney and Gensen, and all the students marching around the Elephant and Castle [district] to call in the lost and fallen.
>
> Four of the Welsh students formed the Welsh Quartette and sang and preached, while the other two preached only. The results were: over 800 conversions—a greater number, it was said, than during any other Evangelical mission ever held at the Tabernacle at any time by any of the great Evangelists of the day and preceding ones.[15]

7
Twenty Wonderful Weeks
in Clwyd

'When the Lord turned again the captivity of Zion,
we were like them that dream'
(Psalm 126:1)

In the early sixties it was still possible to sit by the fireside of men and women who had been personally blessed during the waves of revival that passed over the Welsh-speaking villages of eastern Clwyd. These were the communities that cling to the edges of the moorlands just where they drop abruptly to the Ruabon–Wrexham–Mold–Flint highway. After climbing the steep hill to Ponciau, Pen-y-cae, Rhos and Coed-poeth I had the privilege of speaking with a number of these people, including the widow of the Mr Evans whose voice can be heard on the record *Jiwbili y Diwygiad*, and Mr and Mrs John Powell Parry in their home at Plasbennion. They had all felt the flames of revival and had seen their villages swept by a great breathtaking wind. Their minds were filled with rich memories, yet the pictures they drew would lack a frame if we did not have that rare book of W. S. Jones, Ponciau, *Y Diwygiad Crefyddol yn Rhosllanerchrugog*. This brings together the reports published in the *Rhos Herald* by this man who must have been only a cub reporter at the time. In later life he was to become an elder in his local church, an editor and a spokesman of spiritual status, though not as much a public figure as others of his family. Thanks largely to him, the narrative of the awakening in the Rhos district is a rich store of fragrant memories. Turning to the other Clwydian districts we have nothing like this. The present writer knows only of a minister's testimony, a farm-maid's memories, and a handful of press cuttings.

Blessing first came in the third week of June, but it came only to a few 'prepared' churches. It began at a preaching service in Ponciau on Sunday morning, 19 June, in which Rev. J. R. Jones of Pontypridd preached on 'the impossibility of believers in Christ being lost'. In the afternoon meeting, as Rev. Thomas Shankland of Rhyl spoke on 'the Cross and its meaning in the life of the believer', a strange stirring was felt. Then, on the Monday evening, speaking from Isaiah 55:11-13, J. R. Jones felt moved to call on people to 'Come on in', a watchword which would often be heard again in the revival.[1]

When Mr Evans of Rhos was interviewed by Aneirin Talfan Davies he spoke clearly of the outbreak of the main revival in November 1904, beginning at Penuel Chapel:

> An incredible influence took possession of the congregation and I can only describe it in the words of the Day of Pentecost: 'This is that which was spoken by the prophet Joel; . . . your sons and your daughters shall prophesy, and your young men shall see visions, and your old men shall dream dreams.' At the end of the service many were coming down to the vestry—some backsliders and others coming for the first time, and others who were already in the church, coming to consecrate themselves anew to the service of the Lord of the vineyard. On Friday we moved from Penuel to Capel Mawr ['Big Chapel']. The chapel was filled to the brim and there was not enough room for everyone to come in.[2]

The story is taken up at this point by a minister writing for the Baptist monthly, *Y Greal* ('The Grail')—but after this we shall rely on W. S. Jones's eyewitness accounts.

> On Sunday morning 13 November, R. B. Jones preached in Penuel to a full chapel of listeners, from John 15:16. A service with the dew of heaven upon it. Sunday afternoon, at 3.30 o'clock, a meeting was held for the young people. This was announced for that time so as not to interfere with the Sunday school, and also to give an opportunity for the young people of the district to meet together in a religious meeting. Some of the adults remained to see and hear what kind of a meeting it would be, thinking there would be sufficient room for them, but the chapel was quickly filled to overflowing by the young people of the neighbourhood, so that the older ones had to give up their places for them. This was the meeting that set the young people of the locality on fire. The missioner did not preach, but spoke for about twenty minutes. He set before them the importance of total consecration to the Lord in the flower of their days. He recounted his own experience of consecration, and made an earnest appeal on behalf of the Master for all present to consecrate themselves anew to the Lord. Everyone was urged to pray quietly, and those who were ready to do so were asked to show

110

it by raising their right hands; many were raised, and the place became red hot. Prayer was offered for strength for those who had decided, to carry out their decision; and for those who were halting between two opinions to resolve the argument . . . Many were in tears, and others were astounded.

Sunday night the missioner announced there would be a prayer-meeting in Penuel at two o'clock Monday afternoon . . . At the close of the meeting, a procession was formed; it went along the main streets; hymns were sung, and the missioner spoke opposite many public houses; he stood between two of them, and called them 'gates of hell', and that loudly enough for the landlords and their customers to hear . . . A great crowd came to Penuel Monday night . . .

Tuesday, a prayer-meeting was held at two . . . Tuesday night a sermon was preached on Romans 3:22,23 . . .

Wednesday, a prayer-meeting for the sisters was held, and a large company of them met . . . This meeting set the sisters on fire. By now two great forces in the community had been stirred, namely the young people and the ladies . . .

Thursday a prayer-meeting was held at two o'clock . . . There was a meeting of the ministers of the area the same afternoon, and the missioner attended it at the earnest invitation of the brotherhood. We had from him an address that left an impression on every one of us. Some of us could not restrain ourselves, and found great release in shedding tears. The missioner made an appeal to the ministers to be present at a prayer meeting purposed for the whole of the following day in Penuel . . .

Friday, at ten o'clock, a prayer-meeting began at Penuel that will long be remembered. It continued without a break through the day until the evening service . . . The infallible Spirit had taken possession of the meeting. This was the most remarkable meeting I have ever been present in—praise and prayer alternately without a break, and no one weary. Some had to go out to prepare meals, &c., but others came in to take their place, and those who had left rushed back, in case they missed anything. This was my personal experience exactly: I ran to the house, and I never ate more hastily even when the pressure of business called me. All day Penuel chapel was like a bee hive—some going and some coming throughout the day, except that they were coming to the hive to fetch honey. In and out they went without disturbing the peace of the meeting. Those who were coming in would wait in the entrance until a hymn was started, and similarly those who were leaving. What a blessed time was had—a whole day in which to submit before the Lord, and to wait upon him. It was clearly proved that our expectation was not in vain. Seven indicated their desire to give themselves to the Lord during the meeting. By the time of the evening service Jerusalem Calvinistic Methodist [Chapel] was full to overflowing, so that it was with difficulty that the missioner and I pushed in. The large schoolroom was opened, and that was filled to overflowing, and a meeting was held in the chapel and the schoolroom at the same time. The missioner preached from 1 Timothy 1:15 . . . There were 21 converts. There was no way to reach them because of the crowd. Members sitting near them were asked to bring them to the vestry: so it was; that room became an Enquiry Room, and it was with difficulty that I thrust my way through the congregation to speak with them. This was a novel experience: speaking to so many new converts at the same time. There was nothing to be done but to trust in the Master.[3]

While these wonderful events were taking place at Jerusalem Chapel, W. S. Jones was personally involved in the equally exciting movement of the Spirit at Capel Mawr:

When they removed to Capel Mawr to hold the last meeting of the Rev. R. B. Jones's mission, the expectation of an outpouring of the Spirit had never been higher during the series [of meetings].

It was amazing how quiet and tranquil Rhos was from seven to ten on Friday night,—the streets with no one traversing them, the shops closed, and the dwelling-houses in darkness. One would have had the explanation of this by turning into Capel Mawr to see the gathering there. Never before had that spacious building been so full. So great was the thronging there that it became necessary to open the spacious Schoolroom to hold an overflow meeting. But despite that, hundreds had to turn away disappointed. Inside the building there was one of the most uplifting sights one could conceive. There you could see hundreds of faces with anxiety and expectation engraved on each. The meeting began with a remarkably intense and effective prayer from the Rev. O. J. Owen, Ponciau, who read portions of the third chapter of John's Gospel. Following him came the Rev. R. B. Jones who, after offering a short prayer, announced his text, amidst awesome silence, out of the first chapter of the first Epistle to Timothy, and the fifteenth verse: 'This is a faithful saying, and worthy of all acceptation, that Christ Jesus came into the world to save sinners; of whom I am chief.'

A short sermon, without showing much profundity of thought (as it is said, not because it was not obvious that he possessed this, but because there was no need to darken the Counsel of God by human wisdom), neither was there any attempt at dramatic oratory. It was characterised by simplicity, by the unmixed purity of evangelical doctrine, and by an intimacy which touched everyone, and ensured that not one of the great congregation was unable to understand every sentence. How ordinary he was, but what a lesson to preachers! How devoid of ambition, but what an influence he left behind! How simple, but so overflowing with the riches of the gospel! He did not play at all with emotions, but rather made his way to the reason and conscience of his listeners. What wonder that the effect was so great . . . The vast crowd was swept by a dynamic current or 'shock' which was felt by all. One felt that the Holy Spirit was working mightily through it, and we had proof of this in the number of converts.

After finishing in the chapel he moved to the Schoolroom and there again delivered an address to the congregation there, based on the same words. Following this the meeting was left open for the congregation, and what an anointed service it was! One prayed here; and at his last word, another sang over there, the congregation joining in with complete abandon, and doubling and trebling it; and following this, a number vied to give testimonies; and all was evidently permeated by the Spirit. 'Amens' and 'Diolch Iddo' ['Thanks be to Him'] broke out in showers through the congregation and it was obvious that the majority were in some indescribable exultation and joy.[4]

From thirty pages of detailed reports it is impossible to do more than select a few cameos and try to share the thoughts and feelings of the watchers, as reported by W. S. Jones.

Last Sunday the sound of many blessed services was to be heard everywhere. A gentle incense rested upon the means of grace in this district. A wonderful feeling follows the realization that almost an entire district is simultaneously focussing their yearning petitions, and striving together in prayer on behalf of one great purpose—the saving of souls. There is a power in that thought, and it takes a complete hold of every person who is open to spiritual influences.[5]

* * * * *

In Capel Mawr, [Rhos] on Monday night, as a great multitude gathered together for prayer, the normal form of the service was interrupted by a little girl, hardly twelve years old, rising to her feet in the midst of the crowd, and offering one of the most striking prayers ever heard. A child's prayer it was, for sure, but in its very simplicity it was overpowering. The crowd was shaken like a leaf and their feelings melted into a lake of tears through the eloquence of pure innocence. Strong men trembled like rushes before a breeze, and many a cheek was wet with a flood of tears—cheeks which had been dry in many a worse circumstance. For many that was the strongest impact of the Revival, and the one which affected them most deeply.

* * * * *

In Bethlehem, on the afternoon [of Boxing Day 1904], a similar sight could be seen [to that in the morning meeting]; yet somehow it was felt that the fire had become more of a conflagration. A strange feeling took hold of the congregation when one young man sang the splendid words of 'Berw Bermo' to the American tune, 'Redemption'. This was certainly the most effectual thing in that meeting. There was a kind of indescribable tenderness in his voice, and his feelings were being controlled by a Spirit other than his own. He uttered the language of his soul in every sentence, and the melody came from a heart which had experienced that of which it sang, sinking into the hearts of the hundreds who were listening to him, until they were on fire by the time he came to the last verse . . . The congregation joined in with him, and that was truly wonderful singing! That which they felt in their souls rose up through the rendering and they offered their spiritual praises to Him who inhabits the praises of Zion, in abundance and sincerity.

From time to time W. S. Jones turned his gaze from the activities in the chapels to widely discussed events in the community, such as the decision of the Rhos Silver Band to become teetotal, or the transfer of Sick Benefit Clubs away from taverns, or the attempt to organize a march of witness into Wrexham. It is tempting to stay with these, but it is even more exciting to watch and experience that final, great day of the Rhos revival, one which W. S. Jones considered to be 'the final proclamation of King Jesus':

Undoubtedly last Saturday night stands on its own in the history of the whole movement. In the seven o'clock meeting it was evident that the Spirit was filling the chapel, and that the vast congregation which was in Penuel was entirely under His governance. Quite a disturbance was caused at the end of the meeting when an old man asked the congregation to sing a particular verse of a hymn. When he stood up along with some who had already confessed the Son of God, there was a good deal of questioning as to whether he was a member. When the mistake was realised, and the Rev. R. Jones asked whether he had owned he was Christ's or whether he was anxious to do this, he answered that he was not ready, and a feeling of anguish came over everyone in that place. It was no wonder that the congregation half sang and half prayed again the last part of the verse he had given out:–

> A dywed air dy Hunan
> Wrth f'enaid clwyfus, trist,
> Dy fod yn maddau 'meiau
> Yn haeddiant Iesu Grist.

> [And speak a word Thyself
> To my wounded, sorrowing soul,
> That Thou dost forgive my sins
> Through the merits of Jesus Christ.]

The march which followed through the streets of Rhos was very impressive, because the people watching could see on the march dozens who had been in the public houses a week earlier. A meeting was proposed for eleven o'clock that night, and the first hour of that service was a most remarkable prayer meeting, with earnest thanksgiving for the past months combined with fervent desires for the blessing to continue into the new year. Prayer followed upon prayer with no singing at all. This continued until past twelve o'clock:

Soon afterwards Dr A. J. Parry, who was the chairman, asked for indications from those who desired to yield themselves to Christ. The usual custom was changed slightly, as all who were coming for the first time were asked to raise their hands. He had scarcely asked for an indication when he saw a hand raised in the gallery, followed by another, and a third and fourth. By now the congregation were as if on tiptoe with expectancy, and obviously under strong impulses. Till then nobody on the ground floor had given a sign, but in an instant a hand was raised under the gallery, and the name of a well-known character ran like lightning through the congregation. Some were seen jumping in their seats, unable to restrain themselves in their great joy. Scores were weeping copiously and the congregation did not rightly know whether to rejoice or to weep. They tried to do the first, and began to sing . . . but this was a failure; there were tears in the singing. Perhaps however those tears of joy were the highest form of rejoicing.

Right in the middle of the tumult another hand was raised in the centre of the chapel. When they looked, it was the hand of that old man who had given out the verse in the first meeting. The congregation just could not hold back:—It was shaken as by a strong wind, some influence rushed across them, sweeping them along, the embankment of their emotions was broken, and they were hurled to the ground, as it were, by some turbulent force. His son and daughter leapt to their feet at once, crying out loudly, having lost all control of themselves for the moment. Some unusual wildness flashed from the daughter's eyes, and there was a strange look as she stood on her feet screaming, 'He's my father', her hands stretched out towards him. She burst into prayer, and having released her feelings in this way, she quietened down at once. So great was the effect on the congregation that it was feared that they would become completely crazed, and that the meeting would become unruly; but through the influence of others who had kept their self-possession this was prevented. High emotions were quite natural, and can be easily justified when one takes into consideration all the circumstances which worked gradually and inevitably in this direction throughout the meetings. Certainly this was the meeting of the series which had the greatest impact upon the congregation, and in this one only was there anything like ungovernable excitement, and that lasted only a few moments. The meeting broke up at this point, and everyone moved off to their homes quietly and without fuss. Surely this meeting will never be forgotten by those present.[6]

Powerful emotional upheavals of this kind did not go down well with all the ministers and church leaders, and the excitement slowly subsided throughout January and February, although the *Rhos Herald* could still note some outstanding services. For their annual preaching festivals most chapels invited known revival preachers. Both R. B. Jones and J. R. Jones returned, Joseph Jenkins came to Holywell, and D. M. Phillips to Oswestry.[7]

Though there is much to say for John Powell Parry's conviction that Rhos chapels were ripe for revival because so many humble, prayerful people had prepared for months, yet one can accept the confident view of schoolmaster J. T. Jones that the awakening there had been directly caused by the Spirit's taking hold of the traditional preaching. This is his verdict on the visit of R. B. Jones in the first weeks of the Rhos revival, which coincided exactly with events at Loughor:

[R.B. Jones] came as a man inspired . . . My main impression of him is the impression of EARNESTNESS . . . a sense of vocation, of being called to a special work. His whole appearance . . . was EARNEST . . . Generally speaking, the prevailing atmosphere of church life at the time was indifference, but R. B. was a flash of divine lightning let loose into our indifference . . . His real theme was HOLINESS and the CALL TO HOLINESS. He made holiness REAL, he made holiness TERRIBLE. How shall I describe it all? . . . It was consuming fire. The preaching completely lacked the usual preaching histrionics; R. B. himself was a CONSUMING FIRE and so was his MESSAGE. And the preacher's fire *consumed* the congregation . . . What I heard at Penuel [Chapel], Rhos, in November 1904 was not a theologian but a flaming evangelist, passionate, seraphic, CONSUMING . . . What the preacher dispensed to my soul was not formulae, but life . . . It was the sweep of his passionate conviction that carried all before it in the Revival years.[8]

A number of other godly preachers in Clwyd were also given special vigour and authority at the height of the revival. However, it was the converts who were entrusted with the next stage of taking the fire into all the surrounding villages. They and the local preachers had many a thrilling, blessed day. Here is the testimony of the Presbyterian minister, J. Ellis Jones, recorded long after:

Glynceiriog was near enough to Rhos to be within reach of the breezes, and on the evening of the last Tuesday in November they were carried in our direction. It was the *Seiat* evening and the Man Himself was there in the midst. At the close one of the brethren who remembered '59 came to me, and said: 'You have often asked what is a revival, tonight you know what it is.' The following Thursday the Rev. H. Henlyn Owen, Dinmael, Corwen, was our preacher. The Chapel was full before the time came to commence. The preacher himself was full of Revival fervour, and there was a wonderful anointing on the service. Yet he was unable to finish his sermon. A young man sitting near the door rose to his feet and began to recite a verse of Gwilym Hiraethog's—one of the great hymns of the Revival –

> *Dyma gariad fel y moroedd,*
> *Tosturiaethau fel y lli;*
> *Tywysog Bywyd pur yn marw –*
> *Marw i brynu'n bywyd ni.*

> [Here is love, vast as the ocean,
> Loving-kindness as the flood,
> When the Prince of Life, our ransom,
> Shed for us His precious blood.]

The young friend walked down the aisle to the Big Seat, with a heavenly look on his face, continuing to recite the verse –

Pwy all beidio â chofio amdano?
Pwy all beidio â thraethu'i glod?
Dyma gariad nad a'n angof
Tra fo nefoedd wen yn bod.

[Who His love will not remember?
Who can cease to sing His praise?
He can never be forgotten
Thro' heav'n's everlasting days.]

The hymn took hold of the congregation. Rather, the Prince of Life took hold of it, and to the strains of 'singing His praise' the service ended. Next evening Mr Owen was in our Class Meeting at Tregeiriog. His visit was concerning a particular matter, but his theme was the previous night. The breeze descended here also. And although most of the members were elderly, their youth was renewed. One of them rose— Einion Ddu, from Tregeiriog—and with his face towards the window, he began to recite the verse –

Dros y bryniau tywyll niwlog,
Yn dawel, f'enaid, edrych draw,
Ar addewidion sydd i esgor
Ar ryw ddyddiau braf gerllaw.
Nefol Jiwbil,
Gad im weld y bore wawr.

[O'er the gloomy hills of darkness
Look, my soul; be still, and gaze;
All the promises do travail
With a glorious day of grace:
Blessed jubilee!
Let thy glorious morning dawn.]

My task on the Sunday—the first Sunday of December—was to examine the [Sunday] Schools Meeting at Nantyr, but instead of the question and answer session it was far easier to turn it all into a prayer-meeting. I was to be there all day, but I felt a voice calling me to go down to Glynceiriog that evening. I didn't know why, but that Sabbath evening a man gave himself to the Lord.[9]

One part of Clwyd has close affinity with the mountainous districts of Gwynedd. It is this area to which we turn next. The blessing spread slowly eastwards from Bala and from Dolgellau where, according to the

North Wales Guardian, there had been united prayer meetings, processions and open-air services.[10] It also spread westwards from Rhos and Ruabon towards Llangollen. A special committee meeting of the Welsh Free Churches decided to invite Evan Roberts to Wrexham, but meanwhile the usual pattern of revival meetings appeared.

At Corwen in early March special thanksgiving services were 'attended by nearly a thousand people from all parts of Edeyrnion'.[11] There were blessings and baptisms at nearby Carrog, and at Cefn-mawr to the east of Llangollen; yet there were difficulties at Llangollen itself, where there was some opposition to open-air witness. Even as late as July 1905 there was an incident when a procession, led by the dignified R. B. Jones and other highly respectable ministers, had to stop its hymn-singing because the Town Band was playing nearby and refused to give way.[12]

The first signs of blessing in Llangollen occurred during the week of prayer at the start of 1905. There were processions every day to different parts of the town; there were women's prayer meetings in two or three chapels and there was a special young people's prayer meeting full of lads late Sunday night. A week later there was an even larger procession and this time Rhos converts joined them and gave their testimonies in two chapels. Many Llangollen chapels gave a hearing to sympathetic preachers. The *Llangollen Advertiser* became more and more favourable and the following tribute shows why:

> Every Church in the town is revived, and has witnessed many conversions, the number in this small town being already about a hundred— many hundreds, counting the surrounding district. Sectarianism is now almost annihilated. Committees give way to prayer meetings, organisations are baptized with a holy unction, the atmosphere of the Church becomes more spiritual . . . This Revival works towards righteousness; it is a social elevation as well as a great renewal in spiritual life.[13]

Despite the intense conservatism of the Welsh-speaking families on the moors between Dee and Conwy, there was a gradual acceptance that the Spirit of God was doing something unique within the four walls of their chapels. However and wherever it began, it reached its flash-point in the prayer-meetings that were held at the end of the year. These usually began just after Christmas and attracted large numbers as New Year's Eve approached.

Elizabeth Williams, an aged lady of Gwyddelwern, near Corwen, little dreamed in her youth that she would be a valued witness to that which had stirred her so deeply. Mrs Williams was interviewed during an Oral History Project in 1978 and told of those far-off days when she and her sisters worked hard on a smallholding—water-carrying, milking, baking, haymaking—until the Sabbath, on which day the whole community went to worship. She was asked about her memories of the Revival:

That was the year I went to Maes-gwyn farm as a maid-servant. We were allowed to go to chapel, regularly, to the prayer-meeting on Monday evening, the *seiat* ['fellowship meeting'] on Wednesday evening and the reading-class on Friday evening. We were allowed to go to these. And then we heard from some lads who had gone to the South to work that Evan Roberts the Revivalist was able to do great things and that the chapels were filling up . . .

We went to chapel one Monday. I don't remember who opened the meeting. Four prayed and someone was to speak, but in the end the chairman for that month rose and said, 'Will someone give out a verse of a hymn. It's getting late.'

Someone in the congregation, old Edward Hannan, got up. 'Late!' he said. 'Salvation is needed here tonight'. He took his cap and went out. I thought he had taken offence and had gone out, but then he came back saying 'Save John Roberts'. There the two were, coming arm in arm—the door opened and they were both there arm in arm. Hannan went to his place, and old John Roberts tried to go further, but it was on his knees he went, thanking God and shouting, 'Thanks be that the door of mercy is open'.

Then somehow everyone was praying; but then it quietened somewhat. Then Edward Hannan stood up again and said, 'Thomas Lloyd needs to be saved'—just like that. And out he went. Well, we knew then that something great was happening. Everyone was singing and praying. I was praying, and the other girls—everyone was praying. Something had come.

We saw the door open, and we could see nothing apart from a great light. It was blinding us. The first thing I remember is that we were all on our knees—everyone praying. I remember hearing a man singing *'Golchwyd Magdalen yn ddisglair'* ['Magdalen was washed a brilliant white'], and everyone was praying. I don't know how long we were on our knees, but then we got up and were singing. I think now that it was the Holy Spirit who came. That was the light. It's in the Bible, isn't it? It says there, 'They were all with one accord in one place. And suddenly there came a sound from heaven' [Acts 2:1-2]. And He came like that. It was lovely, you know. We lost ourselves. I'm sure we were full of the Holy Spirit, you know. I'm sure.

Then we went out. I don't remember saying a word to anyone. Some were turning in all directions. We turned down through the village, and as we were going through the village and coming opposite the tavern, we could hear singing and then laughter. Old Janet Evans said, 'Let's sing.' We turned and begin to sing:

> *Dowch o'r dafarn; dowch o'r dafarn;*
> *Dowch o'r dafarn 'r awr hon;*
> *'R awr hon, dowch o'r dafarn;*
> *Dowch o'r dafarn 'r awr hon.*

['Come from the tavern now . . .']

Then we sang,

> *Mae E'n galw, mae E'n galw;*
> *Mae E'n galw 'r awr hon:*
> *R awr hon mae E'n galw;*
> *Mae E'n galw'r awr hon.*

['He is calling now . . .']

And then it was,

> *Deuwch ato; deuwch ato;*
> *Deuwch ato 'r awr hon;*
> *'R awr hon deuwch ato;*
> *Deuwch ato 'r awr hon.*

['Come to Him now . . .']

After we had finished, the tavern door opened and the landlady came to the door and said, 'There's nobody here. They have all rushed out of the back door.' And we began singing, *'Diolch Iddo byth am gofio llwch y llawr'* ['Thanks be to Him for ever remembering the dust of the earth']. What had come to the old tavern, I thought. Well, the Holy Spirit had come there. He had 'destroyed the resting place of obnoxious sin'. The old tavern remained closed for years, with no talk of it.

The Holy Spirit had taken hold of everyone—the young people, the sick, young children in school. He had gone to the school and they had formed little groups during their lunch hour to pray, and those who heard them said they were excellent. But it was the Holy Spirit. It was wonderful.

One man said a little while ago in a meeting, when someone asked

121

the question, 'What was the Revival' . . . 'Oh! it was a flash,' he said. But dear me, he ought to know that it was not a flash. It was the Holy Spirit . . .

There is talk sometimes that some turned away after experiencing the Revival, but I did not see any. Those at Gwyddelwern held, anyway. After the evening of the tavern, there was a prayer-meeting the following evening, and who should be there but some who had been in the tavern the previous evening, praying and giving thanks for being set free from sin. I know that they remained true to their Lord.[14]

All Clwyd was clearly in the grip of the Spirit, but what of Gwynedd? Had the new forces gained the victory in that stronghold of tradition?

8

Prayer-meeting Revivals
in Gwynedd

'And when they had prayed, the place was shaken where they were
assembled together'
(Acts 4:31)

Evan Roberts seems to have sensed that the Sovereign Lord was going to use quite different channels for the outpouring of the Spirit in North Wales. At the end of January 1905, when a Bala College student asked him to come to the north, he was told that up until then he had felt no guiding impulse as to visiting North Wales and had made no arrangements further than the end of February 1905. Then he wrote a short message to send around the North Wales churches, ending with the words 'Forward, forward, forward.'[1] It was not until the summer of 1905 that he reached north-west Wales, by which time the tide was beginning to turn.

David Matthews suggested that Evan Roberts was hindered in the north by differences in dialect, attitude and temperament. Of some of Evan Roberts's meetings in North Wales, he says:

> Somehow there was a heaviness and reticence that must have seemed strange to the revivalist. Quick responsiveness and a ready spontaneity were lacking . . . Enthusiasm—such as they were capable of—ran high when sinners walked down from crowded galleries to make their confession of Christ. But it certainly was not the same kind of enthusiasm.[2]

On the other hand there were some revival preachers who had great success in Gwynedd. Already by the beginning of November 1904 the brothers Seth and Frank Joshua were holding interdenominational meetings in Llandudno Town Hall and were taking converts out into the streets to invite friends in. Their prayers to the Lord to have compassion on the people bore fruit, according to a Welsh newspaper. Again at

Clwyd Street, Rhyl, there were very many converts, and people crowded in to share the spiritual blessing.[3]

Another minister whose efforts were signally rewarded was D. M. Phillips who brought his niece to sing in his special meetings at Blaenau Ffestiniog and Pwllheli. Most beloved of all was Joseph Jenkins who came up with Florrie Evans and Maud Davies on more than one North Wales tour. He was remembered with reverence by those who saw and heard him in the Nantlle Valley, from where he went to Caernarfon and Bangor. On that journey he had a moving welcome:

> An impressive prayer meeting was held without prearrangement at the Caernarvon railway station a day or two ago. The Rev Mr Jenkins of New Quay and two of the young lady missionaries of the revival were passing through. At the request of the railway officials they willingly spent half an hour in prayer and praise with some thirty or forty railwaymen in a waiting room.[4]

Things did not go so well for him at Bangor, though 1500 filled Twrgwyn Chapel. In fact one of the young ladies exclaimed in an impassioned voice, 'Oh what hard people you are. Here has Mr Jenkins been preaching to you for an hour and not a single Amen. You are no friends of Christ.'[5] After Joseph Jenkins returned to his church work, both ladies carried on through North Wales to Llangollen, Ruabon and Coedpoeth where they are interestingly described as 'former advocates of the great revivalist'.[6] Such sentiments indicate that they were distancing themselves from the later stages of Evan Roberts's work. Even sympathetic ministers felt the Word was being dethroned and the singing too exalted. They feared lest 'the deep and holy thing that they had experienced shall lose its strength and charm in a superficial feeling without fruit or continuation'.[7] However, there were many districts where the flame blazed.

In the slate-quarry districts of Gwynedd the fires of revival broke out during the Christmas holiday prayer meetings. The Holy Spirit used the first meetings in each chapel to work mightily among the Lord's people. 'The wind bloweth where it listeth', and no one knew how widespread was the mood of expectation. Even before the workmen and students returned home for Christmas bearing startling news of what they had seen and heard in the south, certain families and chapel meetings had been moved by letters sent home by those who were on short contracts in that region, letters such as the one (in Welsh) from Evan Jenkins of Church Street, Blaenau Ffestiniog, to his wife:

I have arrived here [Treorci] safely. I am writing this at midday. There is a great revival here, praying and singing in every chapel, and it is as if nobody here is working at all. Singing and praying all night through, almost, and all along the street. The colliers come from their work in the morning and sing all along the road. I went to chapel at 10 o'clock this morning; I've never seen such a place in my life, praying and singing— the women and everybody praying and shouting 'Hallelujah' and 'Bendigedig' ['Blessed'] and 'Diolch iddo, byth am gofio llwch y llawr' ['Thanks be to Him for ever remembering the dust of the earth']. It was a great effort for me to keep myself from shouting with all my might 'Hallelujah' and 'Bendigedig', and so on. It was very easy to shout out, and it seemed to me that there were angels at the top of the chapel, because the place was so heavenly . . . I thought I was in the fair at Llan when I first went into the chapel and heard everyone speaking at once, but I soon saw I was not in a fair, but was hearing everyone sing like angels . . . Everyone giving out a hymn and striking up the tune himself. The next meeting is at 2 o'clock, and then at seven. There is not half enough room, with hundreds outside the chapel failing to get in. They go to the chapel at 5 o'clock, two hours before time. I am thinking of going there tonight.

> *Pwy a ŵyr na olchir finnau,*
> *Pwy a ŵyr na byddaf byw.*

> [Who knows but that I may be washed,
> Who knows but that I may be quickened.][8]

There was a second factor preparing North Wales for revival, namely the newspaper correspondents' accounts. It is reported that, in the 1859 Revival in the USA, telegrams were sent from city to city, free of charge, containing messages of such power that they inspired more revival prayer-meetings. In the winter of 1904–5, the main newspapers in Wales became the bearers of good tidings of great joy which electrified North Wales:

> With us at Bangor there is a rush for the *South Wales Daily News* every day on its arrival. Scores if not hundreds try to get the earliest glimpse of it in order to know what is being done among our brethren in the South. And the influence of this is apparent at our ordinary religious services, which are beginning to be permeated by the Spirit whose mighty works are recorded in the *South Wales Daily News* . . .
> We have hundreds of young people here from various parts of

South Wales . . . Very many of them have the paper sent them daily by post either direct from the office or by friends. The paper is sold by two newsvendors here . . . Every South Walian who gets the paper has a dozen North Walian friends as eager as himself for the news.[9]

All these influences reached their highest point in Christmas week when northward-bound trains rang with joyful hymns as the exiles came home:

Glamorganshire, where the enthusiasm and fervour have reached their greatest height, is largely populated by immigrants from rural West Wales and from the northern half of the Principality. Many of these have returned to their native homes, carrying with them the fervour of the revival scenes in Glamorganshire, and thus assisting to set the rural districts ablaze.

North Wales in particular is benefiting by this. At Carnarvon, for the first time within living memory, Boxing Day . . . was devoted to religious services in the form of public prayer meetings. The first of these was held in the morning at 10 o'clock at Salem Congregational Chapel, all the denominations of the town, including the Church of England, being represented thereat. The meeting was conducted on the same lines as some of the most successful revival meetings in South Wales . . . [Among the speakers was an ordinary working man from Cilfynydd who] created a sensation by walking up to the set fawr [big seat] and announcing that he was compelled to tell of the great and wondrous deeds he had witnessed in South Wales . . .

Then he burst forth into rough but eloquent prayer.

'O Lord,' he cried, amidst resounding Amens, 'the people of South Wales cannot be more dear to Thy heart than these Thy people in the North. Christ gave His life for both alike. Restrict not, O Lord, Thy present favours to the South, but pour Thy blessing also upon the North. Sin is as rampant in Carnarvon as in the Rhondda in some respects even more so, as I know and as Thou knowest. O sweep Carnarvon also, dear Lord' . . .

At Machynlleth, where the Aberystwyth and the Barmouth portions of the train had to be divided, all the passengers from both congregated on the platform and an impromptu prayer meeting was held, earnest supplications being offered up that each person might carry the sacred fire with him to his destination, and there assist in setting his own district ablaze. How the prayer has been answered a dozen widely-scattered localities in the Northern counties can already testify.[10]

The slate town of Blaenau Ffestiniog, at the head of the narrow-gauge line well-known to North Wales tourists, was hit by gale-force winds of revival in the Christmas and New Year period. These reached a first climax in the traditional week of prayer held immediately after Christmas and a second climax in February. One very detailed account by one who was present is given below, followed by another more general narrative. These have been translated from Welsh and portions of each enable us to form the following composite story. The sequence seems to be heart-searching, with sorrow first, then rejoicing and ecstatic praise:

> The church and congregation at the Tabernacle was one of the first in the district to be reached by the full flood of the Revival, and it arrived with marvellous power. For some weeks before its coming there was a rumour of it in the distance. The sound was coming nearer us and the spiritual atmosphere lightened at the close of the year 1904 . . .
>
> On the first Sabbath in December the evening service was on the text, 'And, being assembled together with them, he commanded them that they should not depart from Jerusalem, but wait for the promise of the Father, which, saith he, ye have heard of me . . . These all continued with one accord in prayer and supplication' (Acts 1:4,14). Before this preaching service at 5.30 on Sunday afternoon, there was an officers' meeting in the big seat of the chapel to take counsel together what we should do with a view to having an experience of the Revival which we had heard talk of in parts of the country. Present in that meeting were John Davies, Rich[ar]d Griffiths and R. R. Morris. Nothing definite was decided upon, except that we ought to make every effort to ensure its coming, and that we should invite it warmly to visit us.
>
> Now at the close of that Sunday evening's sermon we sang with great warmth hymn number 900.

> *Paratowch y ffordd mae Duw yn dod,*
> *I'w enw glân rhowch uniawn glod;*
> *Mae swn cerbydau aur y nef*
> *Yn rhwygo bryniau daear gref.*

> [Prepare the way, the Lord is coming,
> To his pure Name give all due praise;
> The sound of heaven's golden chariots
> Rends earth's strongest hills.]

> It is likely that while singing that verse on that evening that we had the first visible flash of the Revival.
>
> On Monday night, 5 December, we held a prayer-meeting in the

vestry. Mr Cad[waladr] Owen was the leader that month and he called upon four to take part in the prayer-meeting, instead of three as was the custom, and a new little 'resonance' came into the meeting . . .

On Wednesday, 7 December, there was a *seiat* ['fellowship meeting'] and prayer-meeting. That was something new again.

Thursday evening, 8 December, prayer-meeting.

Friday evening, 9 December, prayer-meeting and a young people's prayer-meeting afterwards. That was the first. And after it was announced, a great crowd very readily remained behind.

Saturday evening. Two prayer-meetings. The same throughout the following week and the last week of December, with the temperature rising gradually. Five people came anew to the *seiat* during December.

The year 1905 came in bright and cheerful, like a summer in the middle of winter, like sunshine after tempests. On Wednesday evening, 4 January, a very special *seiat* was held. Evan Evans commenced it. D. Jones of Four Crosses listened to the children. Then Ed. Thomas, Lord Street, was received into membership—into full membership immediately, for he was at the time on a bed of serious sickness unable to come to the means of grace. Next, after Rich[ard] Griffiths the president for the month had said a few words, a number rose up with great willingness to speak of their experiences . . . Then H. Rowlands stood up in the top end of the vestry to testify, and he spoke of the most remarkable and most glorious experiences that were ever heard of. He depicted how he had been given the victory that very day after a long battle. It was the most remarkable *seiat* we ever yet had.

This was followed by a young people's prayer meeting. Like the seiat, this was owned of God. For over a week there were prayer-meetings and preaching services where the influence of the Spirit was remarkably evident. Every *seiat* was in flames.

Friday evening, 20 January, saw the first procession, a procession from Trefeini to the Tabernacle, singing hymns along the way.

Monday evening, 23 January. A procession from Hafod Ruffydd past Tan-y-graig and [passed] through the vestry [into the chapel]. Dr [D. M.] Phillips was here that night to preach and he was to be here all the week, he and Miss Jones his niece . . . On Tuesday and Wednesday Dr Phillips preached excellently and a number stayed behind each night, and feelings were rising higher each night . . . On Thursday evening there broke out a universal rejoicing with a host praying at the same time for about half an hour. That Thursday evening was the first night for fervent exaltation to break out. Everyone left the chapel about 10.40 and went to the vestry. There was singing and rejoicing until one o'clock in the morning.

From that date until 11 February the diarist R. R. Morris notes processions and prayer meetings, ending in a long prayer meeting for young people on the evening of Sunday, 12 February—full of intense fervour and rejoicing from 9.30 to midnight:

> The week which began on 12 February and ended on 18 February was the most remarkable week of all of the Revival in the Tabernacle. Rejoicing in the vestry every night of the week until Friday evening without any break. On Monday night rejoicing broke out in the last prayer-meeting about 10 o'clock and continued for a long time. That night a host of wives and young girls were praying on one side of the big seat in the vestry, and a host of men and young lads were praying over on the other side—and between both sides, it was very fervent there for hours . . . [One person] attempted to take his coat off and one of the boys alongside him asked what he was doing. 'Oh', said he, 'pulling up the sleeves of my shirt in order to praise Jesus Christ'.
>
> It was the same until 12.30 on Tuesday evening and the same on Wednesday night. That night the vestry was full to overflowing, the crowd pressing into each other over the top of the benches. Never before had there been such a multitude in the vestry—and the rejoicing was universal, scores around the big seat praying at the same time. And the singing did not quieten them, nor did anyone want to quieten them . . .
>
> On Wednesday evening there were two prayer-meetings—one at Trefeini and one in the vestry. Then a further prayer-meeting in the vestry, which was almost brought to a close at about 10 p.m. But at that time a number came in from the Trefeini meeting and the fire rekindled even higher . . . There was fervent rejoicing until 12.10.
>
> Friday evening. A most remarkable prayer-meeting—the second meeting. About a score of young boys prayed at the same time, and several young girls too . . . The crowd were on their knees for about an hour.
>
> We had excellent meetings after that amazing week in mid February, and many an hour of rejoicing in Trefeini and in the vestry, but we did not have a complete week of that kind after that. Two prayer-meetings were held for weeks, and the second continued very late.[11]

The second account, by a chapel elder, was given several years after the revival, but is a valuable picture of how it all began at Bethel Chapel among the Tanygrisiau cottages beneath the slate cliffs of Blaenau Ffestiniog:

It is very interesting to look back for early portents of this gracious stirring. Certainly the roots were spreading out for years. But it was in 1904 the shoots and the fruit were seen. Let me take you as far back as the year 1895. In that year was commenced a young people's prayer-meeting in Bethel. It flourished from the outset and came to be a great influence in the life of the Church. The faithful found strength to keep the prayer-meeting alive throughout the whole period. About 25-35 were attending, but in 1903 (it was in the summer) a number of us felt some stronger influences than normal quietly at work in our hearts. A very unusual resonance was heard at that time in the prayers of several . . . Many a time they failed to carry on because of their tears and their broken feelings.

Everything was flourishing remarkably. In the singing we felt a remarkable inspiration. A meeting was held after the Sunday evening service on 27 November 1904. Feelings ran so high that night that the minister who was engaged to speak in the circuit that Sabbath (if I remember correctly it was the late Rev. Griffith Owen, Rhos-ddu) said that he could almost guarantee that the revival would break out mightily in our midst within a fortnight . . .

Now come with me to 4 December 1904. In the prayer-meeting at nine o'clock on Sunday morning it was resolved to ask the officers to arrange a series of prayer-meetings for the following week. So it came to pass. There were uncommonly solemn and earnest meetings on Monday, Thursday and Friday evenings. During these meetings several young people came forward in tears to bend before the throne of grace—until every meeting was bedewed with tears.

That same week a *seiat* ['fellowship meeting'] was held on Wednesday evening, one which was very different from the usual. There was no pause in the relating of experiences, and that without anyone being asked by name to do so. It was over *two hours* before that *seiat* could be brought to an end, so great was the fervour . . .

That following week was one to be remembered for ever . . . *Almost every night* some new ones came forward to take part, having been overcome by their emotions. On Wednesday evening the *seiat* continued for two and a half hours, and a remarkable *seiat* it was, and then the prayer-meeting was held afterwards until 12.30. It was impossible to break up the meeting. One brother stood up *six times* in order to come forward for the first time, but he failed totally to get an opportunity because everyone was so pliant to bend.

Among the events which were fixed for ever in this man's memory were the following three evenings—the first being on 8 January when Rev. David Hughes of Trawsfynydd preached, and by the middle of the sermon a great 'Amen' went through the congregation. Some young people could not restrain themselves from leaping to their feet, shouting and giving thanks. The second was on 28 January when the Assembly Rooms in Blaenau Ffestiniog were filled with about 2,500 people in a united prayer-meeting, with the converts 'breaking down earnestly and joyfully before the throne of grace'. The third occasion was the Easter Preaching Festival in April when Dr Wynne Davies of Rhos was speaking of 'the floodgates of the eternal love being opened', and could not make himself heard in the great rejoicing which broke out. Neither could he stop the ensuing prayer time when dozens were 'on their knees, praying in tears and praising on the top of their voices'. The faithful veteran ended his report with a personal testimony and thanksgiving, 'Blessed are those who felt and saw God's mighty works.'[12]

Some letters which highlight features of the revival at Blaenau Ffestiniog in early 1905 have been preserved at the National Library of Wales. For example, Lewis Lloyd wrote to D. M. Phillips on 27 February to keep him abreast of events at Blaenau Ffestiniog:

> It has been exceptionally good ever since you left us. It has been very lively in all the chapels especially Tabernacle. The week before last was a remarkable week there, and the same was true of Bowydd. It is estimated that about seven hundred have been converted since your visit to the place. It is hardly necessary for me to say therefore that you have immortalised yourself in Blaenau.
>
> I happened to visit my home a week ago and, just as at Christmas, I was obliged to give the story of the 'Revival' in Blaenau to them on Sunday night. I reported what you had been instrumental in accomplishing in Tabernacle and Carreg-ddu . . . Mrs Jones of Egryn is in Tabernacle tonight and in Bowydd tomorrow night.[13]

Two other letters to D. M. Phillips speak of events at Pwllheli, which he also visited. The first is written by Robert Isaac Jones on 14 January 1905 and contains the sad story of a young man who had been listening and enjoying the meeting on the previous Friday night but had been killed that morning 'by a runaway horse whose dray ran over him and killed him on the spot. Isn't this a very solemn thing? Mr Rees made use of this serious accident to try to bring men to consider how suddenly death comes to some "like a thief in the night".' The postscript reads, 'The tide is rising.'[14]

The other letter is a valuable testimony from James Griffith of Ffactory, Pwllheli. First he tells of a Town Hall meeting on Saturday night where more than 1,700 turned up, and of a prayer meeting there which lasted from 7 p.m. until after 11 p.m. Then he speaks of an extra special 'second meeting' after the Sunday morning service, convened because an elderly man desired to remain behind. Then, after giving an account of a children's prayer meeting in the afternoon which lasted from 1 p.m. until 4 p.m., with 6 to 13-year-olds praying like old people, he proceeds:

> At six o'clock [on Sunday] the Rev. Robert Williams, Graig Arfon, was due to preach. After starting the service in the usual manner (Mrs Williams says it was not in the usual manner either, because I already felt, as we went into the chapel, that there was something there that I had never felt before). As they were taking the offering someone began to sing, 'Dyma gariad fel y moroedd' ['Here is love, vast as the ocean']. When they had finished a young man rose from his seat in the front of the balcony and shouted out, 'There's my father sitting on the ground floor in front of me. He has hardly broken a word with me for fifteen years. Will you forgive me, father?' His father turns towards him and says, 'I will, my boy.' Then the young man runs down to his father and the two embrace each other, with the congregation in a rush of tears and then singing 'Diolch iddo, Diolch iddo' ['Thanks be to Him, Thanks be to Him'] for a long time. After a short interval Mr Williams attempted to preach but he failed completely even to find his text. Twice he said to the congregation, 'I am standing in a terrible place.' The meeting finished in praise and prayer.[15]

In September 1905 O. J. Robinson, secretary of the Pwllheli Free Church Council, gave a report at the annual meeting of the council which recounted the chief events of the revival in their district.[16] According to him the first step towards revival in the town was a decision made by certain brethren to hold united prayer meetings every night in connection with the visit of John Williams and John Hughes, two Calvinistic Methodist ministers from Liverpool, to preach in the Monthly Meeting at the beginning of December. Then it was decided to hold a district prayer meeting throughout December, and to seek out someone to come and conduct preaching meetings for two or three nights every week in various chapels in rotation. The secretary reported that these meetings had been memorable, with evident signs of the Lord's presence. They were meetings where 'brothers and sisters were baptised in the Holy Spirit'. The full effect of all this was seen in January when processions began, and large open-air meetings were held at Pen-y-Cob.

By Thursday, January 12th—a never-to-be-forgotten night—the meetings had risen to a high point in popularity so that Salem was far too small to hold the congregation. It was decided to hold an overflow meeting in the vestry. That dear brother, the Rev. Simon Evans, was present that night and he went with the Chairman, Henry Rees, and hundreds of other brothers and sisters to hold a prayer meeeting in the vestry room above. Miss Jones [D. M. Phillips's niece] also came there and sang in a sweet heavenly fashion. Soon after the meeting started the room was filled with the 'powers of the Eternal Spirit'. The divine dam was broken and the blessings of heaven flowed into sinners' hearts. The spirit of prayer and praise descended on everyone and we remained there a long time singing and praising Jesus. Oh, how blessed was that task! It was a little of heaven on earth. For hundreds in our town it was a night to remember.

Now the news reached the chapel where Dr Phillips was holding a meeting, and scores came up to the vestry, and Dr Phillips with them. When there was a short interval it was decided to go singing through the town. That was a blessed procession, a lovely sight that evening. The devil's castles were shaken and were crumbling at their bases. After going through the town they went back to Salem which was full to overflowing. That wonderful meeting continued late into the evening . . .

On Easter Monday, the Rev. Llewelyn Jones and Miss May John visited us. Oh, what a blessing to see so many young brothers and sisters from surrounding villages coming with us to enjoy the health-giving breezes from Calvary! It was a means of grace in itself just to hear some of them thanking the Lord for visiting them in revival. Miss May John sang 'in the Spirit and with understanding' and we shall not forget the wonderful influence following on her singing, when she shouted at the top pitch of her voice, 'Forgiveness! Forgiveness!' Yes, over and over, she said—'Forgiveness is freely given and He washes white as snow even the blackest.' Oh how fervent she was as she pleaded with sinners 'Come to Him now, right now.'

The prayer-meetings continued in fervour and strength until there came two young revivalists from the south—Mr Sidney Evans and Mr Sam Jenkins. This was at Whitsun and some of the meetings were remarkable. Hundreds of young people from the countryside came to join with us in glorifying the 'Man who had been on Calvary'. Special influences accompanied young Sam Jenkins's heavenly singing, especially at Penmount where he also sang those words about 'Forgiveness' . . . A great impression was created when he sang in Welsh and English about 'Saving a rebel like me'. Perhaps this was the most remarkable meeting during the revival with the chapel crowded, the ardent prayers and singing and the Holy Spirit descending in mighty power.

The report also mentions the night when a political rally in the Town Hall had to be turned into a prayer-meeting. The two speakers, David Lloyd George and the Honourable Bradhurst, enjoyed the service and spoke briefly on the revival in Wales.[16] Further east, from Bryn Afon, Llanfairfechan, comes a letter from the minister of Horeb Chapel. Dr D. M. Phillips left Llanfairfechan at the end of an afternoon service on 10 February 1905. The letter was written to Dr Phillips the following day, and begins by describing a meeting in the chapel the previous evening:

> The chapel was filled just as on Monday night. The heat broke out into mighty flames early in the meeting, just as in the afternoon. The shouting was more general. News of the afternoon meeting travelled quickly through the neighbourhood. That was what awaited the workmen on their way home from the quarry. Therefore their expectations had been raised high; and they regarded the unction that had been received in the afternoon as an answer to their prayers in their work-place during the lunch hour. By and large it was the brethren who took part in the evening meeting, but some sisters also insisted on coming forward. You saw a large number of boys in the afternoon; they had taken half a day off work in order to be at the meeting . . .
>
> We have decided to cancel the *seiadau* ['fellowship meetings'] tonight in order to have another united meeting.
>
> I have to go to Nebo, Amlwch, for two nights before the end of the week. But I don't know how to leave this place.[17]

There is an element of humour in the next account. This also is related by a minister, Rev. G. Wynne Griffith. The story describes how he found himself suddenly in charge of a meeting which came close to chaos:

> The spacious John Elias memorial chapel, Moriah [in Llangefni, Anglesey], was full to overflowing long before the start of the service. There was not the slightest chance of getting in through the front door. But

because I was a preacher of sorts and accustomed to going with the elders through the back door into the chapels of the County, I went down to Moriah's back door (which is a floor height lower than the chapel floor), then I went like the wind up the stairs and gradually worked my way into the chapel. It was obvious that others had seen my scheme because a great crowd of them came running after me. Soon I was thrust into the Big Seat and found a place to sit upon the lowest step of the pulpit. But there was no continuing city there; a crush of people pushed in through the floodgate which I had opened and in front of this flood I was pushed, step after step, up and up till I found myself in the pulpit! A brother Minister was behind me and he was also pushed to my side. So there we were like two Association preachers facing one of the largest congregations that had ever been in Moriah. But two things distinguished us from Association preachers, apart of course from their gifts, namely that we had not been invited and that we were not needed.

Up till then the meeting had not commenced and it was as though all were waiting on each other. Suddenly I noticed that someone was calling upon me to give out a hymn and start the service. Without thinking what I was doing I found myself on my feet, I opened the hymnbook and my eyes alighted on a great hymn. Without considering that hardly anyone had a hymn-book, I announced the number and gave out the first verse. But not more than a tenth part of the congregation knew it. Then someone struck up a tune which not more than one in twenty knew. The singing began and those who knew the tune and, probably unconsciously, wanted to show this, tried to continue to the end. But before they had sung half the first verse the other part of the congregation, which formed the vast majority, had completely lost patience, and I heard loud voices cutting across the tune 'Give us something easier!' After the minority had reached the end of the first verse and were content with that undeniable evidence of their talent, from the midst of a bath of cold sweat and nervous trembling, I had recovered some of my senses and led the hymn, 'Iesu, Iesu, 'r wyt ti'n ddigon' ['Jesus, Jesus, all-sufficient']. I heard a deep sigh of relief and joy sweep over the crowd. And now there was some singing! I do not believe Moriah ever heard such enthusiastic singing before or after. It seemed to me from the pulpit that every soul there was singing with all their might. I read some verses and tried to lead in prayer, but I had no idea what words came out. I could only hear the orchestral sound of 'Amen' and 'Diolch iddo' ['Thanks be to Him'], and that sound drowned the sound of my words.

The service then went on, the most remarkable service I attended in a chapel during the Revival period.

Soon after we had sung one or two hymns, the congregation divided into two sections on the gallery and four on the ground floor. The centre point of each group was a brother or sister standing and praying with remarkable passion. The group round each one was 'feeding' the praying one and joining in with him. I have often looked with wonder on a number of powerful whirlpools in a river full to the brim, and the waters divorcing themselves, as it were, from the mainstream and concentrating, each one, on its own whirlpool.[18]

Some of the more notable events of the revival in Anglesey were recorded in the form of a diary published in *Yr Efengylydd*. The author of the diary forbade the editor of the magazine, Nantlais Williams, to reveal his identity. From his writings, however, it is evident that he was a minister, a married man, and something of a scholar. The diary includes the following extracts:

January 1905

January 6 (Friday).—Sisters' prayer meeting; 50 present. God visited his people.

January 18 (Wednesday).—Religious convention in T–. Ground floor full by 2. Chapel full by 5. Two very young girls took part publicly for the first time. Some recited Scripture verses and verses of hymns, but failed to finish them because of the strength of their feelings. What a blessed time it is when people break down as they pray. 'Jesus Christ who died for ME' is the great theme of the Revival. The 'absolute surrender' of Jesus for our sakes causing 'absolute surrender' unto him from our side. One girl said in prayer, 'Pour out the Spirit upon us in showers this minute.'

January 24 (Tuesday).—A man from — died in a tavern in this town tonight. After they removed his body they went about business as usual. This when Revival temperature was at its height.

January 29 (Sunday).—Mr Jenkins, New Quay, and two young girls with him were here all day. Great exultant praise in the evening. 'Take these young men by the hand,' said one brother in his prayer, 'and show them the names of the streets in the New Jerusalem. "The Lord is my Shepherd"—that's the name of one. And give them strength to go over the white stile of the Ten Commandments with its ten steps.'—(That man of prayer was a cobbler and he made me think of Jacob Boehme.) At the *seiat* ['fellowship meeting'] the following Tuesday one sister said, 'I am giving myself to the Lord altogether tonight.'

February 1905

February [3].—W. E.— was closing the *seiat* and he said, 'Thank you for that which we have done, and thank you for that which we are going to do.' . . . 'I used to dream terrifying things,' one young man said, 'but thank you Lord that now I pray before I sleep, and pray while I sleep, and pray after I wake up.' (This supplicator is still alive, a tender husband and caring father and a faithful deacon with the Congregationalists.) . . . In one *seiat* a young man was present who had just come out of prison, and after I had spoken to him, another brother—one who had been in gaol himself—went to pray on his behalf . . . This month I finished reading [Handley] Moule's *Christian Sanctity* for the eighth time.

Wednesday, February 8.—A respectable burial service for a poor woman. The husband was a sober man but lazy and had been cruel. Over £3 was collected in the funeral. The great gospel is improving society through and through . . .

Wednesday, February 15.—. . . I often don't know what to do in the prayer-meeting, whether to laugh or cry, but the boys and girls are entirely honest. Hypocrisy has received a mortal wound in this blessed Revival.

March 1905

Saturday, March 11.—The experience of full salvation is given attention in this revival. This is the same experience as that which is called 'perfect love' or 'Christian perfection' taught by J. Wesley and J. Fletcher and [Williams] Pantycelyn, so why need we fear and avoid it? . . .

Wednesday, March 29.—Received 16 new members in Ll—, and all want to be teetotallers, and almost all members of the Sunday school, and all promised to attend. They can all read—the majority not having read anything of their Bibles yesterday. A number prayed in public. This was the old custom in Wales—to take part publicly immediately after being received as full members.[19]

In addition to Blaenau Ffestiniog, four other districts closely connected with the quarrying industry experienced much blessing—Llanberis and Dinorwig, the Nantlle Valley, Bethesda, and Port Dinorwic. Whatever happened in the town of Llanberis, there was a great deal of revival fervour in many nearby villages such as Llanrug, Cwm-y-glo and Deiniolen, where a few surviving 'children of the revival' could still be heard many years afterwards in mission halls or in tiny chapel prayer meetings. In the neighbouring Nantlle Valley there lived four or five veterans who loved to share their memories in the mid-1950s with the present author, then a young schoolteacher in the area.

One of these remembered Joseph Jenkins as being 'very quiet and sedate', with many taking part in his services. He also remembered people flocking to hear the local young schoolteacher, Evan Lloyd Jones of Nebo, speaking and singing. The district was really set alight by Evan Lloyd Jones, who amazed everyone who knew him when he became so bold and fiery.

The same person also told the story of how one young man had accused an older godly man of quenching the Spirit and killing the revival, because he wanted to hold a Sunday school not a prayer meeting. 'Go on, my boy, flame away,' was the older man's reply; 'but my fire has been red for years.' 'Like many others,' said the informant, 'he didn't think the churches here needed revival because they were well-attended, with good prayer meetings; yet there was much secret sin.' One example he gave of this was of a chapel-goer who, after being converted in the revival, gave up a good job collecting insurance because he said it was so easy to be dishonest at that job.

Another person told of how a drunkard had been completely changed during the revival, and also recalled how the Revs John Williams of Brynsiencyn and T. C. Williams of Menai Bridge came to preach there. She knew of at least one man who tried to get out of that meeting, but failed. An old lady remembered two farm-girls who would have nothing to do with chapel but had come to faith during the revival and were then praying for their father to be saved.

Another lady told a moving story about her sister, who was in much demand as a singer. One night she went to Llanllyfni 'where a great crowd was expecting to hear Evan Roberts speak. They went on singing and praying, but some began to murmur. Suddenly my sister got up and cried out, "Why are you waiting to begin praising until Evan Roberts comes? Jesus our King is here already." And at once a great time of praising began.'[20]

The outbreak of revival at Bethesda aroused great interest and excitement because everyone in Wales knew of the great strike of the quarrymen there and of the explosion of hatred, suspicion and strife it had caused. For many months the little town was split into a score of parties and it seemed that the strike would leave permanent, livid scars upon the community. Although J. T. Job, then a Calvinistic Methodist minister in the town, does not cover over the cracks, his news of revival, family reconciliations and deliverances from satanic forces was widely reported:

What!—the Revival in Bethesda? Yes, sure enough: 'That which we have heard, which we have seen with our eyes, and our hearts have felt,'—He is here—Jesus is here. Multitudes of young people in this place have been tremendously gladdened by the sound of His feet walking among us! . . .

The adversity of the long strike here had a very great effect on the place, and especially on the churches of the district. The saints began to grow restless, and to feel the need for a visitation of the Holy Spirit. There was a quiet but earnest 'chirping' during recent months at the Gate of Heaven. The Free Churches resolved to have a mission here, and engaged the services of the Rev. Hugh Hughes (Wesleyan Methodist) to assist us. He preached on four nights . . . to huge crowds in Jerusalem chapel; and there was a remarkable vigour in the message about Jesus! But most remarkable of all are the prayer-meetings—a prayer-meeting lasting an hour before the sermon; a prayer-meeting for young people lasting for quite three hours after the sermon; along with a prayer and experience meeting for sisters, old and young, each day at 2.30 p.m. There are around 500 sisters in the latter every afternoon; and Oh! what a sight!—women and young girls on their knees pleading for forgiveness, and saying the most remarkable things ever heard. The whole place a flood of tears, and the sighings overwhelming—and the burdens cast down at the foot of the cross . . . 'Thanks be to God' forever—for remembering poor Bethesda! . . .

Up to the present it is *in church circles* that the effects are visible. And *therefore* we are expectant. We expect many 'from the world' shortly. But there is a need to heal the *exceptional* wounds in the churches of the district first of all . . . No one but the Spirit himself can thoroughly heal our wounds as churches; and we have great joy in testifying that the Balm of Gilead is already falling copiously on our wounds—old bad feelings and old contentions: they are already vanishing before the breath of the Eternal Love! Oh, thanks be to God for remembering us! Our hearts as ministers of the district are leaping with joy! . . . This place is one great prayer these days. Oh, come, Lord Jesus!—nearer—nearer—nearer—until you are truly known by all this populous locality.[21]

A tramway used to bring the prepared slates from Bethesda, Dinorwig and other places across the bleak moorland down into harbours such as Port Penrhyn and Port Dinorwic. Behind the quays stacked with lines of gray and blue slates rose the slate walls of houses and the carved slate frontages of a dozen chapels where revival next struck, on New Year's Eve. It is from here, in Port Dinorwic, that a letter was sent over the Atlantic by a man who had the thrill of sharing in tremendous days of revival at a chapel in that village. In the letter, written on 21 January 1905, this man, who was to die six months later, first explains as follows to his brother, William Evans, who was abroad at the time:

> Although many of the details have gone from memory, yet I believe I shall never forget the principal incidents.
>
> What I am about to relate is an abbreviated account, and that of two outstanding meetings; because the marks were never attained, no, nor anything like them, after those occasions. They were like two great spring tides, although we have had lively and fervent meetings since.

The report then begins, starting with the interdenominational prayer meetings held every night during the last week of 1904:

> On Saturday night, the 31st, no prayer-meetings were held anywhere, on account of the Watchnight service held by the W[esleyans], and the new year slipped in with no celebrations of any kind, it being Sunday morning.
>
> On that Sabbath an exchange of pulpits had been arranged between the denominations, and at five o'clock the young people held a prayer-meeting at M_; and after the *seiat* ['fellowship meeting'] all went to E_ soon after eight. I slipped into the house to have a hasty snack, but by the time I reached the chapel the place was fairly full, however I managed to get a good seat on the front of the balcony.
>
> At that moment L_ J_, an elder of M_, was leading in prayer, and he prayed on for quite a long time, but yet very fervently and tenaciously until he was perspiring, and several times when I thought he was about to finish he would start off again, and there was a lovely atmosphere as we listened to him. The meeting was then thrown open for anyone who wished to take part, without inducement. W_ R_ O[wen], of B_, further told them not to wait one upon one other, nor to aim at any particular order; and if by any chance things happened to get out of order, they need not be troubled; that in the South matters had got out of hand long ago, but that the apparent disorder was really perfect order in the sight

of heaven . . . There were some other ministers present that night, but none of them took any part in the meeting.[22]

After references to repeated hymn-singing and fervent prayer, the letter describes the remarkable surrender and penitence of a number of young people. He then continues:

The S[tation] M[aster] (an excellent man) rose to his feet in the body of the chapel, when it appeared as if there was a measure of hesitancy to come forward, if I remember rightly. And he prayed for the Lord to be very evident among them through an outpouring of the Spirit, and that many might be kept, and that salvation might come to certain persons he had before his mind and for whom he had previously been exercised, and to the delight of himself and everyone this prayer was answered within of two or three nights. They were the staff who were in his charge at the S[tation].

Before long a lady came forward—[it was Miss E.]. I could not hear a word she said, but I gathered that mercy was the burden of her prayer. Shortly after her, Miss A. [the blind lady] stood up under the gallery and, as she prayed and gave thanks for what was taking place, she poured out a heartfelt and eloquent plea for the Lord to save R. G.,—a dear friend of hers . . . This prayer, like the others, hit the target, and that before many days.

About this time a little boy of about ten or twelve made his way to the big seat and waited his turn (there were a number already there waiting), and before long he piped out in his clear treble voice as follows, almost word for word: 'I thank Thee, O Lord, for saving my two brothers. Although I am but small, I have a lot of sins which need to be forgiven. Will you forgive them, O Lord,' etc. He paused there, but before he could compose himself and finish his prayer, fervent singing broke out again . . . The two brothers had been praying just before the lad, and had themselves been previously the subject of prayer, I think.

A short while after someone beside me on the gallery stood on his feet in his place, and his particular plea was that the Lord would save his father and his brother. He said how ungodly they were, and how hitherto every effort to change them had been in vain, and how both of them had caused him considerable anxiety . . . Well, strange to relate, about two nights afterwards, he came to the big seat to say that his brother had submitted. When he was returning from his work the previous evening, who should be waiting for him but his brother with his little children, having surrendered in another meeting, and asking if he would come with him to the chapel. He prayed for his father a second time that night, with what result I do not know.

By this time (to continue with the account of the first of January) the people were very sobered, their feelings long gone to pieces. Close to where I was sitting, a lady was weeping greatly, and groaning. A stout-looking man near her had also broken down and little girls near me were crying unrestrainedly. I had noticed that J. Tŷ C_. was restless in his seat and that his feelings had got the better of him for some time. When others had taken part he rose suddenly to his feet and made his way to the big seat, and I thought was on the point of giving out a hymn, but others could be seen hurrying after him, and they had begun to pray before he had a chance to open his mouth. There he remained for a considerable time awaiting his opportunity, and at last he flung himself face-down on the table and plied his pocket handkerchief, his feelings boiling over until his eyes were red. Eventually he got to his feet after long restraining himself, and instead of praying, he testified that he had had a view of Jesus Christ that night such as he had never had before—a sight of the love and infinite grace that he had shown to him as a sinner . . .

The sight of so many on their knees at one time drew from W. R. O[wen] the remark that it was pleasing and becoming to see young people in such a posture; they could do nothing so worthy of themselves, at the beginning of a new year. Bearing in mind the fact that most of these professed to be Christians, it certainly did seem strange to hear them accusing themselves as they did. There would be no end to recounting everything, even if I tried. They confessed sins of almost every kind, as if conscious that no man heard them, only God—and I understand it is thus everywhere. Certain forms of earthly pleasures were ruthlessly attacked. Several brought unsparing accusations against football, and vowed that they would never have anything more to do with it. Similarly with drinking, unseemly language, impure thoughts, card playing, Sabbath breaking, etc.

When the meeting was halfway through, a lame man came forward, one who used to sell newspapers, begging for mercy. He said that he was tired of hearing those dirty stories which his mates told at work. He did not want to tell them or hear them any more. He promised by grace to try to resist the practice, whatever his acquaintances thought of him. He had heard that his Lord by His Spirit went down the mines with the colliers, and that He taught them to sing praise, pray, and to stop swearing, and he pleaded with all his strength that He would come to the men to the hold in the ships, and he said, 'I shall be going into that boiler tomorrow morning with my mates to clean it. and they will begin to tell their old filthy stories in my hearing as usual, but You come with me into the boiler, Oh! Lord, and help me not to listen to them, nor to take part in their talk, and make them stop telling them. Let me be pure,' etc.

Another one prayed that the Lord would save the men on one of the ships (after acknowledging his own wickedness and pleading for forgiveness)—he knew well how they behaved when they were away from home, and what evil places they frequented . . . Then he asked that the ships might be made temples of Jesus Christ, and not lodgings for the devil. Listening to the young men confessing their faults as earnestly as this, E. H. E_ a stevedore, stood and remarked that he rejoiced to see them with their open wounds, that they might be healed by the Great Physician.

On hearing one lad with a broken voice acknowledging his sins and saying that he felt weak, and fearful lest he be enslaved again by his former bad habits, up jumped W. R. O[wen] at once, saying that grace alone had brought him to that place to plead for mercy, and to see himself as he was. He asserted that the boys on their knees before him were bound to hold fast—'being confident of this very thing, that he which hath begun a good work in you will perform it.'[23]

Mass penitence meetings are always a problem because the pressures produce strange effects on people. In later years some warned that these moods could be Satanic deceptions if they bore no lasting fruit. Over in Anglesey the experienced R. B. Jones warned the meeting leaders against asking repeatedly for forgiveness. They were to believe that sins were pardoned as soon as pardon was sought. They were not to air their doubts and fears continuously in public.

Despite these flaws the Port Dinorwic, Bethesda, and other revivals amongst the quarrymen deserve to be recognized and recorded as part of the mighty awakening of Wales in 1904-5. They are authentic signs of the Holy Spirit's threefold ministry as defined by our Lord himself in the sixteenth chapter of John's Gospel.

9
The Voices of the Visitors

'It was a true report that I heard in mine own land . . . Howbeit I
believed not the words, until I came,
and mine eyes had seen it'
(1 Kings 10:6-7)

Strangely little has been written about the crowds of visitors who came
to the scene of the blessing as soon as they received a glowing report or
read a journalist's essay.[1] Such was the interest that some churches
arranged extra weekend services for those who could not share the blessing because of the language barrier.

They came from every part of England, Ireland, Scotland, Western
Europe, South Africa, Canada. There was no precedent in any previous
revival, though people in the pre-railway age had ridden long distances
to the field-preachings. Few understood the significance of this world-
wide surge of interest, and even the revivalists were slow to see the
universal and permanent impact of this Holy Spirit visitation. The equiv-
alent today would be British Christian leaders humble enough to go out
speedily to the West Indies or Korea or East Africa to be 'ignited', if and
when revival flames broke out, and thus bring fire back to frozen
churches in our lands.

People came for very mixed reasons and even the most distinguished visitors confessed to new experiences. Among these were Mrs
Baxter of *The Christian Herald*; F. S. Webster, vicar of All Souls',
Langham Place, London, and one of the founders of the Church Army;
Hugh Black of Scotland; Ferrier Hulme of Bristol;[2] a son of William
Booth and a son of C. H. Spurgeon, along with several London businessmen. All these came originally to watch events but were consequently
caught up in them. G. Roberts Hern, a minister who came to Caerphilly
early in December, wrote:

> I have been with the revival for a week . . . and I confess that I thank
> God with a full heart for the great experience . . . I have tried to detect

any human element—personal magnetism and psychic effects. We cannot in anything deny these powers, *but* these have only the slightest place, if any, in the great wave of blessing over South Wales. It has come of God . . . It has struck dumb even those who desired it most . . . It is naught less than . . . the breath of the Holy Spirit palpably subduing the human heart . . .

Said a minister who had passed through a rapturous time: 'If all my experience of the past, and all the knowledge I have gained were obliterated from memory, I should need nothing to be added to the experience of three darkly solemn and mysterious hours I had in my prayer meeting' . . . What has affected me more than I can tell . . . has been to see any number up to a hundred, some silent with tears of joy or memory streaming down their faces; others with faces buried in their hands and bent before them in deep reflection or prayer; the white tense looks of men and women, with eyes gazing steadily, as if on the beatific vision . . . or the silent moving lips of men and women in advancing years.[3]

Thomas Phillips of Norwich gave the readers of the *Baptist Times* his impressions of the revival:

I expected a great deal, but I saw and felt more than I counted for. There were some things which jarred upon taste and feeling, while it was also evident that the movement was fraught with great dangers . . .

It is not engineered or arranged by a committee . . . No one could foretell its nature and form, and no one seeks to direct its energy . . . The power veritably moveth as it listeth . . .

There were strong men with bowed heads crying for mercy all over the place . . . A young girl sang two hymns, which stirred and subdued me as no sermon ever did . . . She sang . . . with a naturalness and reality, an artlessness and power which were irresistible. At no hallowed Communion Service did the love of Jesus seem a more glorious reality.[4]

Nobility was represented by a Lady Wimborne, who was deeply influenced. The same was true to an even greater degree of the prominent Baptist leader, J. W. Ewing, who was overwhelmed by some meetings. His article in the *Baptist Times* entitled 'Impressions of the Welsh Revival' seems to have circulated very widely. It is a kind of testimony in that he tells why the last week of 1904 was a 'marked epoch' in his own life:

My ignorance of the Welsh language was partly met by the kind interpretation of my friend, Rev. Thomas Stephens, B.A., and by the occasional English prayers, hymns and testimonies, but for the most part I

145

was listening to an unknown speech . . . And yet I found that the spirit of the meetings appealed to me without the aid of language. There was an indescribable influence present which stirred me to the very depths of my soul, and without words I was made to pass through the varying moods of the assemblies . . . I found that among those Welsh believers the Spirit of God was so mightily present that my own spirit, conscious of His nearness, could only bow in worship. I was not a spectator of Revival, but a participant in its blessings.

One of my deepest impressions was of the presence of a convicting power which acted upon conscience with overwhelming effect . . . There were awful moments during which the soul could only lie prostrate at the feet of God, humbled and broken. I understood then in my own heart what was the power which is shaking Wales . . . One night in Clydach, after a melting prayer of penitence, the whole congregation broke into passionate strains of a Welsh chorus,

O that I were like Jesus!

Again and again, and yet again, rang out that cry from the heart of the multitude for purity, for reality, for truth, for all that Jesus represents. And I was swept along with the tide.

And it is from this overwhelming sense of sinfulness that the rebound of joy arises, when faith in the Crucified has brought the assurance of pardon . . .

If we would see our Churches revived and becoming centres of magnetic and soul-winning influence, let us betake ourselves to the mercy seat, there to confess and abandon sin, to seek the spirit of purity and love, and to await the coming of the Divine power . . .

The breeze has come from Calvary,
I have felt it.[5]

The following autumn he addressed the Baptist Union Assembly and told them, 'My first meeting, at Loughor, perplexed me for an hour. There was such a delirium of joy.' But when he found that scores present were new converts he 'understood their gladness and forgot its rough expression'.[6]

This testimony of an evangelist was heard at a Rhos chapel by W. S. Jones, who found one of the speakers had come from Buxton, Derbyshire:

He had been on his own (except for the Salvation Army) for the last thirty years, preaching in the open air, with very little visible fruit. He had received new inspiration, he said, from the meetings in Rhos, and

146

he could face the same work with much more boldness now that he had seen what he had witnessed. At the end of his address he begged for the prayers of the congregation on his behalf and on behalf of the work in Buxton.[7]

Letters written to Mrs D. M. Phillips reflect the experience of two earnest young ladies, one endowed with poetic gifts, who came in with a party from Stone, Gloucestershire, seeking the power. The letters speak to us of a humble, sensitive soul emerging into new life and vigour when touched by the Spirit. One letter was written on 4 April 1905:

Dear Mrs Philips

I thought I should like Mr Dan Roberts to have the enclosed lines before he leaves Tylorstown. They were written by my friend with whom I am now staying. I am feeling tired & depressed. I wish I could have attended a few more meetings, they caused me to hope. I have for years been in fear of my salvation. Altho' I stood up, I beg to have assurance. I know I long to possess all that God has given to His children but I feel too unworthy . . .

Again thanking you
I am
Your's gratefully
Amelia A. Green

Another letter followed on 11 April:

My dear Mrs Philips

Thank you for your kind letters. I have taken the message as coming direct from God. I need it just now, when I am thinking of returning home and confessing the Lord Jesus. I feel sure some friends will drop me, others will wonder what has happened to me! I confess I feel too weak not to feel this most acutely.

I beg that I may be remembered in your prayers & those of the dear little friend whom I saw with you. If you care to have the verses of my dear friend here, I have much pleasure in sending a copy of them (written by herself) to keep for yourself.

I cannot find words to express my gratitude to you for your kindness to me when I called, as I was *quite a stranger*. I thought it so very sweet of you both . . .

I am
Your's very gratefully,
Amelia A. Green

The poem, written by her friend, Lucy A. Bennett, was published in *The Christian* and is a beautiful expression of their desire to be fully consecrated to Christ:

> Lord, bend me, as the golden grain
> Bends at the breeze's faintest breath.
> Before Thy Spirit's gentle reign
> O bend me, Lord, for life & death.
>
> Oh, if this treacherous heart decline
> To own Thy Spirit's tender sway,
> Come as the fire, O Power Divine,
> And burn the barriers all away.
>
> Lord, bend me, as the ocean wave
> Is bent before the tempest's roar,
> Thine all-compelling Power I crave
> To break in blessing on life's shore.
>
> Lord, bend me, as the bleeding vine
> Is subject to the gardener's skill,
> Thou blessed Husbandman divine,
> So bend me, at Thy sovereign will.
>
> Lord, bend me; as the river's track
> Is traced by an Almighty hand,
> Thy guidance may I never lack,
> For everywhere is thirsty land.
>
> Lord, bend me! of this worthless clay
> A chosen vessel Thou canst make.
> Mould, heavenly Potter, mould to-day
> For I am Thine, to bend or break.[8]

A favourite experience of the visitors was to be taken to a furnace or a coalmine to witness one of the workers' prayer meetings. Crouching in cramped quarters, deafened by the clash of metal or the thunder of trams, they scribbled down the songs and prayers they heard there, and sometimes managed to produce a remarkably vivid impression, such as this one in a pit in Pontypridd:

> In a few minutes we were descending in the cage. The water from the sides of the shaft dripped steadily on us, and soon we were at the bottom, more than a thousand feet from the surface. We were led along a passage

to a central gallery, from which branched out various galleries leading to all parts of the mine. Soon a number of men passed us, and about 6.15 a collier rose and started the hymn, 'Guide me, O Thou Great Jehovah.' At once it was caught up by a large number of voices, and the music was simply awe-inspiring. Then another rose and offered up prayer that God would bless them and keep them all day, and that He would put pure thoughts and good desires in their hearts, and help them to do their day's work for His sake.

After that a Welsh hymn was sung . . . By this time several hundred men had gathered in the various galleries, and altogether . . . there were more than three hundred colliers, out of nearly five hundred employed in the pit, at the prayer-meeting. A lad recited with exquisite effect the fifteenth chapter of John, in Welsh, and the melody of his utterance came like a musical ripple on the air. From out of a gallery, like a voice from the unseen, came an address on the power of God to keep and save; which was followed by the hymn, 'Come ye that love the Lord' . . . One felt the joy of the Lord surging through the hearts of the colliers.

A Church clergyman from Durham prayed in English, and cited the 139th Psalm . . . When he came to the words . . .

'The darkness and the light are both alike to Thee' –

then the presence of God overshadowed us as a glorious blessing, and though in the gloom, lit up only by the feeble lights of the Davy lamps, we could scarcely distinguish any features of man, we felt that we were in the hollow of God's hand and full of joy unspeakable . . .

It was an awe-inspiring sight to see the lamps gleaming out of the blackness of the galleries; to hear the echoes of the musical choruses of the Welsh hymns ringing through the pit. Promptly at seven the service ended, and the colliers wended their way down the tunnels into the darkness, singing with gladness praises unto God.

When we reached the top of the shaft, day was just coming in over the mountains, and we felt that a newer day had dawned in the darkness underground, whose light was the Lamb.[9]

Unfortunately some visitors from other countries began to create problems as time went on. Evan Roberts never knew quite what to do with the Boer War veteran, the American lady with her sweet little son-preacher 'Lawrence', the woman with a divine command to pray that revival hit the royal family, the coloured actor, and the robed M'Taggart.[10] Yet it was not they who aroused anger but the credit-takers and the would-be planners. Dr F. B. Meyer found himself in hot water with the patriotic Dr Cynddylan Jones and with Dr Campbell Morgan by suggesting that the Keswick-type meetings in Wales had been and still were a positive source of the revival.[11] When the journalist W. T. Stead dreamed of a 'Converts League' or similar organization, Dr Cynddylan Jones reacted strongly:

> Wales has never had professional missioners . . . To all these I say, in the name of Wales: Hands off! Come and see and get the blessing; return home, and pass the blessing on.[12]

In more moderate tones, Awstin said this growing opposition was not because Welsh people resented the use of English, but because of 'the occupation of the pulpit by English visitors who seem to think that their speeches are more important than prayer or praise'.[13]

The most attractive visitors were those who came or who were sent to Wales to make intercession for their own towns and counties. They were humbly content to sit in the main body and join in worship until asked to stand and say a few words. The Swansea minister, Penar Griffiths, went to a revival meeting in Porth 'for inspiration for his Sunday's work'. A Rossendale pastor requested prayers for Lancashire and explained that he had also been charged by a brother minister to ask prayer for Manchester with its 1,500,000 people. A Sheffield minister solicited the people's prayers for that great Yorkshire town and said he would be talking to over 2,000 people at Sheffield the next Sunday about the revival. Clark Gibson of the East Suffolk Mission asked for prayer for his county.[14]

Other prayers heard included one for 'a moving among the dry bones' of Birmingham. A Welshman ministering in Ipswich asked for the prayers of the Welsh people for his town; an elderly gentleman from Devonshire remarked that 'showers of blessing' had already fallen there; a chaplain made prayer requests for soldiers in Africa. Some returned with words of encouragement and exhortation. Through the Principal of Spurgeon's College Evan Roberts sent a message to the students, 'Tell them to live very near to God. That's the best life—near to God.'[15]

In some cases the visitor had been almost mandated to speak for his church members and workers. One of the Rhos meetings was addressed by a Manchester minister who said that he had read an essay about the revival in Rhos in the *British Weekly*. When he had read this to his congregation they took to it exceptionally and a longing was created in them to become fuller partakers. They called a Prayer-meeting as a result, and their testimony was they felt something they had never felt before in a Prayer-meeting. But after coming to Rhos, and seeing for himself, he had something new to say to them. He longed to take the account to his people back home, and he believed for certain that they would have a blessed time as they went over the events.[16]

Some people checked the results of these requests by compiling a 'map of revival blessing' in various parts of England and Scotland. The *English Churchman* mentions evangelistic services in St Paul's Church, Onslow Square, London, led by a bishop, and then by Barclay Buxton the Anglican missionary and Prebendary Webb-Peploe the local rector.[17] The *Baptist Times* reported a revival-inspired conference in Edinburgh followed by a march headed by the 'Hallelujah Brass Band'.[18] Nottingham, Leicester and Manchester are named in late January; Exeter, Nottingham, and Newcastle in March.[19] A mission in Gloucester was led by two students who had a rough ride from town gangs.[20] In Reading, Carey Baptist Church and an Anglican church took action together. The full effect of the visits and the intercessions can be known only when the late Dr Edwin Orr's rich resources are analysed.

Overseas visitors caused ripples of excitement because no previous revival had drawn in so many. Awstin said this had been accomplished by the newspapers and by thousands of pamphlets sent to each country, thus spreading the enthusiasm and the yearnings:

There are many of us who believe that Isaiah's references to 'the isles' are meant for the British Isles, and that we are destined to fulfil the prophecy by sending the Gospel from here to the furthermost parts of the earth, and no one who knows what is going on in Wales to-day can deny the peculiar applicability at the present time to our own country of the verses –

'Arise, shine; for thy light is come, and the glory of the Lord is risen upon thee.

'For, behold, the darkness shall cover the earth, and gross darkness the people; but the Lord shall arise upon thee, and His glory shall be seen upon thee.

'And the Gentiles shall come to thy light, and kings to the brightness of thy rising.

'Lift up thine eyes around about, and see: all they gather themselves together, they come to thee; thy sons shall come from far, and thy daughters shall be nursed at thy side.' (Isaiah, 60th Chapter—1st over 4th verses.)[21]

The *Western Mail* Supplement recorded the pleadings of a Turk, an Armenian, and a German lady with a French interpreter, among others.[22] Perhaps the best-known was Pastor Cadot de Chauney of Aisne, France, whose experience at Tabernacle Chapel, Cardiff, was related in Chapter 4. He asked people to pray for 'the struggling little Protestant churches which he represented'.[23] He moved on to Swansea where he was often seen, with outstretched hands, pouring out his soul in prayer, his supplications eliciting many fervent cries of 'Amen':

> [At Nazareth Chapel, Tonna, near Neath he] re-called an incident when he had saved his wife's life, and though he burnt his hands in the effort, so great was his joy that he did not feel any pain. So, too, in an infinitely greater degree was the case with the Saviour of man—the pains of Gethsemane and the Cross were more than counterbalanced by the happiness which He enjoyed at the salvation of man.

At Aberdulais in the Neath valley he testified to his own conversion before asking for prayers for a visitation to his 'dear benighted country'.[24]

Before long reports were coming in that the revival was spreading into northern France and Belgium.[25] A conversation with Pastor Reuben Saillens at the Baptist World Congress in July 1905 told of evangelical pastors taking the revival flame from Maesteg to France and of how the French Baptist Conference had debated whether to free one of their number to 'carry on the revival work'.[26] About a year later the Welsh Baptist paper *Seren Cymru* included a long letter from a contributor from Seacombe with the initials R. M. P. It said that a number of revival hymns had been translated into French, and some examples were included in the letter. It also noted that the revival was being felt in a number of places in France.[27]

The world-wide repercussions of the visits have been observed by Mrs Jessie Penn-Lewis and Dr Eifion Evans, among others. Our only concern here is with revival outbreaks triggered by missionaries and visitors from Wales. Mrs John Roberts, J. Pengwern Jones and Sidney Evans formed bridges between the Welsh scene and the Welsh Calvinistic Methodist mission field in Assam in north-east India. There had been much prayer for revival on the mission field during 1904, and some showers had been felt at a meeting of church leaders in Cherra in February 1905, but nothing compared to that experienced at another such meeting in Pariong in March:

The 'spirit of the living God' was moving to and fro through the Saturday meetings, and there was an anointing on all the activities. The Sunday preaching was in power and in the Holy Ghost, especially that of Babu Olik and Babu Joel. The afternoon meeting was drawing to a close, the people having been greatly blessed yet feeling that they had not received that which they were expecting. There was a sound of someone praying in the midst of the congregation—'Oh! Lord! do not let us go from here in our starving condition. Pour out the blessing *now—now!*' Then there were tens, yes, hundreds uniting in the prayer. In the twinkling of an eye 'all the fountains of the deep' broke. Rain . . . fire . . . what? The great blessing, and the huge congregation face to face with God melting in repentance, confession of sin, acknowledgment of guilt, and rejoicing in the assurance of forgiveness. The Pentecost of the Church on the [Mission] Field! We were there for hours—no talk of finishing now; some in distress, others freely rejoicing, and the congregation finally lifted up to heavenly places on the wings of the great hymn of the revival in Khassia, as in Wales, 'Here is love, vast as the ocean.'

At the end of March there was a further anointing in the village of Nongsawlia, with the full blessing coming after a young girl spoke and prayed until there was much weeping—and then suddenly the flame. The Welsh missionary, Dr John Roberts, who was present at the meetings, rejoiced to see the same signs here as in his own land and played a key role in the intense evangelistic work that followed.[28]

Jonathan Goforth of China also said he had been much influenced by contact with a revived Wales. All these seem to be confirmations of Mrs Penn-Lewis's words:

In the darkest, loneliest, furthest corners of the earth, the most isolated child of God may share in the world-wide blessing, as the life currents from Him who is Life eternal circulate freely throughout the Body of Christ . . . May all be given anointed eyes to see the vision![29]

Ilsley Charlton, the CMS missionary on furlough, must have been one of the bearers of good tidings back to India, since we know that when he visited a revival meeting, he jotted down in his notebook an itemized account of the service he attended:

First, a man offered an earnest prayer, then the whole congregation, standing, sung for some minutes.

This was followed by a most fervent prayer from a young woman in the gallery, after which the congregation sung a hymn sitting down.

Then a young man rose and called upon God with great eloquence, accompanied by many loud 'Amens.'

He was soon joined by a second, and the two prayed on, seemingly unconscious of each other. Then two women joined in, until the congregation rose and burst into singing . . .

Gradually this hymn changed into another hymn to the tune of 'Do not pass me by,' the congregation now sitting.

The alternating of prayer and hymn-singing continued for a while:

Then the Pastor . . . began to say something, and his voice was drowned by about a dozen prayers at once. He seemed quite content to be interrupted, till soon about twenty were praying together! The meeting was getting very vehement and seemed as if it would boil over, but it never did. Just at the critical moment, as an earnest tearful prayer of a little boy added still more fuel to the fire, a hymn burst forth from somewhere . . .

Then two young men began to exhort (or pray) together and were joined by a young woman in the gallery, and again there was a volume of earnest calling upon God, and again the great meeting seethed with emotion and fervour, and again almost seemed on the point of boiling over, but once more a sweet hymn came floating over the congregation, and all settled down again . . .

Then the Pastor asked for 'silent' prayer which evidently meant murmured prayer, as the whole congregation murmured softly their petitions to God.

At this moment a young woman in the gallery was weeping, and another by her side praying for her, the congregational murmuring giving way to, 'I need Thee every hour' . . .

The young woman in the gallery again prays by the side of the weeping one, till the weeping gives way to testimony of having received the Lord . . .

Then the first young woman gives thanks for her converted friend, and the congregation sweetly sings to the tune of, 'To the uttermost He saves.'

There were numerous more exhortations and several more hymns and prayers before the meeting was tested and all church members asked to stand. Finally, 'the Pastor says a word or two . . . and the meeting dissolved after three and a half hours duration.'[30]

No one had ever seen meetings of this kind before and it is little wonder that the many visitors were fascinated. One can share the feelings of that aged man who called out, 'I came three thousand miles to this meeting, but I would go round the world to see such as this.'

It is impossible to end this survey of the visitors without a brief mention of those who afterwards wrote books about their impressions. Ilsley Charlton's conclusions have already been noted. The best-known of the others at the time was the London journalist, W. T. Stead, whose professional life was filled with drama from its beginning to its sudden end in the sinking of the *Titanic*. Londoners took him very seriously, and he was noted for his lengthy dialogues with Evan Roberts which satisfied the longings of many Englishmen to know more about this youthful revivalist. His reports and the conversations appeared under the title *The Revival in the West*.

The Welsh community in London had first-hand accounts of the revival in the industrial valleys from H. Elvet Lewis, whose long pastorate at King's Cross Welsh Congregational Chapel gave him a commanding position. As the title of his book *With Christ among the Miners* suggests, he was particularly fascinated by the instant change in manners and morals and language as Christ through the Holy Spirit visited the miners.[32] Altogether different was the contact made by the novelist Allen Raine, who modelled one of the characters in her novel *Queen of the Rushes* on Evan Roberts.[33]

There were other visitors of some distinction who tried to interpret the revival. Mrs Penn-Lewis of Leicester sought to relate many of the events she had witnessed in the great outpourings of prayer which she regarded as the 'hidden springs'. On the other hand, Dr Fursac of Paris accounted for much of the revival in psychological terms after he had interviewed a number of converts and presented their case histories.[34] Perhaps some visitors saw only what they wanted to see.

Finally, there appeared a volume which has already been quoted, *The Afterglow*. This was the work of an Englishman, M. Holyoak, who came down to Wales in 1907 to talk with a number of ministers and laymen in order to discover how enduring were the effects of the revival. He made very careful enquiries and his recorded observations will have direct relevance to Part Three, since that section of the book will be chiefly concerned with the transforming influence of the revival upon worship, ministry and public witness, as well as upon individuals.

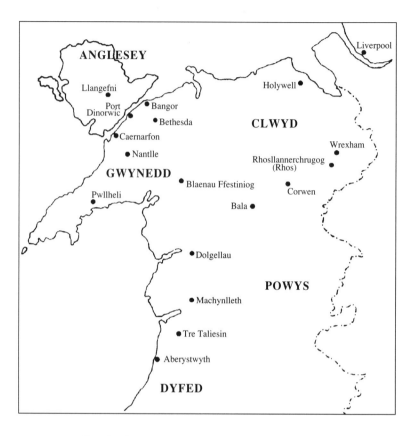

Revival centres and other places mentioned
in North and Mid Wales

III. TRANSFORMATION

Jesus' blood exalts the feeble,
  Makes their victory complete;
Jesus' blood brings down the mighty,
  Lays them humble at His feet.
    Heavenly breezes!
  Breathe on me from Calvary.

William Williams, Pantycelyn (1717-91);
tr. by William Edwards (1848-1929)

10
The Sound of Victorious Praise

'Her saints shall shout aloud for joy'
(Psalm 132:16)

'Both young men, and maidens; old men, and
children: let them praise the name of the Lord'
(Psalm 148:12-13)

The sober, sedate Calvinistic congregation that gathered in Mount Seion that morning received a shock. They looked askance when they saw their minister's place occupied by a young man, accompanied by such youthful maidens. Instead of announcing the customary hymn for the commencement of the service, one of the young women burst forth in a spiritual song expressing her new experience, tears streaming down her cheeks. The whole congregation gasped! . . . What did this mean? was the question on every lip.[1]

Thus wrote David Matthews who saw at first hand the revival in its early days at Trecynon, Aberdare; and the story was continued by Thomas Williams of Parc, Trecynon, who saw the strange things that happened in these same chapels during that November week when mighty new forces had been released into the churches:

The divine assaults of the Eternal Spirit were seen striking down men like corpses all over the floor . . . The unanimous testimony of those who experienced them is that they were pierced as by a sword or an arrow, or struck as though by a shot from a cannon . . . One knows of some meetings where there were reasonable grounds for believing that something like an impairment of the senses had taken place in them; and not a few were frightened at the sights they saw . . . I know of a man of lukewarm temperament, and of a cold and precise philosophical turn of mind, on the spur of the moment being set ablaze like a bonfire; and all who saw him going wild, clamouring, and bounding like a hart back and forth from the ground floor to the gallery, and from seat to seat

159

through the chapel, thinking that he had for certain taken leave of his senses . . . His opinion and experience to this day is that the Spirit of the Lord in a supernatural way was moving him from the narrow circle of his reason, his understanding, and his knowledge, to the wide world of the spiritual.[2]

Ways and means of worship which are commonplace today were breathtakingly revolutionary to them, as the eyewitnesses confess. The coming of the Spirit revitalized public and private means of grace. David Hughes summed up what he saw as the 'Lasting Blessings of the Revival'. He noted four novel features—informality, diversity, exaltation, and prayer and testimony:

> *The first continuing blessing that we observe is, the successful and beneficial way found of raising the meetings out of formalism.* The constant complaint was that the meetings had fallen into this mechanical formalism. That was heard in our prayer that we 'might not come out of form and custom.' There is no greater danger to a spiritual institution such as the Church of Christ than cold formalism. Of course, there must be form; but we must leave the Spirit of Christ shape the form . . . Our spiritual labour as members of Christ's Church requires order, but it ought to be Holy Spirit order . . . We saw that the seeming disorder when in His hand was a blessed order. We were personally at four meetings . . . from six in the evening till four the following morning . . . [On every one of those nights] the spiritual work of the meetings proceeded without any leader all through the night . . . All the formalism had gone, yet with nothing untoward happening . . . This was the Church of God at its climactic moment receiving feasts 'of fat things full of marrow, of wines on the lees well refined' [Isaiah 25:6] . . .
>
> This new way was, and is, a blessing to many thousands in the churches—the way the Spirit has of leading His people who are in His hand by the 'means of grace' of the meetings of the Church . . . Once they have been on this new and living way . . . religion becomes a new thing to them . . . God is new, Jesus Christ is new, the Holy Spirit is new, their own kingship and spiritual priesthood are new. Yes, sin—the devil—everything from the depths to the heights have become new to them, and are realities more vital than ever before . . . This is a priceless blessing, and will remain, whatever use is made of it.[3]

The principles of informality and diversity can be illustrated from the records of different denominations. Within the Anglican Church the new ways penetrated even to the sacraments through the efforts of Vicars Pritchard, Williams, Rice, and others. They made a serious attempt to reach out to their revival-thirsty parishioners without dispensing with the liturgy. The Vicar of Llanddona in Anglesey persuaded Evan Roberts to give an address in a 'service of reconciliation and preparation for revival'. Meanwhile:

> The Dean of Bangor paid an unexpected visit to Loughor, and attended an overcrowded meeting at the National School. The Rev James Jones and Canon Williams addressed the gathering, the latter gentleman putting these questions to his auditors:–
>
> > 'Have I given myself to God, or when am I going to do so?' 'Do I read some portion of the Bible every day, or shall I now begin to do so?' 'Do I hold family prayer at home, or shall I begin?' 'Do I pray for others, or am I only concerned for my own soul?' 'What am I going to do to help to bring others to God?'

After having repeated these questions, the whole congregation fell on its knees in fervent prayer. The Dean of Bangor then addressed the gathering, and said he had come all the way from Bangor as he had heard so much about the revival, and was very anxious to see for himself what was going on. Since he had been there two things had come home to him. The first was that in order to win souls they wanted nothing new. They wanted no new Gospel—the old one was in power. They did not want a new Bible, Prayer Book, Creed, or Church. 'But,' the speaker continued, 'we want to feel more and more the power of the Holy Ghost working through these things.'[4]

At a later meeting in the National School at Loughor:

> an address was delivered in a most eloquent, earnest, devotional, and fervent manner by Rev. the Hon. Talbot Rice, Vicar of Swansea.
> A strange feature of this meeting, too, was the irresistibility of the Welsh element which broke out, though it was conducted in English, and overwhelmed both preacher and congregation with its depths of emotion.[5]

Equally remarkable was that service at Pontarddulais when the Vicar of Gors-las, Anthony Briton, invited the people to stay behind, descended from his pulpit, gave out some hymns, and delivered an earnest revival address.[6] Finally, there is the story from the nearby Amman Valley about the vicar, E. A. Davies of Christchurch, who distributed a special leaflet of penitential collects and hymns for use in matins:

> The great congregation seemed to enter heart and soul into the special prayers, and, with solemn utterance of sentence by sentence after the vicar, between 300 and 400 voices blended into one. Instead of the ordinary discourses a series of simple appealing addresses were delivered. At the end of the evening service the vicar from the chancel steps made a final appeal for decision. Then followed a stirring scene. One person after another from different parts of the church stood up and walked up the aisles in the presence of all into a special penitential seat, which had been kept vacant for their accommodation in front of the pulpit. As the vicar stood continuing his appeal, the seat accommodation proved too limited, and ten converts were counted, all being adults. This result was obtained without any noise or confusion, and without the slightest departure from Church of England formularies. The singing of canticles and special hymns throughout the day was unusually stirring and impressive.[7]

From North Wales comes a correspondent's story in the *Wrexham Advertiser* of a Bangor vicar sharing with a nonconformist minister in an experiment:

> An interesting ceremony took place in 'Yr Afon Cegin' (the River Kitchen), near Bangor, on Tuesday afternoon, when a young man and woman were baptised according to the rites of the Church of England. They are to be confirmed shortly. They had not been baptised as infants, and it was at their own request that they were thus baptised. The Revs. W. Edwards, senior vicar of Bangor, and Owen Evans officiated, the actual immersion being performed by the latter. The congregation numbered about seventy, all but three of whom were women.[8]

A minister's diary mentions a house communion service in which one of the church lads spoke as led by the Holy Spirit. He described also a communion service on 5 June 1905, when the people began to recite verses and chapters—'as in the time of Richard Owen the revivalist'. And again there is this entry in the diary for 23 May 1905:

> The seiat at 7 was turned into a communion, which was a new thing in Ll_. Two brothers prayed to begin with . . . [The service] was chaired by a dear old respected minister, and two of us took the elements around . . . The *seiat* was alive with intense, tender and serious feelings,

and we delighted in singing, 'Ni buasai gennyf obaith' ['I would not have had a hope']. Such communion is better than at the end of the Sabbath when everyone is tired.[9]

Welsh Nonconformists, and Presbyterians in particular, had their own ideal vehicle for more flexible forms of revival worship. This was the long-established weeknight meeting (already prominently featured in this account) known as the *seiat* ('fellowship meeting'), which had grown out of the experience meetings of the Methodist revival of the eighteenth century. Thomas Williams, also known by his bardic name 'Parcwyson', gives two striking pictures of this type of meeting at Trecynon, Aberdare—one where a converted poet spoke so imaginatively and earnestly that all were dissolved in tears; the other when the stammering James Mathias recounted his experience in his strongly colloquial Welsh.[10] The writer who signed himself 'Christian Worker' tells us what happened in one of his churches:

> It was very difficult to have a society meeting because the spirit of prayer had so taken possession of people that every meeting turned into a prayer-meeting. Yet we did have some very blessed and unforgettable societies, the most notable being the one when fifty were seeking membership . . . A lovely sight worth remembering was when all the converts were present and the majority told their testimonies. Some of their sayings abide in our memory till this day. One question asked formerly was how to hold a seiat in a way which would be profitable and edifying. It was difficult to get anyone to say a word. By now, things have changed greatly. No older member got an offer to say a word because the converts were so ready to tell of their experiences and to bear witness to the work of God's grace in them and upon them.[11]

For Baptists the greatest event, and the most challenging, was the mass baptism of converts. This was followed by their reception into membership, usually at the next communion service, where they filed up to the pastor to be given the right hand of fellowship. The *Wrexham and North Wales Guardian* has a fine picture of such a baptism in the icy cold waters of the Dee at Carrog near Llangollen, witnessed by a large crowd standing on the bridge, and accompanied by massed choirs on the river bank who sang well-loved revival hymns.[12] A detailed picture was given by a *Llanelly Mercury* correspondent, who saw 92 converts celebrate the New Year by 'breaking away from sin' symbolically by immersion in the river Lliedi at Felin-foel. This is what he saw:

The people came from 'all the regions round about.' Hundreds walked from Llanelly, while the entire population of Felinfoel appeared to be present. The spot chosen for the baptism is at the further end of the village, where the river runs under a bridge that carries the main road across. Hard by is the picturesque 'God's Acre' of Holy Trinity Church. Above the trees stands out the tower of Westfa, while nestling on the hillside are the humble dwellings of the colliers . . . The weather on Sunday was fine, but cold, a keen north wind blowing along the high ground. Down in the valley, where the baptism took place, this was not felt much, and the spectators forgot all discomfort (if there was any) in the fervency with which they sang well-known hymns while the ceremony lasted. Mr Humphreys began the morning's work with a brief address, followed by a prayer, after which he walked into the water up to his waist. Then the long line of converts wended its way down the steps, and the singing of 'Diolch Iddo' ['Thanks be to Him'] heralded the first immersion. Included among the converts were several females, but the great majority were young men, who in the future will become, let us hope, pillars of the cause at Adulam. Included among them were men whose past life has not been all that could be desired. Now, however, they have thrown off the 'old Adam' and begun the new year on the side of Christ.[13]

One of the remarkable documents that have somehow survived is a broadsheet bearing a picture of Hermon Chapel, Fishguard, and its well-known minister, Dan Davies. Underneath is a poem entitled 'Bedydd Mawr y Diwygiad yn Hermon, Abergwaun' ('The Great Baptism of the Revival at Hermon, Fishguard') composed by one 'W. Rees', who used the bardic name of 'Arianglawdd'. After mentioning the gifted preachers and memorable experiences Hermon Chapel had witnessed in bygone days, the bard sings of the days of revival it was now experiencing, and especially the mass baptism of ninety-two converts baptized by Dan Davies in the river Gwaun on 15 January 1905. With so many men and women being baptized in its waters, the bard pictures the river itself as entering into the spirit of praise that broke over the heads of the onlookers, whom he compares to a 'cloud of witness'.[14]

One of the characteristics of these baptismal services was the practice of making an appeal by the side of the river or pool. People were invited to decide on the spot that they too wished to 'die with Christ', or 'follow Christ', or submit to some such watchword. The report from the 'mini-revival' at Ponciau, near Rhosllannerchrugog, in June 1904, of a nervous young man responding to such an invitation and stepping down into the baptistry to make a public witness, is but a foretaste of many such occasions during the Revival.[15] In the light of experience it was later thought wiser to hold instruction classes first.

*   *   *   *   *

The second novel feature of the revival according to David Hughes was diversity:

> *The means of grace are richer for everyone when a variety of age, sex and gift yield themselves to glorify Christ through those means* . . . Was there not a cry here and there in the land for a greater variety in the form of public worship for its own profit? And surprisingly, when the Revival came to the land, it led this variety in like a high tide; and without exception the experience was that the blessing was possessed by a greater number than before.[16]

Nothing moved people's hearts more than to see children joining in the praises of Zion, just as Jesus had once been stirred. They watched them going out in processions, not so much as Sunday-school classes on parade, but as channels of prayer and testimony, having their own revival hymns. A correspondent from Penmachno writing in the Blaenau Ffestiniog newspaper, *Y Glorian*, said that seeing and hearing children of three years of age upwards marching through the village was a most moving and glorious experience.[17] There were touching and curious scenes in the school playgrounds of Rhos and other villages where young children could be seen at prayer in some corner. Reports came from Aberdare and Treorci of older pupils bringing repentant sinners to Christ. From every part of Wales came first-hand reports of children's meetings for prayer and praise, like this one from Pwllheli:

> At one o'clock each Sabbath afternoon we have a meeting for children and a number of young men are there with them. Last Sabbath a meeting was held as usual, but somehow, no one knows how, that meeting was turned from one which catechized children into a children's prayer-meeting. It developed that way imperceptibly; no one can ascribe it to anything but the Spirit of God. We had a prayer and singing meeting from 1 to 4, which no one present will forget. Children of 6 to 13 years of age were praying like old people, weaving together verses of Scripture and verses of hymns in their honest and childlike way, until it drew forth amens and tears in showers. When the adults' school understood what was going on in the children's school, the people were flooding in there.

165

It was similar in Penmount school, in the children's school there. A class of boys started singing 'Ar ei ben bo'r goron' ['On His head be the crown'] and could not be stopped. They rose up as one man and walked like a regiment of soldiers, still singing, into the adult school, where there was tremendous singing and praying.[18]

The renewed devotional life of the young people also broke away from traditional forms. The thing that struck observers most of all was the almost unbearable intensity they showed. One of them from Tanygrisiau, Blaenau Ffestiniog, remembered those weeks when there was no shortage of young volunteers to do every possible task, including wholehearted involvement in prayer:

All the mind and will of the young people was upon the chapel. Scarcely could the day finish soon enough because of so much eagerness to be found in the sanctuary. This was the testimony of most of the young people—that 'the zeal of thine house hath eaten me up'. After a warm, earnest prayer-meeting in the chapel on Monday, 12 December, certain of the young people went into the vestry to plead for a more abundant outpouring of the Holy Spirit in our prayer-meetings. That was the most *terrible* meeting (forgive the word, but that's the word I have for it) that I have ever been in. Before a quarter of an hour was up everyone was sobbing. Someone led that verse *'Ai am fy meiau i'* ['And was it for my sins'] in a broken-hearted manner and in a quavering voice, his bosom swelling with emotion and with an abundance of tears. As he went on from line to line and idea to idea, the weeping became extraordinarily bitter and the sighings even more burdened. No one thought of singing the verse but others went on reciting the rest of the hymn, and still no one was able to sing. But after a spell, when everyone calmed down, we began to sing the hymn—and Oh! the emotion that was in the singing. The praying then began again—praying and singing, and lamenting across each other. The scene was terrifying. That meeting broke up some time around midnight . . .

As you know, we had oil lamps with which to illuminate the buildings at that time. Because the meetings were going on to the early hours of the morning, it was needful to clean the lamps and replenish the oil in them quite often, yet there was no shortage of workers for the task. I cannot remember the lamps going out because there was no oil in the vessels.[19]

Equally fascinating was the acceptance of a new freedom and role for women. Sisterhoods and guilds and women's missionary auxiliaries have become so much a way of life now that it is hard to imagine how radical these were before 1904. Yet suddenly, as the Spirit of God touched hearts, the handmaidens as well as the servants began to pray and praise. Two valuable independent observers describe with astonishment these early women's meetings. They have a free experimental feeling about them, though they had to have male elders of the chapel to start the service:

> In the mornings the wives got up with their husbands at half past four in the morning and did daily housework from five to half past eight when they sent the children to school. Then the mothers would go into any chapel if the revival was on there and then they'd go home to meet the children coming home at 12. And after they sent the children they'd go back again (they had finished their housework in the morning). It was throughout the whole town like that for the mothers were so interested. They would go home in the afternoon and prepare dinners for husbands (who washed in the house) and then return to the house of the Lord. It was all praise and worship, and God was glorified in a wonderful way. The people were blessed and life was worth living.[20]

The second comes from the quarry village of Bethesda near Bangor:

> The crown of all meetings without doubt is the Prayer and Testimony Meeting of Sisters (of all ages) at 2.30 every afternoon in Jerusalem vestry . . . This vestry can . . . seat five hundred with ease; and is overflowing every time! Many stream in from quite a distance, and among them students from Bangor University [College] . . . After beginning with singing, reading and prayer (and many—preachers and elders breaking down completely in doing so)—it is announced that the meeting is 'open;' and the meeting is left in the hand of the Holy Spirit. And there are three or four sisters immediately up on their feet! and the verses of Scripture spring up as fresh as the torrents of Lebanon! And Oh! *what* utterances: what a blessed emphasiser is the Holy Spirit. Although we are very familiar with most of the verses, yet—they are today as *new* to us as God. But there—God is new for ever. Hush! there are others on their feet, and the verses come tumbling after each other, weaving like rainbow colours through each other; and Oh! how lovely they appear through the showers of tears that are on the faces of the congregation. Over there, two . . . are on their feet at the same time ('one at a time,' says the president, 'so that we can understand you') with a word of living testimony on the lips of both. 'Oh! Jesus is good,' says one. 'Whom

do I see like my Beloved, lovely and fair' &c. . . . 'I have sat beneath His shadow' &c., says the other. At that point there is a disturbance. A young girl starts leading the song 'Bendithiaist goed y meysydd' ['You blessed the trees of the fields'] until the place is electrified. Soon a girl of fifteen is on her knees and praying heaven down on our heads . . . Now everyone is in a flood of tears; and 'Gwaed dy groes sy'n codi fyny' ['The blood of your cross raises up'] is struck up with overwhelming power . . . A woman gets up over there,—'I am a great sinner; yet I have not been the same woman for the last fortnight; Jesus Christ has taken hold of me; Oh! thank you! A little while ago, God took two of my little children to heaven to Himself. And I am able to see now what He was saying—"You are not a fit mother to rear these lovely little ones—I will rear them myself." That's what He was saying to me.' We were now completely overcome by this last observation. Oh! God was near.

Yesterday (Friday) we had the most remarkable of all these meetings. I can never describe it: but I will remember it for all eternity. It was awesomely divine from beginning to end. Towards the end a young girl of about twenty-four years of age (one of the sweetest singers in the district) burst into prayer—with the most stirring effects we have had here yet.

She was asking the Lord to help her pray publicly for the first time, thanking Jesus for his presence and her mother's counsels, and calling upon her sisters to 'break through' and to tell Christ 'our grievances honestly':

'I have been a bad girl. O dear Jesus—a very bad one too.' ('*No*, my daughter; you have been a *good* girl,' said her mother). 'No indeed, dear Jesus,' (said she—with tears coursing down her cheeks!) 'Oh! dear Jesus! forgive, O forgive! I am a great sinner—O forgive, forgive! Thank you for ever receiving sinners, dear Jesus. Keep me for your service as long as I live. I've tried to sing for you. But Oh! do not let me sing any longer for anyone but yourself, and of Calvary . . . I will sing far more for you yet, Oh! dear Jesus! . . . Thank you for being so kind to me until now. You took my earthly father from me when I was young; but Oh! you have been a blessèd Father to me always. Prepare me to go to heaven to live. I have more today in heaven than I have upon earth.'[21]

Sooner or later the spirit of freedom and informality was bound to affect even the most solemn occasions, such as denominational assemblies and preaching festivals. At Baptist Union Annual Meetings at Aber-carn, the President, Peter Williams ('Pedr Hir'), summed up the revival as 'new wine in the old bottles . . . [which] must prove elastic, that there be nothing lost'. Thursday saw a series of open-air preaching services throughout the day. 'Just as night came on . . .' says the correspondent in the *Baptist Times,* 'a wave of revival swept over the whole of the vast congregation.' When it was learned that several young people had professed conversion at the morning services, there was a spontaneous outburst of harmony:

> At the close Dr. [William] Edwards, of Cardiff, tested the meeting, and in burning words pressed the great question upon the huge gathering. That signal manifestation of the Divine Presence, he said, was the crowning feature of the meetings. He appealed for testimonies, and a large number of prayers came in response. When he asked that everyone who was under Christ's banner should show it by lifting up the hand, hands went up as a forest, and held up spontaneously during the singing of a hymn. It was an intensely solemn incident, and strong men wept like children. Finally, when, after the Benediction, the multitude dispersed, they went in different directions and sang as they went until the whole valley and the hills around resounded with praise unto God. Groups were formed here and there on the way, and prayers and praise were continuously offered up to heaven far on into the night.[22]

It took a little longer for the Spirit to take hold of the preaching festivals, as is seen by this severe criticism by Richard Griffith ('Carneddog') of special preaching meetings at Beddgelert at which two of the most prominent preachers among the Calvinistic Methodists, Evan Jones of Caernarfon and T. C. Williams of Menai Bridge, preached:

> The sermons were very able, but they were delivered too mechanically to stir up or attract the body of listeners to true worshipping zeal, and because of this, no one stayed 'behind', that is, gave themselves to Christ. The Revival has suggested important lessons to ministers as well as to listeners. They must divest themselves of ostentatious conservatism in all its forms. Yes, ascend the holy pulpit without cloak or gloves, and impulsively, and wholly naturally, deliver the words of Life to anxious sinners. That is the opinion and expectation of the common people from Holyhead to Cardiff.[23]

Reactions at the beginning of 1905 varied from that of a Caernarfon clergyman who burned all his professional sermons, to those of certain Rhondda ministers who would not enter the pulpit at all. In some places they broke down when they tried. Again, Thomas Williams of Trecynon,

Aberdare, illustrates this with a story of what happened during a special afternoon preaching service on Christmas Day.

The late and venerable Rev. O. R. Owen, Glandŵr, rose to his feet in the pulpit slowly and unostentatiously and approached [the Bible] in a devout manner . . . It was evident that he was too full of some difficulty to preach any form of sermon without some sort of self-emptying or deliverance first taking place.

Oh! the indescribable intensity! and the unforgettable look on the seraph's face at that transforming hour in the pulpit of Ebenezer, Aberdare, Christmas afternoon, 1904—the great year of God's right hand.

Look at him again:—His hands are outspread on each side of the pulpit desk . . . his two genial eyes like two sparkling fountains casting their crystal contents over his pale cheeks. When the crowd realized that he could not see his text through the flow of his tears, someone struck up [a familiar hymn] . . . The weeping preacher had time to dry his eyes. When the singing ended, a deep and sweet silence reigned. The congregation now waits and listens expectantly; but the preacher remains dumb and stunned. Some could now be seen talking and looking around, trying to conjecture what was hindering the messenger from speaking . . . We heard one old woman asking audibly in her seat, 'What's the matter with Mr Owen today?' but her acquaintances knew the answer. They recognised the breeze. Hush, another bright tear falls from his cheek. The crowd sing again . . . The preacher is still dumb, and the congregation hears a quiet sigh rather than a text. The leaves of [the Bible] are wet, and the text beneath the tears. Penar [Griffiths] is behind him, but he cannot leap into the breach. He has his head bowed on his lap, soaking his handkerchief with tears, and raising his hand for heaven to stay the flood, for the sake of the servant who was before him in the pulpit, unable to speak . . . The quivering and melodious voice of the silver tongue is heard [at last] . . . 'We have long yearned for it to come . . . The Lord has answered us in a blessed manner, praise His name.' Then he read his text:

'Be not drunk with wine, wherein is excess; but be filled with the Spirit'—Eff. v.18.[24]

At a preaching festival in Blaenau Ffestiniog in April 1905, on Easter Monday evening, Dr Wynne Davies, the guest preacher, was well into a sermon on forgiveness. As he spoke of 'the floodgates of the eternal love being opened', suddenly the dam broke:

Great rejoicing broke out, with Mr Davies keeping on in the midst of

170

the rejoicing, almost unconscious of himself. His testimony was that he neither saw nor felt during the revival such a manifestation of the Lord's presence as he saw and felt in that meeting. Then they went to the vestry . . . and Mr Davies in their midst. There were dozens on their knees, praying in tears and praising on the top of their voices. An attempt was made to close the meeting around 10.30. Mr Davies got up and stood on one of the benches to try and silence the meeting and close it. He said a few words but the fire rekindled and his attempt was in vain. At last he got the meeting to sing [a hymn] and the Lord's Prayer was recited, and thus he succeeded in drawing that remarkable meeting to a close.[25]

Even the strict *cymanfa ganu* ('singing festival') tradition surrendered to the spirit of liberty and rejoicing. The accepted task of any festival conductor was of a musical rather than spiritual character. It was to complete the preparatory work of singing classes by bringing the singers to perfection of form and tone. Into this world of dedicated musicians the revival entered like an explosive charge—as in the singing festival at Pontypridd Town Hall at which Dr Cynolwyn Pugh was present along with two thousand singers:

Though the crowd is so large every individual there is as quiet and as reverent in spirit and devotional in appearance as if in a cathedral. And why not? Had they not come there to praise the Lord?

After a reading of Scripture and earnest prayer—and this was not some kind of preface but rather an indispensable part of the service of praise—the singing begins in earnest, one hymn after another, and each hymn, as it were, taking a firmer hold [on us] than the one before. In a little while the conductor calls upon the singers in the gallery to sing one or two of the great classical anthems composed by Handel or Haydn or one of the other masters; these singers had been prepared carefully by local conductors, most of these being ordinary colliers yet fine musicians and living examples of the folk culture of the Welsh nation.

By and by one of the ministers is called upon to give a short address but, poor man, he could not go on! The singing had fired the speaker, and he in turn inspired the crowd, and one felt an atmosphere of rejoicing throughout the place and saw various men and women breaking forth into prayer and testimony. Suddenly there was a young man up on the platform striking up the chorus 'Pen Calfaria, nac aed hwnnw byth o'm cof' ['Never let me forget Calvary'] . . . What is happening? you say. Only that the Lord Jesus is walking in the plenitude of His power through the service of praise. By now the poor guest conductor is sitting in a heap in his chair! The reins are in the hands of the Holy Spirit! . . .

In addition to this, through the power of the great truths which were sung under the might and influence of the spirit of life, men were to be seen being convicted of sin and turning from the errors of their ways . . . The splendid great truths about God and Eternity and the reality of sin and forgiveness and grace were *singing themselves* into the guilty conscience and the bruised heart.[26]

Did the Welsh revival produce any new music of a spiritual kind? This is hard to answer because many of the reports tend to note only the familiar hymns. Mr Webb of Gorseinon remembered singing an old song declaring that 'forgiveness is free', and another about sanctification:

> Kindle a fire within my heart,
> Causing Satan to depart,
> Make me holy as Thou art,
> And lead me safe to glory.

Someone like Kate Morgan Llewellyn might compose new tunes for old themes and the congregation would soon pick up the key lines or improvise new verses themselves. Here is the report of an eyewitness from a Swansea chapel:

> There was a remarkable outburst of singing when someone struck up 'O na bawn i fel Efe' ['O that I were like Him'], and when the ordinary verses of the hymn had been sung the Rev. T. Teifion Richards, Ravenhill, sung . . . striking additional verses of his own composition, the congregation joining with increased and increasing fervour in the refrain.[27]

A great favourite was a Welsh translation of 'Throw out the lifeline' which was found scribbled on a checkweight ticket of a colliery worker and was the work of Daniel Davies of Rhymney.[28] Another old hymn which, next to *'Dyma gariad fel y moroedd'* ('Here is love, vast as the ocean'), became almost a signature tune of the revival was *'Y Gŵr wrth ffynnon Jacob'* ('The Man by Jacob's well'). W. S. Jones of Rhos recalled how the famous London preacher, Elvet Lewis, brought it to Rhos at the beginning of 1905:

> [Elvet said] he was anxious the verse should be given a new lease of life in the Revival; like everything else the old verses were coming back like Noah's doves. He asked them to sing it to the tune 'Bryniau Cassia', and

the solemn yet triumphant accents of that old Hindu tune have sounded in our ears ever since. It would be good if the verse were sung in every meeting as it was sung on Friday evening. Who can forget the heavenly effect felt when Mr Caradog Roberts led a second time on the organ: so tender, so solemn, and so overwhelming![29]

Fifty years later, Aneirin Talfan Davies had no difficulty in finding someone who could sing this ballad of the woman whose soul needed living water. There is another recording from Moriah Chapel, Loughor, of less well-known revival songs remembered by the ageing converts. In their repertoire also was a wealth of traditional Welsh hymns about salvation, centred upon the cross and the covenant, mingled with hymns from the Sankey-Moody tradition about cleansing and yielding.

The *Baptist Times* printed a number of translated revival hymns, most of them translated by Principal William Edwards of Cardiff and Rev. John Thomas of Liverpool. Welsh readers will recognize the originals of 'Ride in triumph, blessed Jesus'; 'Here is love, vast as the ocean'; 'Jesus' blood exalts the feeble'; 'The sound of Gethsemane's groans'; 'Come, old and young, now come'. A favourite in North Wales was an old revival hymn about a ship named *Salvation* being brought safely into Calvary harbour and there being unloaded in three hours for the eternal blessing of all who partake of her treasures. The best-loved hymns echoed the singers' own experience of salvation and had an instant effect on singers and hearers, as this man saw:

> When the people sing of Jesus they know not how to cease. Their love overflows. Their enthusiasm rings out in notes of triumph. One night at Moriah Chapel, Loughor, I heard the chorus,
>
> To Jesus be the crown!
>
> sung, perhaps, a hundred times, and I seemed to see the coronation of my Lord.[30]

In every department of public worship the principles of freedom, informality, flexibility, together with variety of age, sex and condition, all created new and sometimes troublesome problems. Reaction set in and opposition mounted (see Chapter 16) but these features could not be ignored. Evan Roberts himself found the continual outburst of song rather annoying at times, but he defended it against the many critics.[31]

*   *   *   *   *

173

According to David Hughes the third lasting blessing of the revival was exultation:

The victorious proof we have that the length of a religious meeting is an irrelevance when the Holy Spirit comes upon it . . . The spiritual world became so real [during the Revival]: in its light men lost sight of time. The blessedness of eternity was everything . . . A victorious proof has been left by the Revival as a continuing blessing to the Churches that the length of a religious service is an irrelevance where the anointing of the Spirit rests on the meeting. No one is compelled to remain; no one transgresses by leaving before the end, if need be. Everyone is allowed to do as he will, and this is the reason so many remain with no thought of time. To them the Spirit gives joy.[32]

Grawys Jones of Aberdare used to speak of his own experience of this victory and joy in the early days of the revival when he and his colleagues returned to the pulpit to supervise revival meetings after Evan Roberts had left for Pontycymer:

Some most strange joy took possession of the whole congregation. The only way I can describe it is this—as if a great shower were coming down the valley here—I have seen it often—and you can hear the noise of it in the wind, and then by and by a few big drops come, the forerunner of the great shower. Exactly like that it came. I knew that something great was approaching. We could hardly hold ourselves together. The praying continued, and just then, one young man who was a very splendid singer and a very fervent Christian began to sing upstairs. It took hold of the congregation, and they jumped to their feet and sang right on for about a quarter of an hour. Some were shouting for joy, and others praying. We three ministers in the pulpit were crying for joy, the tears running down our faces. We were lost to everything, and forgot all about this world, I think. The joy of it, the immense, untold joy of it was something that I never, never dreamed possible, and I doubt whether I could experience it again. It was something once for all. We never thought of time, or of drawing the meeting to a close. It never occurred to us at all. However, about 3.30 it came to a close of itself, like putting one hand in the other, and we all got up and went home. And out in the roads I could hear companies of people going down to Aberdare and singing, companies going to the east and to the north and to Cwmdar. About 4 o'clock I went home, and I could hear companies in the early morning singing away with all their might. I went to bed but could hardly sleep, and when I did I was laughing for joy in my sleep, and I got up in the morning full of joy.[33]

Thomas Williams's account of the revival at Trecynon includes a remarkable first-hand description of exultant praise at a Boxing-day service at a local chapel in December 1904. Only a selection is translated here:

> Salem was almost bursting with the throng—scores were singing and praying ceaselessly from beginning to end. *Evan Lewis* shouting like a silver trumpet, '*Salem!* Salem! Salem! Blessed Salem! The place of my conversion—where I felt my God forgiving my sins,' &c., and the voice and praise of Miss Lewis, Llwynypia, electrifying the crowd.
>
> Llewelyn Marchant, the man from Bethel, little in stature, in the big seat, taking off his coat to fight Satan . . .
>
> '*Bili bach Welsh Harp*', with his long loose locks playing across the nape of his neck as he leaped over the seats, and his short fervent prayers bringing down the fire from heaven in heavy showers! . . .
>
> In Salem that afternoon the women of the churches of the area first broke out in exultant praise for the Saviour of the world! and there also God first received praises out of the mouths of children. The ministers and deacons of the district were astounded amidst the noise of the fiery torrents. Elvira George exploded in fiery prayer for her father. Tom Bedlicotte sang his song of deliverance. Mr Rees the tailor waxed eloquent as the sea—'About the Salvation that flows relentlessly to shore'. The old pilgrim, James Thomas, feeble and crookbacked, rejoiced and leapt like a fifteen-year-old youth. There we saw Satan arming his servants with all the weapons of their impudence in order to try and silence the sound of Hosanna and Hallelujah! . . . Young men—men and women swooning, and fainting under the strength of the powers. Fear and dread fell on the hypocrites of Zion, and alarm came upon the godless of Jerusalem . . . There Charlie Samuel's tongue was set free to magnify the *Propitiation*! And David Evans, Top-y-cae's lips were opened to pour out the pearls and the thrill of his new experience in Christ! . . .
>
> In Salem the sermon of Mr Rees, the lay preacher from Cefncoedycymer, melted into anointed praise the first Sunday of the awakening.[34]

A Welsh poet from the Garw valley, whose bardic name was 'Brynferch', composed an ode to these days of victorious joy. It was called

'Dychweliad yr Amen' ('The Return of the Amen'). As the title suggests, the poem describes the effect on Wales of this new visitation of the Holy Spirit. Wales, says the poet, has again found the 'Amen'. As a result of God's mighty visitation, all peoples of the world are gazing upon her.[35]

The late John Powell Parry tried to describe how this eager, rejoicing spirit seemed to fill the air outside as well as inside the chapels. Some said that they could feel thrilling excitement of a pure, holy kind even when they were a few miles away:

> In those days there was no traffic, no cars, but just horses and traps and carts taking coal from the collieries. In the afternoon everything was silent and finished, with no traffic. Only throngs of people singing and praising God. And on Sunday mornings when there was no work, the people got up early in the morning as if on a working day—so the chapels were open at 6.00 a.m. They didn't lock the chapels, and you could go to any chapel and they were open throughout 1905 without abating in the least. People didn't want so much sleep in those days for there was life in the air that they breathed. There was power and life and activity. I remember well that I never felt tired.
>
> I remember in mid 1905 there was a little branch line from Wrexham to Rhos, and it was a continuous service with people coming from other places. It was only a fourpence return journey and the train was in continuous service all day, bringing people into the revival zone. The people here were rejoicing as people who came from other districts were saved there and they were going home full of the Holy Spirit and a wonderful experience of real revival in their hearts.[36]

Was this unusual spirit of triumphant joy merely the result of a build-up of expectation? Or is this the natural result whenever God's people are truly cleansed and consecrated? Were they not priests unto God, standing within the inner courts and gazing towards the holy of holies as they sang and prayed? Here are the testimonies of three such men who had been standing in the Presence:

> The praying and singing are both wonderful . . . repentance, open confession, intercessory prayer, and, above all else, this marvellous musical liturgy—a liturgy unwritten but heartfelt, a mighty chorus rising like the thunder of the surge on a rock-bound shore . . . And all this vast, quivering, throbbing, singing, praying, exultant multitude intensely conscious of the all-pervading influence of some invisible reality . . . They called it the Spirit of God. Those who have not witnessed it may call it what they will; I am inclined to agree with those on the spot.[37]

176

Then we have this testimony from David Matthews:

> With my back to the pulpit, I witnessed a sight that made me feel faint. Confronting and surrounding me was a mass of people, with faces aglow with a divine radiance, certainly not of this earth. For one brief moment my faith staggered, and criticism arose in my mind. But it soon vanished. Critical analysis could not survive such a dynamic atmosphere ... With awe and fear I gazed upon this scene.[38]

And lastly, we have this testimony from Blaenau Ffestiniog:

> January 29th ... An ever-memorable Sabbath ... Nothing like it had been seen in Bethel's history since the 1859 revival. The dear, now deceased, Simon G. Evans, B.A., Pwllheli, who was at that time in Bala College, was on the circuit on that Sabbath day. This brother had been immersed in the spirit of the revival. He was a messenger well suited to the heart of the congregation and many earnest prayers were offered on his behalf before he came. There was a prayer-meeting for young people in the morning. In the 10 o'clock meeting, after the service had begun, he made no attempt at all at preaching but left the meeting completely in the hands of the Holy Spirit. One after the other men and women rose up to pray in the very place where they were—some on the ground floor and others in the gallery—simultaneously and cutting across each other. Remember that by now the young girls were as fervent as the boys. They were in the chapel till 12.15. Two stayed behind ... Three quarters of an hour later, at 1 p.m., a Sisters' prayer-meeting was held in the vestry until it was time to begin Sunday school. At 4.30 a prayer-meeting was held until the evening service. In the evening service, no attempt was made at preaching. The Holy Spirit was leading. Prayer was being offered up in every part of the chapel, and the singing was most blessed. After that service the vestry was filled at once with boys and girls praying. Among them were seven sisters yielding for the first time.[39]

Did any post-revival groupings become guardians and preservers of this new-found freedom and informality and boundless joy? Did the women and the children continue to take part? That must surely have been the case in the little gospel halls and mission halls until the coming of the Pentecostal movements which put their own seal on such worship. But it is sadly true that the denominational chapels soon went back to the old, traditional way of prearranging hymns and appointing people to pray, thus blocking new ways and new language and new hymns. Former revival preachers went eagerly to any chapel where they could hear again the ardent prayers and joyous songs, usually in a weeknight meeting. Not everything was lost, however, and there are those who speak of the gains.

* * * * *

It was about the old chapels that David Hughes was thinking when he wrote his final summing up of the revival in 1909:

> Many a corner of the land has found cause to rejoice that the revival has distilled lasting blessing into the means of grace. Holding a meeting today is not the same thing as it was before then. There is a great difference, and that to the advantage of the spirituality of the meeting. It is true that the original perfections, and the spontaneous spirituality which breathed mightily upon every meeting and everyone in it, no longer fill the temple now in all places as at that time. Yet the hearth of every meeting throughout the land that is held along the lines of worship, is closer now to the fellowship of saints and the family of God meeting together to give testimony and to pray, than was the case previously.[40]

The continuity of revival praise was assured as long as that first generation of 'children of the revival' was alive. They were in the pulpits and prayer meetings when a younger generation, who had outgrown the simplicity of their elders, clever, smart, patronizing with all the confident sophistication bestowed by education, derided their odd ways of speaking until suddenly their souls took wing in praise and yearning prayer. Once more Thomas Williams's book of memories of the revival in Trecynon can be drawn upon to illustrate their role. He describes how Tom Howells, who had been a drunkard before his remarkable conversion at the Stag Hotel and Ebenezer Chapel, Trecynon, was still expressing praise and joyful thanksgiving seven years later at a '*seiat*' (fellowship meeting):

> Thank you for this breeze, Lord. I had thought you were not going to breathe on our meeting tonight—but the *Breeze* has come, and we have felt it. Thank you for it: and grant that we may keep it, we will not do much here without it. We have proved that many times—but it is *flat*— it is dry and hard enough, Lord, without the breeze . . . The breeze can pass between a man and his sin—yes, it came between me and the cup, and it brought memories of my mother's prayers on its wing. I felt the

breeze making my spirit tender; and the taverns . . . became images and idols which are hateful to my soul. The breeze passed by our hearth bringing peace, and ever since then there has been peace and comfort in our cottage—instead of swearing, a verse; instead of an oath, a psalm; instead of passion, prayer; and instead of sullenness, a hymn of joy and singing. Thank you for the miracles of the breeze, Lord, let us keep it. *A breeze from Calvary's Hill!* We can swell your praises in the company of the breeze—we can subdue kingdoms—stop the mouths of lions— quench the violence of fire—escape the edge of the sword, and wax valiant in war, and turn to flight the armies of the aliens—we can! says your Word. But we must have the wind behind us.

In another meeting, his prayer went like this:

Gracious Lord, my mind runs back tonight over the seven years of ful- ness I have received from your hand! yes, seven years of your gracious gifts—for that is my age in religion. I am a child born in the midst of revival flame. And Oh! blessed years. From then until now the Lord has sustained me. Blessed be the Great Lord for this sustaining; I deserved nothing. Despite this, I have seen no need of anything from your hand. You have kept me from the cup, and if that were all, it would have been a great keeping, namely keeping my feet from slipping—keeping my lips pure—keeping my temper meek. What a keeping! Yes, keeping my lust under control, and keeping desire underfoot. You have kept my mouth closed against wine and spirits—and away from doubtful and destructive paths. If it were not for this keeping and upholding I would have spent much of my gold and my silver by now. I would have squan- dered much of my labour on the enemy's mess; but through this merci- ful *sustaining*, my strength and health and labour and earnings have been used for a better purpose . . . What a blessed keeping; keep again Lord.

Another prayer-warrior was John Hwmffre who lived alone and was quite a character. He was known to despise all fashions, ceremony and small talk. His large head and bull neck made him look rather frightening, yet every child seemed to know he was gentle and would flock around him. At a Saturday-night meeting in a chapel vestry in Trecynon during the revival:

He sat warming himself near the chapel fire half an hour before time . . . After two of us had entered, and almost before we had time to sit, we heard Hwmffre announcing in his big voice, as if there was a large congregation there, that it was time to begin. With that we saw him rise, and direct his steps to the platform. Having arrived he put on his glasses and opened the old [Bible]; then he asked how appropriate it would be to read one of the chapters about the Seven Churches in the Book of Revelation. 'Very appropriate,' we said. 'Yes,' he said then, 'you must remember that this is a time of revival, and it will not do to read anywhere.'

If the manner of his praying should bring a smile to the faces of those who heard, there was no mistaking the dignity and solemnity with which he prayed. Asked on one occasion after the revival about his public praying he replied that since the revival he had prayed regularly in public:

'I was praying on the last prayer-meeting night. There was a place! The heavens were descending there; I got hold of the prayer of old Habakkuk. Boy, it was glorious.' And then he went on to repeat the prayer—'O Lord, revive Thy work in the midst of the years. God came from Teman, and the Holy One from mount Paran; His glory covered the heavens, and the earth was full of his praise . . . Although the fig tree shall not blossom,' &c., &c., with his rough, unmelodious voice, until all who passed the house stopped to listen.[41]

When men and women of this kind formed prayer groups and waited upon the Lord, the effect could be overwhelming. W. S. Jones, the Rhos reporter, once described what he called a 'Horeb' experience, as if on the mount of God, at a meeting in a Wesleyan chapel in Rhos some time after the revival had reached its 'high tide':

Arriving at the chapel some time before the service began, the first thing that struck us in the porch was the strange silence within, and the sense of a Presence that could be perceived on the threshold. There was almost a dread of thrusting through it, but so desirable was He that of necessity one entered to 'look at the vision.'

When the appointed leader rose to open the meeting, it was easy to see that he felt there was no place for him that evening . . .

Various attempts were made to pray, or to give a testimony, or to sing a hymn—but every effort failed half-way through . . .

After a period of silence, the leader rose a second time and indicated that Dr Owen Davies, Caernarfon, was present, and asked him if he wished to speak. The Dr sat in the seat nearest the door, and took no notice of the invitation. He was pressed on a number of occasions, and eventually, obviously against his will, he arose and answered in the most modest manner: 'I feel that this is neither the place, nor the time, for anyone to speak. There is One greater than all speaking here tonight.'

He sat down, and for a time again, the meeting was handed over to the Great Presence; and so in the midst of the silence every soul was still before Him, to enjoy fellowship with Him, and to hear the secret of His heart . . .

To us, that was the most remarkable meeting of the Revival—a meeting with hardly a word spoken in two hours! . . . And we, poor sinners, although surrounded by the flames of His Presence, possessed by fear without dread; by awe without anguish; by modesty without servitude.[42]

Careful local enquiries would no doubt provide many examples of a continuing spirit of freedom, joy and adoration—but we must end this chapter with a meeting of revival converts which was held annually for many years and was known simply as 'Cwrdd y Mynydd' ('The Meeting on the Mountain'). This was held on the slopes of a mountain on the edge of Llyn Eiddwen, a lake in the hills of central Cardiganshire, half-way between Tregaron and Llanrhystud. It had been started by nine converts in the year 1906. This story of a latter-day revival meeting comes from 1924. After the preparation meetings on Friday night and Saturday morning, which raised great expectations, the blessing fell in the afternoon:

We went to the mountain at two o'clock and there were from 1500 to 2000 people from all parts of the land, some of whom had come in cars; brothers and sisters from the Rhondda Valley, &c., &c. We had a blessed time on the mountain, though the crowd was more mixed there than in the chapel . . . The evening meeting commenced at six o'clock, and it was the loveliest sight I ever beheld; the vast crowd on the mountainside praying to God and there was a strange solemnity in the prayers. Towards the close of the meeting a young boy who had been saved recently began to pray. We sang

> *A'r maglau wedi eu torri,*
> *A'm traed yn gwbl rydd.*

> [My fetters broken,
> And my feet wholly free.]

That hymn was doubled and trebled until everyone felt wholly free! As he prayed he came across that verse again, and the great dam burst so that everyone went on praising until late. After many gave testimony, the day—one of the best on earth for many of us—came to a close.

Blessed be our God for ever and ever, Amen . . . Praise be to dear Jesus' Name for remembering us. The burden of our prayers was that men should be saved everywhere, and our chief desire is: O come Lord Jesus in your glory![43]

Only eternity will show how often that mighty spirit of prayer and praise born of the revival broke out in the countless converts' fellowships, until their earthly voices fell silent in the grave and they were called to sing to the Lamb in nobler, sweeter praise.

11
The Call of the Master

'Let . . . the ministers of the Lord weep
between the porch and the altar'
(Joel 2:17)

Just as the new wine of the revival affected worship in a dynamic way, so it affected the type of man and woman already much involved in church and chapel life but not freed from various defects in personality and doctrine and experience. A 'Bord Gron' ('Round Table') article in the Baptist magazine, *Seren Gomer* ('The Star of Gomer'), said that 'among the host of indifferent and barren people in the churches of Wales in the period before the revival were to be found many who lived faithful to their obligations, and in season, and out of season, sowed the good seed'.[1] Scores of these ministers, deacons and others were filled with joy, boldness and new vision as strange things happened to them and they were humbled under the hand of God. In curious ways the experiences found in this selection of testimonies and reports correspond with the breaking and bending of the revivalists themselves as recorded in the Prologue.

From the many missionaries who claimed that their first inspiration originated in the Welsh revival comes this testimony. It is that of Daniel Thomas, a native of Llandeilo and a missionary in South America, who told *Y Cylchgrawn Efengylaidd* ('The Evangelical Magazine') readers his story:

> I found someone to show me the Way of Salvation, but I did not find anyone to instruct me further in the spiritual life, and this proved a great hindrance to my growth because of my ignorance of the Scriptures, especially regarding assurance of salvation. I never heard anyone use that phrase 'assurance of salvation', but I continually heard in the prayers of the saints about the possibility of falling from grace and being lost; I believed this was scriptural and therefore I lived in fear that I would be lost at the end. Then came the 1904-5 Revival and all doubt

was removed about the security of those whose trust is in the finished work of Christ on the Cross. God was very near in those days and I experienced an abundance of his blessing. It was as if Satan was bound, and it was very easy to live the spiritual life.[2]

Daniel Thomas was not the only one to find blessed assurance and to be set free to be a bold witness to the gospel overseas. The story of Rees Howells is well known but others are unrecorded. A little-known account comes from Cross Hands, near Ammanford, where a young miner named Edward Wilkins had come to the place of decision in an early revival meeting. Sitting in July 1962 in his cottage parlour which looked out on a courtyard full of shell ornaments, this wiry, energetic man told his astonishing story of the effects of revival on his life:

After I was converted in the revival I went to meetings like a bee looking for honey—because I did not know much. We all went to Bryn Seion [Gospel Hall] and there heard about the new birth, full assurance and obedience to the Holy Spirit. There came a day when the Lord told me to go and tell about Jesus to the Kaffirs. My friends in the Lord were ready to support me, but how could I reach these people when I had no training nor much education? I went to the Johannesburg compound for a while but the Lord told me to go and work among the blacks. I had been a miner so I had to work alongside blacks down the gold-mine. It was so hot that we could not wear anything there—but I found a way to speak to them about Jesus. I came home in 1913 and helped found a mission.[3]

Home missioners include Mary Jones of Egryn, near Towyn, and Evan Lloyd Jones of Nebo, to the south of Caernarfon, who were set alight during the revival. Mrs Jones was a quiet, reserved farmwife who began to have mysterious experiences after seeing a strange light on her way from Islaw'r Ffordd to Egryn chapel. Gomer M. Roberts quotes someone as saying:

This shy, modest woman became the mightiest force ever seen in the neighbourhood, and that in a quiet way, with no one knowing exactly how or when. She took the meetings into her own hand, and her words carried deep, strange conviction to the hearts of the people amongst whom she had long lived.[4]

However, some aspects of her work were treated with great suspicion.

Evan Lloyd Jones was a young teacher, poet and deacon who lived in the Snowdonian hills at Nebo where people divided their days between quarrying slate and farming their smallholdings. As news of revival came to Nebo, Evan began to stir up the young people and then came down to a revival meeting at Tal-y-sarn in the Nantlle Valley. Normally a modest and unassuming person, he found himself going up the pulpit stairs and telling everyone that the Spirit had compelled him to come and testify. Each day he went around the quarrymen's villages and was given liberty to lead and speak.[5]

The conversion and commissioning of George and Stephen Jeffreys, evangelists and founders of great Pentecostal movements, were equally remarkable. They were converted in their home church at Maesteg under their own pastor, Glasnant Jones, and they had their full share of the revival fire. According to his secretary-biographer, George responded totally to Evan Roberts's call to obey the Spirit in everything.

David Matthews of Aberdare, the singing evangelist whose main ministry was overseas (after a brief spell as an official Welsh Baptist evangelist), was just a decent, hard-working, religious man with musical gifts when he became impressed by the radiant life of one of his own students after going to an Evan Roberts meeting. He went along himself and afterwards described his feelings as 'petrified', 'tossed about', 'puzzled', 'crushed', 'disturbed', and 'mobbed' with the words of God. Then came a panoramic vision of Jesus moving through a crowd and a blind, beseeching beggar, whom he recognized as himself, pleading, 'Jesus, thou Son of David, have mercy on me':

> A sweet voice spoke within my spirit so clearly, unmistakably, audibly, that the voices of all creation could never succeed in drowning its message: 'Be of good cheer, thy sins are forgiven thee.' Heaven came into my heart that very moment.[6]

This was how one evangelist was born. There was another named Matthew Francis, a Llanelli tinplate worker, who came under strong conviction at an open-air meeting and finally gave his life to Christ shortly after the revival began in his town in late 1904. Ten years later he emerged as an ordained evangelist, spent four years itinerating in a gospel van through South Wales, did valuable pastoral work under the Bethel Evangelistic Society in Bristol and Newport, and finally enjoyed twenty-five years of fruitfulness in Walsall.[7]

From missioners and missionaries to student ministers—and the recorded testimony of J. R. Morgan who was to become a long-serving minister and one of R. B. Jones's supporters as secretary of the Bible Institute at Porth:

As a candidate for the ministry I was expected to give a paper at the mid-week service. My text was, 'Oh that I knew where I might find him!' [Job 23:3]. That night, as I gave that paper it was the cry of my own heart. Between the days spent at Newcastle Emlyn Grammar School and those spent at Aberystwyth University College, I had already spent three and a half years in the course of my preparation for the ministry when the Lord met me on Monday evening, 4 December 1904. O sacred day! Time will not allow for the details; to put it briefly, after some three weeks of direst conviction and wretchedness and my sense of utter unworthiness, I yielded myself to God and had an experience of receiving the baptism of the Holy Spirit and the unspeakable joy of full assurance. O glorious days of the right hand of God! Joy! love! glory! heaven on earth! God everywhere—one's heart lifted up to the heights of delight and satisfaction—filled with wonder at the simplicity of faith.

That same night, after having a baptism of the Spirit which manifested itself in great waves of love which rolled over me like sea billows. I thought, when I raised my head in Bow Street chapel, that all the doors and windows in the building would have been blown out. It was like a rushing wind. Filled with love for the Lord and for others, I went home that night to my uncle's house (he was pastor of the church where I was staying) and going up to my room I was so full of the love of the Lord that I knelt at my bedside and said, 'Lord I'd give anything to show that I love you more than anything else.'

Filled with this burning love the young student gave up all inclination for the young lady he was then courting. Next, he put his full trust in the Lord for healing from a complaint that had weakened him for years, and actually burnt his bandages. Then he vowed to testify to the first person he met in the early morning. 'It was the milkman and I testified to him and told him of the love of the Lord Jesus.' J. R. Morgan never lost that simple loyalty.[8] The same is true of Llwchwr and Morgan Jones who were struck down at Bangor Baptist College, but no other testimonies seem to have survived.

The revivalists were really shocked that so many ministers kept sitting on the sidelines throughout the awakening. They did not object or criticize but they sat silently in the back of the pulpit while remarkable events took place before their eyes. However, there were a number who were deeply touched, probably the first being Thomas Francis of Gorseinon. He was cast into deep confusion by his first contact with Evan Roberts, but a letter from the revivalist to a friend made joyful reference to the blessing which had come upon the minister and his sister. Mathry Morgan of Llan-non was next, so thrilled with the change in his district that he too became a fervent champion of Evan Roberts, as did Penar Griffiths of Swansea who came back from meetings in Trecynon, Aberdare, a changed man.

Dr Cynolwyn Pugh told *Y Drysorfa* ('The Treasury') readers of the dramatic change in his own pastor at Trehafod, Rhondda:

Siloam's preacher at the time was Rev. T. P. Thomas, one of the most lovely and courteous men ever . . . He was considered over the years a substantial but very dry preacher. Perhaps this was a kind of nervousness because in the *seiat* ['fellowship meeting'] he was a completely different man. In that meeting, when he drew near to the people, he was at his best and could open up the riches of the Gospel in a manner suited to the understanding of the most simple Christian . . .

When the revival had just begun Mr Thomas went to the Monthly Meeting in Aberdare; he came home from that meeting as a man set on fire! The spluttering and little cough and all kinds of mannerisms vanished completely; and if one ever saw a man totally possessed by the Holy Spirit and divine fire, Mr Thomas was that man! Our privilege in Siloam was to behold this miracle daily and to rejoice; and the churches of Glamorgan from one end to the other came to know that a notable prophet had risen up in their midst, and they vied with one another for his inspired, precious ministry.[9]

The most notable vessel swept along in the revival floods was a rising young minister at Bethany Chapel, Ammanford, well known in eisteddfod circles. W. Nantlais Williams told his story several times in print. It seems that he went through four distinct crises:

(a) *The mission at Carmarthen*
I remember I was preaching at Carmarthen on one Sunday in those days. A mission was being held there at the same time under the auspices of the town's churches. The evangelist was Mr W. R. Lane, the official missioner of the Free Church Council of England and Wales.

On Sunday evening after the services an 8 o'clock meeting was arranged for him at Water Street Chapel. At the close of the meeting he asked everyone to bow their heads, and if anyone felt need for prayer he was to stand up. I felt at once the desire to rise, but I held back because a friend from Ammanford was sitting by my side. What would he think of me if I stood—I who was the minister of Bethany? Thus I lost the opportunity through my shyness and sinful respectability.

(b) *The week of prayer*

When I came down from the pulpit one of the elders suggested that it would be very reasonable for us to have a week of prayer to prepare the way for Mr Jenkins's coming. With that we all agreed, and we had an answer also in the shower that fell upon us on the following Sunday, and especially the evenings after the departure of the preacher [Joseph Jenkins of New Quay]; for the gentle rain broke into a hail-storm upon us that week. The meetings would go on until one or two o'clock in the morning, and souls would be set at liberty every night. *Yet I myself had not found the blessing.* I spent one whole night knocking and pleading at the door of mercy. That was on Friday night, after an amazing meeting in the chapel. But nothing availed. I was still in fetters. On Saturday night in the chapel the multitude came together again, and the new-born ones sang triumphantly, *'Diolch iddo byth am gofio llwch y llawr.* ['Thanks be to Him for ever remembering the dust of the earth'.] I decided within myself to join in the singing; though I had not myself received the blessing, should I not rejoice that others were free of their bonds? Yes, I broke out to join in the praise, and in that act of giving thanks for others, like Job of old: 'And the Lord turned the captivity of Job, when he prayed for his friends.' Yes, I began to experience the liberty in the meeting, and after I reached the house and meditated, I saw that it was through *believing* that the blessing comes, not through the worthiness of any effort of mine in deed or prayer. 'By grace ye are saved through *faith.*' I realized now by experience what the way of salvation was.

(c) *The surrender of gifts*

Then came the time to understand more of the Christian life. It is one thing to receive Christ as Saviour; it is another to live for him day by day . . . What were the obligations of the new life? . . . I had a *pryddest* [long poem] on 'Forgiveness' ready to be sent to the secretary of the Meirioneth Eisteddfod in Dolgellau. What should I do? I saw that I could not live for the sake of competing in eisteddfodau and spend all my time and talent in Christ's service—and my calling was to serve

Christ. In short, my eisteddfod interest was thrown overboard, together with much else of the ship's quite legitimate tackle.

(d) *The crucified life*
I chose to be out of sight and shun a host of 'big meetings', and live in insignificance, so to speak, in my own church. This cost me a great deal . . . The doors of many chapels were closed to me, [but] . . . the Lord turned this into a great blessing to me, and to my church. I was forced to give all my time to the church in my care. And O what refreshing and glorious times we had![10]

Many of these changed ministers were never promoted to any denominational positions. Another kind of humbling happened to the leading church laymen and especially to the deacons, who dominated Welsh chapels in those days. This had inevitable consequences for their power to witness.

Some of the press were always on the watch for conversion stories involving church officers. The chapel-goers were just as bad, calling out, 'Here's a big fish caught' when they saw an elder or deacon in distress of soul. The earliest testimonies come from deacons who lost their stiff dignity and began to weep like children as the Holy Spirit worked. Evan Roberts wrote to Sidney Evans about the surrender of Daniel Davies at Moriah, Loughor, and was overjoyed at this sign of blessing: 'I told him that he had received the Spirit . . . He laid hold of me as though he were beside himself, and kissed me.'[11] This reminds one of Gomer M. Roberts's story about a Pont-rhyd-y-fen elder known as 'a dry stick':

[He] would mumble inaudibly when about his public work. No one doubted his godliness and his ability, but he was rather dry in the *seiat* ['fellowship meeting'] and the prayer-meeting. But early in 1905 he was set ablaze and he was seen more than once jumping up and down in the big seat, and shouting at the top of his voice, 'Nail the flag to the mast-head, boys!' One night in the *seiat* he said: 'I had a strange dream last night—I dreamt I was in heaven. I was led up to the great white throne, where the Father was seated in his eternal glory. The Holy Spirit came to me and dressed me in the Son's righteousness. When He had clothed me in white raiment He introduced me to the Father. "Here he is for you," said He to the Father, "what do you think of him in the Son's righteous-ness?" Yes indeed, Dafydd Parker clothed in the righteousness of the Son! Hallelujah! Thanks be to Him!'[12]

J. Vyrnwy Morgan had many doubts about the revival phenomena but was deeply impressed by the change in the life and witness of a church officer who was zealous, pious, and highly moral, yet was in the habit of drinking and smoking. He was transformed from being a prisoner of such habits, and struggling and failing gave way to freedom and triumph. His old desires vanished when he became a new man in Christ.[13]

One newspaper printed a report about 'a pillar of his chapel' who had nevertheless behaved badly towards the widow of a near relative:

[He] is a man of some position and an employer of workmen. He had behaved cruelly to the widow of a near relative who had died through his harsh action. The widow had been deprived of a good deal of her money, and actually turned out of house and home.

But now in the revival he came under conviction:

Struggling to his feet, he confessed before five or six hundred of his neighbours, including some of his own workmen, the wrong he had done, and with tears in his eyes begged for forgiveness.

It was a terrible moment for all who listened to the heart-broken confession, but the scene of sorrow gave way to one of great joy when the penitent man sank to his seat, and the hundreds of people around him raised their voices in a psalm of praise.[14]

Often it was a sudden vision of their unclean condition in the light of the holiness of God that made the most unlikely men cry out, 'Woe is me! for I am undone; because I am a man of unclean lips.' The sensation and the stares of amazement may be imagined when, one evening in a Rhosllannerchrugog chapel, a very devout and moral man suddenly shouted out:

I tell you to your face, Paul, that you are a liar! . . . You, Paul, the chief of sinners? No, no. I, George Jones, am the chief of sinners.[15]

Robert Ellis, Tŷ-croes, describes someone called Dafydd in his church who had always been cultured, amiable and blameless of character. His friends expressed 'surprise that Dafydd spoke of his second birth; they all felt he had been born spiritually privileged the first time'.[16]

Thomas Williams of Trecynon, Aberdare, has a long and dramatic account of a chapel friend who was a poet and a religious man, yet who needed to be touched with the revival power. Like many others before him, this poet had often used scriptural allusions in his poetry, and gospel themes as inspiration and material, yet had never been affected personally until the fires of revival came and changed his life. A number of pages are devoted to his intense sufferings as he moved slowly to the hour of decision and was at last transformed. Those who knew him after the revival recognized traces of that painful baptism of fire in his many personal poems (he wrote no hymns), and thus the question arose as to why God had treated him so severely and what was his secret. Williams's view was that although the poet had been well taught in the Scriptures and had been keenly religious, he had never seen himself as a lost sinner and had never experienced cleansing and forgiveness. After this terrible crisis he was able to speak of his sins and to testify to the greatness of Christ's atoning sacrifice. This was the poet's testimony:

> I was full of sin, a greater sinner than anyone. I was full of selfishness, and cared nothing for those who were more deserving of respect: I cherished disobedience. I succeeded in hiding envy. My lips were not always clear of slander—nor would I say I was free of untruth, nor clear of hypocrisy either. I refused to give charity—I nurtured covetousness. I behaved inconsiderately towards weaker brethren, without caring for their feelings: I spoke roughly and foolishly to those in distress. I was so keen to find faults in others, yet I myself was bent under them. I read dubious books.[17]

Williams concludes that the poet was only gradually set free from these blemishes because it was the nature of grace to work gradually. But from then on his gifts were all for God, and the influence of the baptism of fire was seen clearly on his poetry.

Mrs S. M. Saunders, who wrote a remarkable book called *Y Diwygiad ym Mhentre Alun* ('The Revival in Alun Village'), had been in the midst of a village revival, living among people who nearly all had chapel backgrounds. In her book, in slight disguise, these people illustrate the effect of the revival, 'which came as a storm of lightning and thunder'. One of her comments is penetrating:

> Hardly a week passed without our hearing some of the main pillars of the sanctuary confessing, in anguish and intense lamentation, their unfitness to be even members of the church; and many of these would name their sins publicly, and ask for the prayers of the Lord's people. Salem, Pentre Alun, was a terrible place in those days.[18]

Her story of Mrs Powel of Tyn-rhos shows that the lightning did not spare respectable female do-gooders, who were such a tower of strength in chapel, Sunday school and Bible class, and such a fount of help for those who were sick or very poor and in distress. Mrs Powel had heard reports of the young Evan Roberts in South Wales, but she believed the church needed depth, not noise, and did not approve of young people staying up late and being unfit for work the next day.

Then suddenly she was absent from chapel and the village buzzed with rumours of a mental illness, especially when she told some visitors that 'she was not religious at all, but that she had had an appearance of piety for years, and that she had committed the unforgivable sin'. After two weeks of failing to eat or drink, and of lying in bed from morning to night, groaning because of her sin, Mrs Powel suddenly began to testify that God had forgiven her and filled her with joy. Certain friends treated this as a new turn in her illness, but all this talk reached its peak when Mrs Powel announced that she would take part in a *seiat* ('fellowship meeting') and break her own rule that women might visit the sick but never proclaim truths publicly. What happened on that Thursday evening is best told first-hand by someone who saw her enter and marvelled at the way her face shone:

After beginning the meeting, the elder, William Griffith, asked,—'Is there something on someone's mind?' In an instant Mrs Powel was on her feet. 'Yes,' she said 'there is a lot on my mind.' Her voice was clear and penetrating. She turned to the congregation, and began to speak,— 'First of all, let me confess that I have been a member of this church for 35 years; I have professed to follow the Lord, but it was all a lie. I wasn't fit to be a member,—hypocrisy and deceit have ruled my life. A month ago I had the first sight of my condition; my corruption reached up to heaven, and I was ashamed to look up. Five weeks ago tonight, if one of you had asked me,—"Are you afraid of Exodus 20?" I would have said, with confidence,—"No, I keep every one of the commandments." But when God opened my eyes, I saw I had broken each one of the ten over and over again. You have probably heard that I went close to the mad-house. You heard the truth, I was very near to going there. The corruption of my heart was so great that I could not believe it was possible for me to receive forgiveness. Many times over the years I have studied the way of salvation. I believed, certainly, that I had gone down with Adam; but I also believed (quietly) that if other people had sinned as little as I had, there was no need of the Sacrifice of the Cross. But a month ago I altered my opinion; and what tormented me night and day was a fear that there was not enough merit in the Blood of the Cross to wash my sins away, let alone others! Oh! my hypocrisy, my pride! . . . My self,—my self has had all the respect and the honour! For a full fortnight I have been living in the midst of my sins, seeing nothing but my corruption and filthiness; I saw my sins like mountains around me. On my right a great Snowdon of my sin; behind me a great Cadair Idris of my sin; on my left a great Plynlimon of my sin; and in front of me I thought there was a great Himalaya of my corruption! That was where I was for a whole fortnight, living in the midst of these mountains; and there was not even a narrow path between them whereby I could flee. But one morning, in my distress, I cried out,—"O God I know that I must go to hell,—I am not fit for anywhere else, and I am ready to go; but before sending me to eternal damnation, let me have one sight of the Man who died for me." In a moment, the mist cleared, the darkness fled, and there was my Saviour standing before me! I do not know how long I gazed upon His glory, perhaps hours,—I have no idea. But at last I remembered I had promised to go uncomplaining to hell, and I was determined to keep my vow. I shut my eyes and there I was again in the midst of those old mountains; in a while I opened my eyes to look at them, but, O the wonder of it! Every mountain had vanished out of sight, and a river of Blood ran between them! Now I began to rejoice,— and the old bed was dancing under me, and by now, the doctor and the nurse were running up the stairs, and taking hold of me. "Be calm my good woman, be calm," they said. "Calm indeed!" I said, "with the mountains of my sin having been dissolved in the Blood!" And I have been rejoicing ever since,—rejoicing in my dear Saviour, and in His costly death. O Calvary! Calvary! Calvary! I will gaze at you now for all eternity, and sing of the great victory. Thanks be to Him! Thanks be to Him! Thanks be to Him!'[19]

When she finally sat down no one could speak for half an hour. Then slowly and silently people left their seats and made for their homes, 'feeling the place to be full of God'.

Two further examples come from the Gorseinon and Loughor district and concern people who were not yet called to office in the church. First there was a minister's son who had come to the chapel to take his Sunday-school class. When he arrived there he realized that it had been turned into a prayer meeting, and just as they were singing a hymn of dedication, he fell under conviction and felt guilty, not of being immoral, but of being too religious:

He walked across to his father and said, 'Dad, some strange thing has happened to me, as if I had been born again. Is there time for me to go home and bring back my wife?' His father broke down, and I had never before seen him cry.[20]

Then there is the confession of Mr Webb, an earnest youth worker:

> What came about was that the Holy Spirit revealed to me that I was a lost sinner. A very big shock it was, and there was no one there to tell me things or to lead me. The Holy Spirit was glorifying the Son and showing Jesus crucified on Calvary for me—He did it all. I remember my eyes being fixed on some spot in that corner of the chapel over there, and I seemed to be seeing it all. I remember going into Old Seion [Chapel] and, as I was opening the door to go into the chapel from the lobby, the Holy Spirit met me like the wind. I'll never forget that coming across us; the place was full of God . . .
>
> You ask why I saw myself as a lost sinner although I had been such a religious man. It was sin in another sense and it looked different because I had been stripped of everything. Before the revival, if you went to meetings and did the Lord's work, you were all right. But the Holy Spirit has given a different revelation; it is not through such things that one is saved, but through faith and grace. It's nothing of self, but is God's gift.[21]

A different kind of transforming experience was to result not in the humbling of existing leaders but in the calling and commissioning of new ones. Here the Spirit of God fulfilled another promise made by Jesus, that he would give his followers the power to speak with boldness (Matthew 10:20). It was these people that Mrs Saunders had in mind when she wrote in her foreword about Christians who had never realized what resources they had:

> They had, for years, perhaps, lived in the King's palace as hired servants,—fulfilling religious duties faithfully and lovingly. But during the Revival, they heard, for the first time, the Father's tender voice inviting them to the feast, and they received 'the best robe, the ring and the shoes' there and then through the Blood of Jesus.[22]

Our next group of testimonies and reports illustrates how the divine Spirit removed the hindrances from people and gave them a tongue which no man could withstand. At Clydach Vale in the Rhondda Valley in December 1904, Awstin saw a man shouting at the top of his voice, exhorting and warning the people and praying. A local minister, W. E. Davies, told the congregation that

the man standing in the 'big pew' was, like those upon whom the Pentecostal fire had descended, filled, not with wine, but with the Holy Ghost. A month ago that man could not be prevailed upon to say anything publicly, but a change had come over him, which had transformed a timid, retiring member of Calfaria Church into what they now saw and heard. Of the genuineness of the transformation there could not be the slightest doubt.[23]

Grawys Jones of Aberdare told Holyoak what happened to two local teachers:

a) We have just lost one of the best workers; she has been a Sunday school teacher for forty years and was sixty years of age—an excellent worker but one who had never taken part in public prayer until the revival. I was amazed at the gifts which she had unearthed and which had been lying dormant so long.

b) A man in the seat next to me—a schoolteacher and a very good man—leaned over and asked me, 'What is this great thing?' 'It is the true revival,' I replied. 'I should like to feel it myself,' he said. 'Have you not felt anything?' 'No,' he answered, 'I cannot say that I have felt it.' 'Have you asked the Lord to bless you specially in this revival? Ask,' I said. 'Go on your knees here and now. I will go with you.' And we both knelt down, and prayed fervently. And when I got up I could see this man shaking all over, and weeping like a child. 'Thank God,' he said. 'He has rolled away the burden from my shoulders. I have seen the light.' 'Well,' I said, 'if you have had that of the Lord you must do one thing more. You must stand up here and now, and declare to these people what the Lord has done for you.' 'I can never do that,' he said. 'O yes, you can, and you must do it,' I replied. He got up and began to speak, and as soon as he opened his mouth he did not know how to stop.[24]

This sudden flow of speech is suggestive of two little incidents in rural chapels. At Tre Taliesin near Aberystwyth an old man known to be totally illiterate began to recite Scripture verses and hymns and explained that when he could not sleep at night, the Holy Spirit would teach him.[25]

In another chapel a lad with an awful stammer was suddenly freed of it and began to pray and testify with great power and beauty. Some of the testimonies recorded in Thomas Williams's account of the Trecynon revival are not just passing wonders but evidence that these men were being equipped for long service as lay preachers and elders.

J. Ellis Jones told his *Cylchgrawn Efengylaidd* ('Evangelical Magazine') readers of a strange incident which showed him how so many shy people found liberty:

> One Saturday afternoon when a young friend was in my house, another friend came in. He was one of the [chapel] members, a man who was quiet, unassuming and bashful in spirit. I knew his excellent qualities of character, but his modesty was almost a snare for him. Yet in the middle of that afternoon conversation, this quiet man broke out: 'Oh! I have seen Him, yes,—I have seen Jesus!' I can hear the tone of his voice now as I write. We saw him grow spiritually, and we were taken to the heights in many a *seiat* ['fellowship meeting'] as we heard him declaring the riches of God's grace. He was one of the multitude without number who 'saw Jesus' in 1904-5.[26]

From north-west Wales comes this letter, dated 22 January 1905, from a modest young wife and mother, Mrs Jane Griffith, who felt a new freedom to testify in the weeks after D. M. Phillips had come with his niece to the market town of Pwllheli and conducted revival services there and at nearby Edern:

> I never before had such power before the throne of grace as I have since feeling freedom a week last Saturday morning. I attribute this to Miss Jones praying for me and I am glad to say it is continuing. Nothing gives me greater pleasure than reading my Bible and secret prayer. My eyes have been 'opened to see the mysteries of His purposes and of His Word. Better for me is the law of His mouth than thousands in silver and gold'.

For some years this lady and her husband, James, were engaged in Christian work in their area.[27]

The celebrated member of the Society for Psychical Research, A. T. Fryer, himself an ordained man, received a number of letters in reply to a circular letter requesting trustworthy information on those aspects of the revival which illustrated or were concerned with the mental and psychical sides of human nature. Some of the replies are full of visions, lights, and voices, but a young man from Glamorganshire told how he had left an open-air meeting to go home, despite 'an overpowering impulse to join the group' holding the meeting:

Along the road I heard an inward voice saying, 'Go back, go back!' whilst I felt uneasy. However, I returned to the group, and remained to the end of the meeting. The following day (Sunday) the words of the preacher and others seemed to have a terrible force, and at night I felt bound to do something. I rose from my seat and spoke a few words, saying that I felt that I had not been what I should have been. After this I often had the desire to speak or sing or pray. I realised that there was a great power on my side, and that I must obey that power.

Another young man claimed that, after he felt that he had said something detrimental to the cause at a meeting one evening and had decided never to speak again, he was not allowed to sleep and heard the Spirit say in Welsh:

You said to-night that you will not speak for Me again . . . I have a message, I want you to deliver it, and that in the most public place . . . Tell them that hypocrisy is the worst sin against Me.[28]

This seems to have been an isolated event in his experience, different from the circumstances which led to a young quarryman, J. Eifl Hughes, starting out on a path that took him into full-time ministry. He was deeply impressed by what he had read of the dramatic events in South Wales and what he had witnessed in his own neighbourhood in North Wales:

I can remember arriving home from one meeting, when every member of the family was peacefully asleep, and feeling strange—I cannot define the experience. I saw myself as a lost and perishing sinner; I fell on my knees on the hearth, and if I ever prayed in my life, I prayed that night. I wept and pleaded for forgiveness and mercy, and then the dawn broke upon me. I thought I saw the Saviour on the cross dying for me, his hands and feet bleeding, and him looking at me from under his crown of thorns. I was like one who had a glimpse of his infinite love. I rose from my knees in the early hours of the morning, and there was a longing in my soul to go out as a missionary.

I went to work that morning with a Bible in my pocket, but before I reached the workplace, in a lonely place on the mountain, I saw the two

197

most heedless men in the quarry waiting for me—not to revile me and mock me but to ask me to hold a prayer-meeting with them. Amazed I asked them to wait until the dinner hour, and they agreed. After dinner I asked if anyone there would like to read a portion of the Scriptures, and to my astonishment one of these two heedless men took it from my hand and began to recite with tears, *'Dyma Feibl annwyl Iesu'* ['Here is Jesus' dear Bible']. Afterwards he began to pray, holding on to the anvil which stood loose on the wooden block in front of him, and he prayed so mightily that he lifted the anvil in his arms though it was so heavy, and tears of repentance were descending on it in salty drops. He yielded himself to his Saviour and served as a Baptist deacon for years.[29]

Thus a rather reserved and unassuming lad was turned into yet another effective witness alongside other missionaries, evangelists, ministers, deacons and church workers whose experiences are on record.

As this chapter was being completed, an exciting opportunity was given to meet someone who had been converted in the revival and was still witnessing and rejoicing at the age of 98. Dafydd Jones of Aberporth, to the south of New Quay where the blessing had begun, sat talking for an hour or more. From him was heard the authentic sound of a 'child of the revival' glorifying his Lord. This is his testimony, compiled out of answers to our eager questioning:

My mother died when I was very young and the greatest influence on me was my godly grandmother who used to give me my midday meal when I went every day to Blaen-porth school. Before each dinner she would read a verse or two from her Bible and then ask a blessing, and this affected me terribly. She welcomed the revival of course. One day in her chapel she stood up and started to unfold the Word of God, and the place seemed to be shaking until I found it was me that was shaking. Our family went to Tan-y-groes Chapel and when the revival began there was much groaning and calling out, which seemed strange to me as a thirteen-year-old. I remember that three sisters from Cardigan went into the pulpit and sang, and then the place was filled with the Spirit and there was much weeping. I didn't realize what had happened to me, but when I went back to the farm, where I shared a loft bedroom with an English boy, the Spirit came upon us there. I began to pray for God to save my dad, and he was converted and eventually set free from drink (he went as a bailiff and was Sunday-school superintendent at Tresaith). When I was praying for him, Mr Thomas of Cilgerran, a revivalist, could hear me from the farmhouse and they came out to listen and then went back to pray for us. I cannot remember the exact moment, yet it changed my life-style and took me away from the local gangs. But I offered very few prayers for myself, except when I was in the battles in France, and I became unfaithful to my vows until 1924 when Sister Mary Williams spoke about forgetting God and challenged us to receive the Saviour.[30]

Asked why he thought he and others lost their fire, he said that although deacons and precentors and the like were godly and had some experience of the Spirit, and the minister, M. P. Morgan, was a real preacher whom people used to call *'un o'r hoelion wyth'* ('one of the eight-inch nails'), there was no special teaching of converts and only one convention down at Cardigan. Children's praises soon stopped; women ceased to pray or testify; the young people were not used as witnesses.

Dafydd Jones went to work for many years in South Wales and found fellowship there with the converts in the gospel halls until his retirement. This astonishing veteran continued to preach until his ninety-sixth year, and also wrote a prophetic poem in Welsh about revival, which has had a wide circulation.

The end result of all these different transformations was summed up by the author of an article in the periodical, *Y Geninen* ('The Leek'), as the formation of a new group of fully committed disciples and witnesses, who served well and faithfully in their day:

[There is a group] who are in the midst of the Revival and partake of it. They are men full of the Holy Spirit, seeing visions and dreaming dreams, yes, and full of good works in faith and prayer, under the continuous leading of the Divine Spirit.[31]

Other witnesses lend their testimony to the way these sons and daughters of the King conducted their churches out into the highways and byways to seek those who had never dreamed of being invited into the family of God, and it is to these we turn next.

12
The Public Witness of Churches

'Go out into the highways and hedges,
and compel them to come in'
(Luke 14:23)

The consequence [of revival within] the Church is, that it is made attractive to the world. People cannot help going to church or chapel now. Sensible men, though they may be unsympathetic, talk respectfully about the Church of Christ to-day. Moreover the Church is aggressive. Awakened itself to its own needs, it has at the same time been awakened to the needs of the unconverted and unregenerate world outside. It can be said of the Church in Wales . . . that great grace is upon all. There is the grace of love and of consecration.

Those are the words of Luther Davies, pastor of St Mary Street Baptist Church in Newport, Gwent.[1]

To some extent the involvement of certain churches in active evangelism was inspired by the suggestions made by Nantlais Williams of Ammanford, Cynog Williams of Aberdare, Thomas Pritchard of Rhos, and others. To some extent it was a consequence of the brave pioneering efforts of Christian Worker teams and students, as pictured in an earlier chapter. But the main stimulus to church-based evangelism was surely the pleadings and the challenges of Evan Roberts himself. Listen to him at Bala in July 1905:

What need is there here to-night, friends? The need of prayer. Yes, it is prayer that raises our heads. It is possible to go to destruction singing. Let us pray for saving the people. Show the Saviour to the people, there is plenty of room for all in His kingdom, and plenty of welcome. Is there anyone ready to come in? Here is a splendid place to accept the Saviour. Pray for the Holy Spirit. Everyone ought to pray for His coming. Pray for bending the people. Offer Jesus to them. There is not half enough working here . . . Is there anyone in the audience working now? That must be done before we shall have all the listeners in. We want to have everyone in . . . There are people here despising the Son of God. How can we be so quiet then? Certainly, there is something not right. Can it be that there is someone here again not having prayed? We must all be workers and sincere in prayer. It will not do for us to go to heaven by ourselves. We must be on fire, friends, for saving others. We cannot be so without being workers. To be workers will draw Heaven down, and will draw others to Heaven. Oh! that we were filled with the spirit of the Great Teacher—the great love! Without readiness to work the spirit of prayer will not come.[2]

At every suitable opportunity—and some unsuitable ones—Evan Roberts raged at the scandal of a non-praying, non-confessing, non-evangelizing church, crying out that God did not want idle people.[3] By the Spirit's guidance he knew that the churches of Wales were full of priests and Levites, who were sure to pass by on the other side while the needy lay so evidently around them.

Time after time the young revivalist exhorted Christians to prove their obedience to the Holy Spirit by an act of public witness. In his published and much discussed sermon, based on Abraham's obedience to the call of God, there is a strikingly direct challenge to the hearers:

If God calls on you to give out a hymn, or to pray, or to give a testimony, do it. It does not matter if you go into prison, or into captivity, if the call comes to you. — We were talking about sacrifices. There is nothing worth calling a sacrifice. What have we done for Christ? Someone has never said a word for Christ, and he has been in the Church for years. Say a word for Christ. It is not enough to be there. You must be working there by your word and testimony . . . If you find a man who does not say a word for Christ, he has never known Him. The moment you meet Christ you will be on fire; you cannot help speaking.[4]

The response of churches was very patchy because only a minority felt obliged to act. Right to the last Evan Roberts was still calling upon chapel folk to wake up and speak, instead of 'letting stewards take your crowns'. No doubt these frequent probings made many groups and churches more eager to witness. Here is just one more example from a *Western Mail* account of a meeting in Liverpool in April 1905:

Mr. Evan Roberts shortly afterwards rose again, and said he felt that there were many Church members present who were not praying for the salvation of souls that night. Would they pray now? Immediately there was a wonderful scene of simultaneous prayer from the body of the chapel, from the galleries, from men and women, in Welsh and in English, while hundreds more stood with bowed heads and tears trickling over their faces, and when they quieted down somewhat another striking prayer by the Rev. Dr. A. J. Parry voiced the supplications of many more, judging by the chorus of 'Amens'.[5]

Exactly how were the different denominations going to respond to this powerful challenge to be witnesses? To begin with, the Anglican Church in their newspaper, *Y Llan* ('The Parish Church'), reported a number of parish missions at places like Llanerfyl, Llangadfan and Garthbeibio in Powys, the Welsh-language St David's Church in Cardiff, and St Peter's, Pentre-chwyth, Swansea. The mission in Llanerfyl, Llangadfan and Garthbeibio parishes during the week commencing 9 January was led by the Rev. Armon Ellis, Vicar of Rhes-y-cae, and by the end of the week there were thirty-six converts. His practice was to append to Evensong a gospel sermon, which was then followed by a kind of 'second meeting' where converts could offer prayer or testimony. A correspondent wrote:

> By this means, the congregation was made to feel perfectly at home, and free to pour out their hearts on the bosom of Old Mother [Church], so to speak . . . It was announced publicly that the names of any persons wishing to consecrate themselves anew, would be given to the minister of the Church or chapel they normally attended. This was done so that everyone would understand clearly that proselyting would not be tolerated . . . As communicants, let us all do our best to keep those [who have joined us] from returning to their old paths. Let us help them and watch over them. The enemy will be trying with all his strength to get them back into his service. Let us pray continually for them. Let us take care that we will not unwittingly be a stone of stumbling or a rock of offence to any one of them.[6]

No one was more affected by the revival than Thomas Pritchard, the Vicar of Rhos, who felt he had to work out a programme for some thirty zealous converts. In a letter to an English clerical friend he says:

> Instead of an average of 35 or so at Holy Communion, the number was 65 at the last Holy Communion . . . Early Sunday morning prayer meetings have started . . . Most emphatically the great bulk exhibit cheering signs of true conversion—in word and deed—in attendance at services—mission work—institution of family prayer . . . The means are— simple, earnest, and short addresses—but especially prayer and praise

... The revival here is pronouncedly Welsh—Rhos being a Gibraltar of Welsh on the border.[7]

In South Wales, as we have seen, certain vicars inserted into the standard service ways and means by which converts could express their penitence and church leaders could reconsecrate themselves—but news of actual missions is less common.

Even less has been discovered about missions set up by Wesleyan Methodism in South Wales, but fortunately the *North Wales Guardian* mentions evangelistic services conducted by J. R. Gee, a lay evangelist, at the English Wesleyan Chapel in Mold.[8] The same edition describes a mission at Pendref Wesleyan Chapel in Holywell, led by Joseph Jenkins, with the singers Florrie Evans and Maud Davies. At Llai near Wrexham John H. Cooke, an evangelist from London, held evangelistic meetings in February 1905, in which almost a hundred professed conversion, and a follow-up visit in June when five followed suit. In that little village, the Christian Endeavour in the Primitive Methodist Chapel had seventy-three members by June 1905.[9]

How did other nonconformist chapels answer these calls to mission?

At the end of R. B. Jones's ten-day mission in Rhos in November 1904, a meeting of church officers was called on Friday evening, 18 November, to consider how to carry the work forward. They ventured to call a prayer meeting for 10 a.m. the following morning at Penuel Chapel, and further prayer meetings were held at 2 p.m. and at 5.30 p.m. The Baptist minister, Evan Williams, describes what happened next:

At the end of the meeting, a procession was formed and marched through Rhos and Ponciau; hymns were sung, verses of Scripture recited, and short addresses were delivered opposite many of the taverns . . . Most of the taverns on the route of the procession were emptied; those in them were terrified, escaping anywhere they could. We heard that some in the taverns were afraid to come out through the front door into view of the procession, but that they had, in their fear, put out the light and hidden under the tables. This shows what strength and influence the church has when she is awakened. We then went back to the chapel about 9 o'clock, and had a very lively meeting. That meeting was closed just before 10, and the Christian workers were encouraged to go out to watch for those in the taverns that it had not been possible to get to join the procession, and to bring them together to a later meeting at 10.30

p.m. So it was to be. Many went out full of zeal and enthusiasm, and by the appointed time Penuel schoolroom was so full that the chapel had to be opened; and by 11 the chapel had been filled—the ground floor of the chapel was almost full, between those under the influence of alcohol and the Christian workers. There arose in our mind fears as to how we should deal with such persons, and what we should say to them. The only thing to do was to cast our burden on the Lord and fully trust in Him. The meeting was quiet and intense, and there were clear evidences that the Spirit of the Lord was working mightily in the meeting. Those most under the influence of drink were quiet and listening earnestly, and they seemed to have sobered before the end of the meeting. I will never forget the sight when a number of them came to us at the end of the meeting to thank us that someone remembered them and cared for them, since they had thought they were rejected by all. A number of others came forward to sign the pledge, and some of these have remained zealous, despite being in the midst of many temptations. The meeting lasted for an hour; and it was a lovely scene to see so many church members escorting home those who had come to the meeting. A number had come with bottles in their pockets full of alcoholic drink ready for Sunday [when the taverns were closed], but many of these were smashed near the chapel, after the meeting, by their owners.[10]

W. S. Jones was specially interested in the actions of a group of young men who went out witnessing in needy villages surrounding Rhos.[11] But he was also aware that this new spirit of strong desire to win souls was creating another kind of personal evangelism in the quarries, collieries, brickworks and foundry-yards. As it happens we have personal testimony of this from veteran John Powell Parry:

It was a pleasure to go down the pit to work and I remember 1905 when I was working in the mine. There was praising, and everyone was talking about being saved—and the unsaved of course were afraid. It was as much joy to go down to a place of work as to go into a place of worship. The Spirit was in the pits. I remember a manager saying how wonderful it was with no tensions and disputes. People had prayer-meetings down the mine when the hauling and everything was finished. People were praying and praising and some were saved down the mines the same as in the chapel. It was wonderful to be discussing the Lord and the joy and peace which is life in the real sense—Oh! life was worth living. Some were saved down the mine as they were crying for mercy and forgiveness of sins. There was the joy of it all. It was wonderful.[12]

W. S. Jones recalls this delightful story of what happened in Bersham colliery when the ropes snapped and the men could not be brought from the pit bottom for several hours:

> To pass the time one of them suggested that they should hold a Prayer-meeting there. They readily agreed to this, though many of the men had made no profession. Mr. John Jones, Butcher Street, Rhos, was asked to lead, and without hesitation he began to sing 'Yn y dyfroedd mawr a'r tonau' ['In the great waters and waves'] to the tune *Tôn y Botel* as the hymn most appropriate to the situation they were in. It was sung with special unction, and then he asked someone to lead in prayer. Several did this and, in the lightless depths of the pit, there was something strange and unfamiliar about them. Between praying and singing the meeting lasted some hours. The effect on some was fervent; we heard of one going away to hide himself in the workings, being unable to stand in the face of that which had been so long meaningless to him. Another elderly listener testified that it was a blessing that the rope snapped, seeing that it had brought about such a meeting, and as he spoke, the clean tears made furrows in his blackened face. For many there was nothing more glorious during all the meetings of the Revival.[13]

The Independent and Baptist churches were inclined to depend a great deal upon processions as their means of going out into the byways. The model already existed in the form of Easter and Whitsun processions with banners, involving family groups and a host of children. This is the opportunity to mention the schoolchildren of that revival period who found their own ways to reach the unconverted. Sometimes this was in the form of a mass meeting or 'children's revival'; sometimes it was the sudden outflow from a Sunday-school room. At Rhos the passers-by heard children of seven or eight talking spontaneously about Jesus because they had heard so much about him in their homes. John Powell Parry said it was 'not just testifying but saying strange things about Jesus that affected teachers because it was out of the ordinary—it was revival talk'.[14] Before long the children were asked to join the processions and to sing their own favourites. An aged lady rose from her sick bed to tell the author her story, as though she was still under the spell of the revival in Rhos:

> I am a daughter of the Rev. Morgan Williams who died in 1902. I was just a young girl in 1905 but I was often asked to pitch the tune because

I was trained in tonic sol-fa. I believe that local people always arranged the programmes because R. B. Jones was not dogmatic about this. I remember that R. B. Jones spoke to us young people about God's guidance. He said that all members of Christ ought to know how to work and how to pray and how to know their particular task. Almost at once, I was asked to take the primary class in the vestry and I said to myself, 'If I refuse to go, I am not worthy of the Lord.'

The children's favourite game was 'Let's play open-air meetings.' The children were often singing outside the taverns, *'Deuwch allan yr awr hon'* ['Come out now']. We would all shout *'Diolch iddo'* ['Thanks be to Him'] if the innkeeper said, *'Does neb yma'* ['There's no one here']. R. B. Jones did not discourage children's processions nor the children's prayer-meetings.

I can't remember most of the songs I sang but there was one which was introduced by Miss Lizzie Dodd which went, *'Mae'r diafol wedi colli'r dydd, a minnau'n teimlo'n hollol rhydd'* ['The devil has lost the day, and I feel completely free'] . . . I'm sorry but I cannot go on now.[15]

Local newspapers were on the watch for the processions, and the *Glorian* of Blaenau Ffestiniog saw one in the village of Penmachno at the top of the Conwy valley, where even three-year-old infants were joining in the singing.[16] The impact of child witness was described in a magazine article in *Yr Hauwr* ('The Sower') in March 1905, which declared that 'one of the characteristics of the present revival is that children are instruments in God's hand in many hundreds of cases in bringing their parents to Christ . . . There are a great number of examples of little ones breaking out to praise and pray to God in public.'

Inter-church marches through the streets became increasingly popular in the first ten weeks of 1905, despite a flu epidemic. Marchers led by clergymen were seen in the streets of Neyland, Cardigan, Wrexham, Bala, and Newport (Gwent), as well as in rural communities where for so long the Anglicans, the Calvinistic Methodists and the Baptists had stayed aloof from each other.

Before the revival the churches and chapels of Wales did not really embrace open-air witness and personal work. One individual from a North Wales chapel remarked that to do so would have been a revolution because 'before the revival the respectable chapel-folk had never gone out of their way to speak to or to invite the bad people in their village. Now all this was changed everywhere as the love of Christ constrained them.' Chapels with a high percentage of revival converts were not satisfied with hymn-singing processions. If ever those converted became the majority, the church's outlook changed. Once again we turn to eye-witnesses for illustrations of this.

Swansea

A new mission hall was built late in 1904, and in that place about 150 converts embraced Christ during the revival and then went on to join the church of their own choice. David Lloyd, an architect in Swansea, gives this account of what happened there:

> During the first six months of the Revival it was a real pleasure to work. You could catch anyone. They were coming running into the nets. We had wonderful times here in Swansea . . . The public-houses here in this large town were emptied, and the publicans were running about from place to place complaining that they could not pay the rent and the rates. The publican who keeps the public-house now on the corner of the street where our Mission is, had his place fairly emptied for about two months, and he sent a letter to the Mission complaining that it was ruining his house. He wanted a reduction in the rent. We held meetings just in front of the square there every night, and we saw the men coming out of the public-house, leaving their beer on the counter, and kneeling in the ring. The meetings lasted like that for nine months in our Mission Hall, meetings every night, praise and singing into the depths of the night, until we were all tired out. Many of us worked too hard for our bodies.
>
> The grandest thing of all is to hear a big sinner shouting for mercy. That is the very best thing I have seen . . .
>
> Lasting good was done, and the effect of the Revival now is felt in all the meetings around here. We have warmer meetings, and a great deal more reality in the work and more sympathy with the world at large, the down-trodden, and the drunkard. Sin now is manifesting itself again, but not to the extent it was before the revival.[17]

Rogerstone near Newport

Here in 1905 a little mission was erected near the Baptist church and in the shadow of the foundry. Its purpose was to cater for the roughly-clad and ill-taught converts who surged in from 'The Nook' terraces. When in February a great many critics found their voices and condemned the revival extremism, Granville Llewelyn of Rogerstone, a professional man, sent them an invitation: 'As to the revival being a show, the only thing I can say to anyone who has the slightest doubt whatever, "Come to Rogerstone", and see and hear the testimonies of some of our converts—the hard-headed men of the neighbourhood—and I guarantee that the only conclusion they will arrive at is that it is of God and none other.' Five or six of those rough diamonds went on witnessing in slum streets, now redeveloped.[18]

The Hayes, Cardiff

A strange transformation came over the prestigious Tabernacle Chapel, a showcase of top hat, cloak and gloves businessmen and shopkeepers, pastored by the refined, gentle Charles Davies. Suddenly it became a rescue centre:

> The Tabernacle Baptist Chapel, in the Hayes, Cardiff, is the centre of a great rescue movement into which the Cardiff revival has developed. Night after night, the huge edifice is packed, from pulpit to porch, with an eager throng who come to work, to sing, to pray, to talk, to rescue, and to be rescued . . . Principal [William] Edwards has worked strenuously in connection with the glorious work, having been engaged at the Tabernacle every night for the past two months. He seems to revel in rescue work. It is the joy of his life. All sorts and conditions of men and women—drunkards, gamblers, debauchers, prostitutes, prodigals—have been coming in night after night, all of whom the Principal has directed to the Cross of Calvary, where they have found salvation. Many who have been castaways, without a friend in the world, he has assisted in various ways and generously entertained at his own house. He believes that this is the only way by which outcasts can fully be reclaimed. He wrote some time ago for the establishment of settlements in the country for the fallen . . . Mrs. Edwards has taken a prominent part in this mighty movement of mercy. She has thrilled to ecstasy by her sweet singing many hearts that were broken by sorrow and sin, and has helped to feed hundreds of poor starving children, who crowd daily to the Tabernacle.

* * * * *

The present minister of the Tabernacle, Rev. Charles Davies . . . is gentleness personified. His roses have no thorns. No one has ever known him to cherish an evil thought, utter a cynical word, or do a spiteful act in regard to friend or foe . . . He is the Baptist Barnabas in Wales, preeminently 'the son of consolation.' Like rain in August, not March, his ministry is gentle, warm, and refreshing. His central theme is Gentle Jesus, and he wreaths the Cross of Calvary with the lily of the valley.

The Tabernacle is the centre of a great rescue movement into which the Cardiff revival has developed. Over 600 have been converted: many of them saved from the lowest depths of sin. The chapel has been packed with huge congregations night after night . . . Marvellous scenes were witnessed one night. The meeting opened with a conversion—a young man, who said he had been 'on the brink' for some time . . . About eleven o'clock there was a large influx from the streets, and the chapel became very crowded. The meeting lasted until nearly one o'clock on Sunday morning, during which there were thirty-three conversions . . . Impromptu street missions [are also held] . . . Many men and women are met as they leave the taverns, and though the offer to join in a chapel service is frequently rejected with scorn and swearing, perserverance tells, and in a short time there begins to stream into the Tabernacle a motley crowd. Many are the stories heard, many the tales of despair. The earnest, inspired pleadings of the missioners turn many a lost soul towards the light. At one service, which held on until two o'clock in the morning, the majority of fifty or sixty street sinners were willing to seek a better life. The Tabernacle Church has resolved to keep the chapel open for these services as long as any people can be found anxious to attend.[19]

Trehafod, Rhondda

In this valley neighbourhood, young people particularly were encouraged as they saw the fruit produced by their efforts among those whose weekends revolved around the public house. According to Dr Cynolwyn Pugh:

Immediately after Evan Roberts' visit, the Young People of Siloam Chapel began a meeting which was a great blessing to them. It was also effectual, in the hands of the Holy Spirit, in convicting many drunkards and turning them into new men.

For some years prior to the Revival, music was all my passion,—chiefly instrumental music. I had charge of three brass bands, and a small choir also. The first thing that happened was the consecration of the Cornet to the Lord's service. It was decided to hold an open-air service at eleven o'clock each Saturday night,—'stop-tap time' when men were turned out from the local tavern into the road! Between the cornet and the singing there was no difficulty in ensuring a congregation. It is true that a number of the drinkers had trouble in standing; they had to lean against the wall of the shop near where the meeting was being held. But miraculously, many times some of these men were to be seen sobered under the influence of the Gospel, and better still, the occasional person was to be seen dragging himself into the circle and there going on his knees and committing himself to the Lord Jesus; even more marvellous was it to see that person standing straight in the circle the next Saturday and appealing to his old companions to give themselves to Christ and the Gospel! Yes, such things were seen many times: the young people took care to lead the converts to their homes on Saturday night, and how hard it was to persuade wife and children that their husband or son had been changed. The young people would go to those homes again the next day, to bring the converted to the chapel, and it became a custom for the chapel people to welcome these old 'firebrands' to their homes for tea on the Sunday! Some of them had never before sat at a clean tea table with a white cloth on it.[20]

These meetings continued for several years.

Aberdare

Some twenty miles to the north of Cardiff was a district called Cwm, near Aberdare, which then had about fifty houses. The people that lived there were very poor. The local minister, J. Grawys Jones, told Holyoak that many were quite strange to churches and that their children were utterly neglected:

A Sunday School was started in one of these houses by a few friends, people who were much moved during the revival. It was very difficult to work there. The children were so mischievous, they would not be obedient. But we determined to go on with it, and some of the young people from our chapel and other churches around here determined to do what they could. The school gradually increased, but it became impossible to carry it on as before, as the people in the house removed and the new tenants were not in sympathy with anything of the kind. Just then, however, a lady belonging to our church gave £100 to build a chapel or iron mission room in the place. We had great difficulty in getting a piece of ground, but succeeded at last; the place was opened on May 6th, 1906, and ever since it has been crowded. Many of the people of Cwm have become members in different churches. I superintend the work there, and several of our young members, and those from other churches, go there as teachers in the school. Our plan of work is to advise all who give themselves to the Lord at that little Mission, to join one of the different churches. They select what church they prefer, but we insist on their joining some church . . . I preach there every Tuesday night, and there is a service there every Sunday afternoon and evening, and a Women's Prayer Meeting has been formed . . . In that little room we have had most wonderful times. I consider this is the most practical result of any you could have.[21]

Unfortunately some of these enthusiastic efforts to set up missions upset the mother churches so that it became one more reason why revival converts left them and formed gospel halls. John Lewis described the setting up of a hall in the Brynaman area where a former church secretary, John Jones, and John Howells, the brother of Rees Howells, became leaders.[22] The late George Griffiths of Cwm-twrch in the Swansea Valley told the sad story of how the parent church there disowned their evangelism. It was laid upon the hearts of some to provide Sunday-school classes for the very ill-dressed children of the district, and also for their fathers who asked if they could form a class of their own. They explained that some of them could not read, but that did not matter as they knew one another so well. It was this adult class that upset the deacons, who complained the pioneers were neglecting their church, and sent them an ultimatum to stop or be expelled. They prayed and felt they had to persevere with the work which God had blessed:

It is only fair to explain here that we were faithful to all the other services of the church, not only the Sunday services, morning and evening, but also the weeknight meetings, on Tuesday and Thursday nights. And we tried, as conscientiously as we could, to make ourselves useful in those weekly services . . . As a result, although our fathers and forefathers had always attended that church since the beginning of the 18th century, we had no church to attend. We had to meet somewhere and so we had no alternative but to gather in our homes. That was in 1907. I hasten to add, however, that we did not harbour any ill feeling towards the church at that time. We felt assured that we were doing the will of God in looking after those children and we found it easy to forgive the church and all the members for their unkind treatment. Indeed the only possible explanation for their behaviour, as we were soon to realize, was that in Cwmtwrch, as in many other places in South Wales at that time, they objected to our testimony . . .

The enemy was very busy in the meantime doing all he could to discourage us. The talk of the village at that time was, 'What a lot of fools they are, how can they carry on their services . . . They don't belong to any denomination . . . They have no minister . . . They have no means of supporting one either . . . There's not one able man among them . . . Those doors will soon be closed.'[23]

211

The great drive to evangelize weakened slowly during the next three years, yet some chapels still managed to maintain their outreach. Holyoak visited the English Congregational Church at Pontypridd in 1907 and at once noted the very crowded congregation, with whole families sitting together downstairs:

> The pastor is the Rev. Edgar Williams, an Englishman, who settled there some eighteen months ago. At the close of the service a gathering was held in the Lecture Hall for fellowship and social intercourse. Mr. Williams told me that this plan had been adopted specially with the hope of reaching the large number of men whom I had observed in the galleries. They were there week by week, but slipped out as soon as the service was over before the minister had an opportunity of speaking to them. Many of them, however, now remained to these Sunday evening meetings where personal intercourse and conversation were made possible . . .
>
> The deacons at the Congregational Church are certainly 'watchful to entertain strangers,' and as soon as the Sunday evening service concluded I was welcomed by a kindly deacon who had provided me with books and a pew. He asked how I had liked the service, and further as to my business in Pontypridd! . . . From him I learned something of the Mission conducted by Gipsy Smith, which followed on Mr. Evan Roberts' visit to the town.[24]

In the Aberdare district the evangelistic impulse lingered on in Bryn Seion Calvinistic Methodist Church. The minister, John Morgan, had worked out with his officers how to make use of their keen converts as a means of winning others for Christ. The weeknight meetings, such as Bible Class and *seiat* ('fellowship meeting'), were to remain spontaneous but within set limits:

> To a certain extent the churches have left their meetings in the hands of the converts, and then, of course, the older members are shy and take a back-seat and if left to themselves, will be passive elements. So I occasionally ask So and So and So and So to take part first of all, and after calling on some like this, then I throw the meeting open for anyone who feels the Spirit moving him. Our prayer-meetings begin at 7 o'clock and hold on until 9.00, 9.15, 9.30, and even 10 o'clock during the last few months . . . I know this. That the character and spiritual fervour of our prayer-meetings are quite as high now and more pure than even when the revival was at its height.[25]

Not only did the spirit of evangelism and witness continue in Wales itself but wherever Welshmen went. The missions of the Welsh students from Spurgeon's College have already been described. In Charing Cross Welsh Calvinistic Methodist Chapel in London, a dairyman named Ben Griffiths felt led by the Spirit to start meetings in the parlour of his Millward Street Dairy. This mission work evolved into Peniel Chapel, Notting Hill, which accommodated 800 people and became a 'hive of spiritual industry':

> There are no sales of work, bazaars or concerts, but with the key of faith they have access into the unbounded treasures of the Heavenly Father. They spread the gospel daily, and what a privilege it is to enter the ever-open door of Penuel and feel the Spirit of God enabling us to struggle with angels for victory. This crowded assembly is composed of people of every tongue, and has 89 missionaries working the world over.[26]

If and when Dr Edwin Orr's documentary evidence of revival effects in the rest of Britain is collated, it will be seen that the men and women who went home from revival scenes initiated many evangelistic missions of different kinds from Kent to Cornwall and from Hampshire to Yorkshire. The *Baptist Times* alone mentions over forty between January and May 1905. These need to be correlated with the numerous accounts of revival teams sponsored by other denominations and with the new work going on in the scores of gospel halls and fellowships set up in all parts of the United Kingdom.

From 1905 to 1913 one can trace numerous evangelistic meetings in Wales that were sponsored by the awakened churches, especially those that responded to the appeal of R. B. Jones and his volunteer gospel preachers. They themselves were men 'eager to reach needy places in both town and country areas partly prepared for a mission'. The *Efengylydd* printed an appeal by Evan Roberts to the people of Wales to become witnesses because 'the silence of the church is sinful'. One other appeal came from a dying man, W. Ceinfryn Thomas: 'We are all living in debt until we go forward.'[27] The result of all this was over a hundred evangelistic missions plus the journeyings of the 'Gospel Carriage' into the rural areas where the itinerant missioner could often get help from converts of the revival.[28] In addition there would have been scores of missions organized by the stripling Pentecostalist movements in Wales. So the revival spirit became a dynamic force in evangelism also.

It is tempting to go on looking for signs of blessing in the churches, their worship, commitment, and witness. But there is another important aspect of the revival which has to be considered briefly, that is the more general impact on society and culture in Wales. Eyewitness accounts of this are rare but there are enough to confirm the general verdict of interpreters such as R. B. Jones, Dr William Morris of Treorci and journalists such as 'Eilir' of the *Western Mail,* and W. T. Stead.

13
Social and Cultural Overtones

'This . . . went forth throughout . . . all
the region round about'
(Luke 7:17)

It would be a futile exercise to attempt anything other than a general survey under this heading since the topic is covered in so many articles and books about the Welsh revival. A distinction has to be made between unusual and passing effects, and the more normal and enduring consequences discerned by thoughtful observers.

The deeper, more enduring results which were produced in the personal lives of the miners and foundrymen spilled over into their work patterns and their relationships with the owners and managers. These effects owed much to, and were evidenced by, continual prayer meetings such as at Cilfynydd, where 'the miners go down one hour earlier not to trespass on employers' time'. In his book, David Matthews has stories of moral and social changes and tells of a colliery manager named Beynon who, despite being a chapel deacon for twenty-five years, had to admit in the face of a collier's testimony, that he was not saved:

> There and then the rough miner, with his equally rough friends, knelt around their manager in fervent prayer and pointed him to Christ, the Saviour of men. On that very spot he was saved through the instrumentality of these simple men.[1]

John Powell Parry gives this personal testimony regarding changed behaviour:

> I remember now that in the pit where I worked there were ninety little ponies fetching and hauling coal for the colliers from the 'wickets'. That was the mode of transporting the coal in drams holding ten hundredweights. There were ninety in one pit and eighty in the other.

215

Before the revival there were what you might call journey-masters who were slave-drivers driving the young boys—and I was one of them. We only had a pittance of three shillings a day for a nine-hour shift, working non-stop all day. There were two men looking after the ponies in number one pit—father and son, as in many pits. They worked twenty-four hours between them looking after the ponies, to groom them and feed them and look after their gear. Plenty of work. Now before the revival some boys were very wicked and nasty. The slave-masters who were driving the boys had all the wages as was the system in those days; it was tyranny. But when the revival broke out . . . well!

There is a verse that says, 'He that believeth shall not make haste.' It was the same thing down the pit as up in those days. As happy below as at the top, and every boy looked after his own pony. And I remember listening to the old ostler Evan Jones; a fireman or deputy was asking him, 'Well, Jones, how are you tonight, old fellow?' and he said, 'O David, David, David! I'm afraid of losing my job. I'm afraid of the boss getting to know that I've got nothing to do. I don't touch the animals for the boys look after them and clean and groom them and look after their gear and give them food and water—and I've got nothing to do.' So he was weeping, but the fireman said, 'Don't weep. According to the law we have to keep you here even if you don't do anything.' 'Is that right, David? Oh! I've been so upset. I've been afraid of losing my job. But the boys are singing and singing and they are kind to me and kind to the animals. It's wonderful because I have nothing to do.'

Asked if the lads were converted Mr Powell Parry replied: 'Oh, no! but the effects were no cursing, and their behaviour—they all got a touch and many of them were saved.'[2]

The prayer meetings of the shiftworkers and clerks and tradesmen helped to bring social groups together in ways which would later have a healing effect. The *Western Mail* mentioned lunch-hour meetings of dockyard staff and traders in the Bute Docks and elsewhere in Cardiff. Working men, foremen and under-managers who had been engaged in revival witness on the weekend found it easier to gather at agreed times in a foundry, or a brickyard, or a quarry. Only the proprietors seemed to be out of step, and Mrs Jessie Davies, then a domestic servant, said that her employer, a colliery owner, often poured scorn on these meetings. This is a typical situation in Gorseinon where revival began early:

In the assorting-room a few days ago over 200 workmen assembled, the meeting being marked by great religious enthusiasm, coupled with deep reverence. At night, 'between shifts,' a similar meeting was held, workmen all grimy with the marks of their arduous toil, bending the suppliant knee and with tears imploring Divine pardon. One of the lady missioners roused the meeting to fever heat as she read the last chapter of Revelation . . . The scene, indeed, was an impressive one.

All around was the murky gloom of the works, the blackness here and there being relieved by furnace fires, before which stood out illumined the shadowy figures of the men. Then above the whirr of the huge wheels and the heavy lumbering of the rolls was heard the familiar strains of –

> *'Iesu, Iesu, 'rwyt Ti' n ddigon,*
> *'Rwyt Ti' n llawer mwy na' r byd;*
> *Mwy trysorau sy' n Dy feddiant*
> *Na holl gyfoeth India i gyd.'*

> ['Jesus, Jesus, all sufficient,
> Beyond telling is Thy worth;
> In Thy Name lie greater treasures
> Than the richest found on earth.']³

These meetings had not found favour with a Mr Harrap, the manager of Grovesend Tinplate Works, chiefly because there was stoppage of work. Before long a compromise was worked out for the men to have an hour's prayer before the shift began. Mr Harrap should soon have been consoled by another effect of the revival in Gorseinon and Loughor, which John Penry mentioned. He said that men converted in the revival played a large part in setting up a pioneer Workers and Management Conciliation Panel after which the Works had no stoppage or strike for many years.⁴

R. B. Jones noted that for a short time work-patterns were dislocated, but there had been better quality work, reduced wastage and a new spirit because 'men went to their daily toil with a new spirit of gladness and hope'. John Powell Parry claimed that strife and bickering and complaining in his colliery faded away during the revival. An old collier living near Pontypridd, speaking of feuds between Unionists and Nonunionists, said—and this was reported by no less an authority than *The Iron and Coal Trades Review* :

I have seen neighbours refuse to speak to each other, although they had been great friends. I have seen some refuse to descend the mine in the same cage with men who did not belong to the Federation, or to speak to them below ground, except with an oath. The Revival has stopped all that, and the colliers look upon each other, spite of all the differences, as friends and companions. Some of the Non-unionists were among the best of men, and, at the meeting I have just left, one of them was leading the prayers, and the Unionists joining in![5]

There was more dramatic evidence of reconciliation at Bethesda in North Wales, once the scene of a famous Welsh novel about a community torn apart by strikes.[6] J. T. Job writes from Bethesda in December 1904:

There is no stop to the popularity of the meetings—crowds inside, and crowds outside . . . Our purpose here is to keep the meetings *united* for a little while longer—before separating into our different churches. We believe that it is the Spirit who is directing us in this matter also: there is need to cement us together as residents, and for us to 'drink into one Spirit'. The Holy Spirit will soon bring order amongst us again, and I dare to predict a very bright future for Bethesda, though lately it has been through so many pangs . . .

The policemen tell me that the taverns are nearly empty, and the streets entirely quiet, and to hear a curse in anyone's conversation is extremely rare. It is delightful for the police here now!—a splendid holiday to them, I say; and the district is quite happy to maintain them from now on — *for doing nothing!*[7]

Evan Roberts made an effort to promote a mood of reconciliation in families, churches and neighbourhoods. Using the National Eisteddfod cry, '*A oes heddwch?*' ('Is there peace?') he appealed in Ainon Chapel, Treorci, for an end to all divisions. The new climate lasted another decade, but collapsed in the post-1921 strike years when Emlyn Lewis, at the time a much respected lay-preacher from Hengoed in Glamorgan, recalls that much bitterness was created by an inter-Union dispute with chapel members ranged on both sides.

One form of peacemaking was the repayment of debts, which R. B. Jones illustrated from a letter sent to a Rhondda provision firm:

Gentlemen, I have pleasure in sending you the enclosed Postal Order for two shillings. A child of mine received a two-shilling piece instead of a penny as change in your shop eighteen months ago. Lately the child told me of it; and I am greatly pleased to return same to you at the child's request. I sincerely trust that it has not caused you to lose confidence in any of your servants. I remain, Yours respectfully, The Child's Father. P.S. The child is now eleven years of age.[8]

Another extraordinary letter of this kind was published in a North Wales paper. The editor said that the recipient, E. V. Jones of Blaenau Ffestiniog, had two reasons for publishing it, namely to assure the sender he had totally forgiven him and to give the public the opportunity of possessing the truth. The address at the top read, *'Lletty'r Cydwybod, Tref Anesmwyth'* ('Conscience's Dwelling, Town of Unease'):

Dear Friend,—Perhaps you will be surprised when you receive this note, but I must tell you how I came to write it to you.

You probably remember that once, long ago, you lost a half sovereign in the Fall at the Oakley [Quarry], and the Evil One persuaded me to keep it quiet, and one day one of my workmates told a story about an uneasy Conscience, after doing an injury to someone as I did to you, and my conscience awoke at hearing the tale, and I can't ask my God for forgiveness, whilst remembering that I kept the half sovereign while knowing it is your property. My conscience could sleep quietly in the cradle of indifference after deceiving for many years like this, but it awoke at last. The simple truth is that I found it on the ground, and kept it, but I repent greatly, and I want you to forgive me so that I can have a quiet conscience to ask my God for forgiveness for the grievous sin. I greatly hope that you will receive it forgivingly. Well, I have taken advice from more than one friend on how to get peace, and they suggested I sent it like this anonymously, pleading again for your forgiveness with this fitting name—'REPENTANT SINNER.'[9]

The story is perfect proof of R. B. Jones's verdict that 'revival brings conscience to something like a new birth; at least, it uncovers its eyes, releases it from its gag, and gives it new tone and vigour'.[10]

From the report of a meeting of the Machynlleth Board of Guardians comes further evidence. The Master of the Workhouse submitted a letter from one of his 'old boys' sent with money to pay off contribution arrears.

I am writing these few lines to you hoping that you will forgive me for being so long sending the money and causing you so much trouble. It is very likely that you have heard of the religious revival in this part of the country. It has done me a lot of good and has drawn many young men to profess the Lord Jesus Christ in public. I hope it has reached you all.

Forgive me for not writing to you. I am in Merthyr Vale close on four years and I have not written to you, but I hope you will pray for me and forgive me for all I have done to you and my father. I hope God will forgive me. It is the song of everybody everywhere. Ministers come from America, Ireland, and all parts of England to see and hear our young revivalist, Evan Roberts, and to hear the Welsh prayer meetings. I am sending two postal orders for eight shillings.[11]

Such a sum would be a week's wages for a boy.

The spirit of reconciliation was also at work within family life, changing attitudes of husbands, wives, children, parents. An NSPCC inspector in the mining valleys of Glamorgan told one reporter about another great change in habits:

> Homes that I have had under observation for some time have undergone a complete transformation through the parents having been brought to a better life through the Revival. The children throughout my district are now kept in a much more clean condition, and it can be confidently said that in my line things are decidedly slack . . . This time last year I was compelled to prosecute at the rate of two a month. Now I have had no prosecution since November.[12]

The Poor-Law Inspector for Wales addressed the Guardians at Ffestiniog. He told them he would be the last to scoff at the revival. He believed it to be an instrument of great value for good, and hoped that one effect would be 'to wake up some to their responsibilities to their parents'. This was greeted with applause.[13] A Swansea headmaster noted the improved honesty among children and a Llanelli man noted how diligent workmen became.

One factor that had much to do with the improvement in family life was the fierce attack made by revivalists and converts on 'strong drink'. Reports came in from all over Wales of the dramatic results in homes and in workplaces when men were set free from the slavery of liquor. The converts' remarks show this sense of relief. One said:

> This is the first Christmas for me to be sober since I was married, and I want to spend this one at home and have tea with my wife and children.

A wife was heard to testify:

> Family life has altered. I feel now that the kitchen is consecrated. I can rear my children without trouble now—it was the devil who was often

here before. I used to think that I was worse off than everyone else, but I will never murmur again.

A child was heard to say:

> What's wrong, mam? My dad is praying at breakfast time, and praying at dinner time, and praying at tea-time, and a great deal before going to bed.[14]

Various schemes were devised to keep men away from drink. All local magistrates were persuaded to reduce the hours for drinking and to close down many public houses. Many social and cultural activities were removed from rooms in public houses and even the sick benefit clubs were moved to neutral halls. In many cases the benefit officers and insurance agents were encouraged to do house-to-house collections instead.

It is far more difficult to measure the effects of the revival upon cultural life, especially as the national culture was already in decline in many districts and doomed to virtual extinction in such areas in the next generation. Those who came into Wales noticed that there were restraints upon many forms of entertainment. Music halls, dance halls and theatres had always been regarded with suspicion. Many writers claimed that the world of entertainment was deeply affected by the great stirring which changed the face of Wales:

> The most thoughtless became serious; those whose entire pleasure was in amusement were now drawn into the services; Sabbath breakers not only began to keep that day holy, but they were also present at mid-week services, turning workdays into Sabbaths; there was more in the Prayer-meeting and *Seiat* for those whose interest had been previously on sport and on the football field; in a word, almost everything in the locality was revolutionised.[15]

David Matthews described how comedians lost their charm, stages their glamour and concerts their audiences for a while. He insisted:

> It was not the result of thunderous denunciations by some preacher. Neither was it in consequence of anyone aggressively demanding the giving up of such carnal pursuits . . . It was the undemonstrative voice of the Holy Spirit quietly influencing daily conduct, turning thought into new channels, producing the instantaneous results that no other power could have accomplished.[16]

The trouble was that when people began to disobey the Spirit again, the converts fell back on a legalistic 'thou shalt not' to keep themselves and their children from all sport and entertainment.

There was a cleavage between religion and sport as men heard that their football club had cancelled all fixtures or had disbanded because all members were converted and the club captain was now a preacher. There is an allegation in the rugby history, *Fields of Praise*, that 'the Revival singled out rugby as a rival deserving of condemnation'.[17] In over 600 pages of revival reports and press-cuttings, there is no talk of a revivalist leader or preacher sermonizing against sports. Actually, there was very little sermonizing of any kind. Instead it is the converts' prayers and testimonies which are sprinkled with angry words against the violence, the blasphemies and cursings, the drunkenness, and the immoral ideas which they had picked up while attending matches. In this field of sport, as in the world of entertainment, the revival converts protected themselves and their children against dangerous influences by forbidding them to go to such places.

What was to be put in place of these activities to occupy the minds of converts was a subject much discussed even before the revival ended. There was the warning of the Lord's parable of a room which was swept clean but left empty. The debate was long and complex and need only be briefly mentioned here.

Some writers and groups commended training classes and local conventions, whereas Pentecostalists invited converts to receive a Spirit-baptism which would free them from any left-over habits and problems. On the other hand, some church leaders claimed that sound pastoral care and tender love would be enough.[18] After the *Wrexham Advertiser* ran an 'open column' at the beginning of May 1905 addressing the question of how churches could deal with revival converts, a plea was entered on behalf of the Christian Endeavour movement because:

> There is no limit to the scope of a Christian Endeavour Society. It is not bound by hard and fast rules, although it is ruled by the highest and best principles. It seeks to meet all the needs of one who desires to make the most of life. It is just what converts want, it is what all churches may have, and its claims should have the careful consideration of all who are anxious for the welfare of the many who have been influenced by the revival.[19]

A few bolder spirits, such as Dr William Morris of Treorci, in an article in the Baptist monthly, *Seren Gomer* ('The Star of Gomer'), called for a new programme of religious education, character building and culture to save the young people from degraded entertainments. It had to cater for the needs of the whole person—physical, mental, moral and spiritual:

> Our young people's recreation must be completely free from the tavern and drink, from the immoral and that which is dangerous to the body, mind, and spirit, clear of what is doubtful, consistent with the teaching of the Bible, and with the spirit of Christ. The four principles of Dr. Pearson in his *Ethics of Amusement*, set the matter on safe ground . . . Amusement should be
>
> 1. Active, rest being found in variety of activity rather than in idleness.
> 2. Recreative, sought not for its own sake, but as a means to an end.
> 3. Elevated, imparting a higher, not a less tone; refined rather than gross.
> 4. Conscientious, consistent with purest morality, and leading up to a higher plane.
>
> In order to achieve this culture and legitimate amusement, it is important that the means used should be consistent with ethics and religion . . .
> The converts in this present great revival have spare money that they used to spend either on the playing field or in the tavern, with the bookman or in the drinking club, and they ask: Where shall we go? . . . We have evenings during the week when there are no meetings in the chapel; we have young workers . . . who have a holiday on Wednesday or Thursday, yes, and Saturday night free. Where shall we go? What shall we do? How shall we spend our time? Show us. Houses are filled with lodgers near the works . . . On a wet, cold and stormy day, where will they go? The chapel is shut. The church authorities do not dream of keeping it open every evening, and especially on Saturday evening, the evening of terrible temptations . . . No, on Saturday night the chapel must be kept clean for the following day. Many think more of the dust than of souls, and of the spider more than the salvation and preservation of our youth. No wonder so many young people are falling. The drinking club, with its expensive comfortable seating, and its handsome furniture, its sparking fire and . . . its enticing music . . . is wide open every night of the week, and parts of Sunday. The tavern is open, and has every attraction that can be devised to entice people in, while the chapel is closed to them . . . Suitable buildings connected to the chapels should

be provided for young people in industrial areas and towns . . . Provision should be made for a number of Bible classes for both sexes . . . for a variety of lantern lectures, for times to sing and pray, and to deepen the spiritual life. Also a good library should be provided . . . I see from the rules of a number of social institutions in England which I have in front of me, that the opening times noted are from 6 to 11 o'clock at night . . . [and] a Christian atmosphere is sought [in them].[20]

Quite a few halls were built as some churches rose to this challenge, but little was done to meet the urgent needs of the converts. Many family, community and work relationships were profoundly altered and stayed in new moulds for two generations. But generally, sport and amusement and culture ran back into the usual channels, as did social life, until the coming of a murderous war which hundreds of converts experienced in all its shattering effects. Vyrnwy Morgan's lament is unfortunately a true estimate of how the revival lost out nationally:

Vital religion has not been made more effective in our industrial centres, agricultural districts or coal regions. By 'vital religion' I mean, not conventional phrases about getting to heaven, but vital religion in the sense of curbing the passions of the great masses of the people, in purifying their common speech and in eradicating their criminal tendencies . . . A disenchanted nation remains neither stimulated in thought nor enriched in character. Its very language is being gradually driven out of its chapels by 'pigeon' English; and with the language goes its spiritual atmosphere.[21]

A gloomy view this, until one remembers rather singular men and women who in old age displayed a lively energy and astonishing grace and sincerity and humility. That had been the imprint of the Holy Spirit upon them ever since the day that each one was captured and utterly changed. It is of these, who were salt in society, and cities set upon hills, that the next chapters will speak.

14
The Cry of the Rebel

'To the Lord our God belong mercies and forgivenesses,
though we have rebelled against him'
(Daniel 9:9)

During the service I sang, *'Am achub hen Rebel fel fi'* ['For saving an old Rebel like me'], and the message was carried by the Spirit of Truth into a host of hearts in the service, and while I was repeating the words, *'Mi ganaf Ei glod'* ['I will sing His praise'], a man stood up in the front of the balcony and cried out, 'Rebel! Rebel! Is there hope for a Rebel like me?' 'Yes,' I said from the pulpit, 'there is hope for a Rebel like you.' 'But you don't know me; forty years of sinning against God. Is there hope for a Rebel like me?' 'Yes,' I said again, 'The blood of Jesus Christ His Son cleanses us from all sin.' 'Yes, but you don't know anything about me. I have wearied every deacon in the place; I have caused grief to every minister I ever knew, yet it was freedom I was seeking,' he cried at the top of his voice. Then a girl in the centre of the ground floor said, 'Didn't you know what freedom was?' 'No, I didn't,' replied the voice from the gallery. And the girl said again, 'If the Son shall make you free,' and a host of voices answered as if they were reciting together, 'you shall be free indeed.' 'Well, Lord, it's tonight, or hell for ever,' was the next cry, and he fell into a heap in the pew. I was told later that he shone like a bright star for the rest of his life.[1]

This strange incident at a Calvinistic Methodist Association meeting at Llan Ffestiniog in North Wales, recounted by Sam Jenkins, is only one of many hundreds of scenes where strong and violent men were brought crashing down. That same mighty Holy Spirit who caused such great upheavals in church worship, leadership and witness, was well able to crack open the hard, cold shell of the atheist and smash the brazen moulds of the rebel. Often the Spirit seemed to pursue the ungodly and pierce them with his arrows and watch them all resisting and struggling until at last, in some appointed hour and place, they would surrender.

Listen to their own testimonies or the reports of close friends, some of which bring to mind a strange prophecy in Jeremiah 16, 'Behold, I will send for many fishers, saith the Lord, and they shall fish them; and after will I send for many hunters, and they shall hunt them.' It came as a kind of vision to old Jonah Hughes of Rhos who went to the prayer meeting one Saturday night after being out in the fields watching the local gentry shooting game. 'Let us be like those hounds,' he said, 'and go out after those who have been wounded in this meeting.'[2]

May the following accounts of rebels brought to the place of surrender awaken in those who read them a sense of wonder. They bear eloquent testimony to the divine compassion, and are an unsurpassed exposition of that gospel which is 'the power of God unto salvation'.

The man who burned his books

A member of the Trecynon Ethical Society, which was composed of secularists and unbelievers, happened to be a good singer. He went into the lobby of a revival meeting to hear the singing, and returned another night. So affected was he that, when he came home, he tore up all his books and burned them:

> As the flames shot up the chimney and the blaze increased his wife said, 'Tom! Tom! what's the matter? You've lost your balance. You'll put the place on fire.' 'Nothing of the kind, my dear,' he said. 'The Master who has kept us safe through all these years while those cursed books were under my roof will certainly take care of us tonight while I am destroying them.' Altogether they were worth a few pounds, and so keen was he on their destruction that he afterwards said, 'As I was watching them I was under the impression that the angels of God were there blowing the bellows and fanning the flames for me.'
>
> The work of destruction over, he said, 'Now I am going back to the chapel to give myself up to Christ.'
>
> 'Tom! Tom! do be cooler and act like a reasonable man.'
>
> 'No, no,' he said, 'I've been a so-called reasonable man long enough, and now I've lost my reason entirely, as people will tell you, and it's time I did' . . .
>
> 'Tom, dear,' said his wife, 'instead of going back to chapel let us sing like we used to do in former days before you got those books.' And once more Tom Hughes was 'fetched' by singing, and he and his wife and children sat singing till three o'clock that morning . . .

When he went to work on Saturday morning one said to him, 'Tom, bach, you are a converted man at last—welcome to Brynseion, your old chapel. The doors will be wide open to receive you back.' He instantly replied with his well-known sprightliness that has always helped to make him popular, 'If the doors were not open, I would come through the window. And if the windows were barred, I would take a ladder and get on to the roof and come down through that, for come I will!'[3]

The convicted commercial travellers

The following story comes from Tabernacle Baptist Chapel in Cardiff:

One night in a hotel here four men were sitting around a table smoking and gambling and drinking, and they were talking about the Revival, and making all sorts of fun about it. A commercial traveller, a Christian man, was sitting close by, and it went like an arrow to his heart to hear them speak as they did. And getting up he said to the older of them, 'Don't make fun of the Revival. It is the work of God.' But the laughter grew louder, as the other returned, 'Is there a God? And if there were, would He be doing things so foolish as are attributed to Him?'

The good man sat down and finished his letters, and about five minutes to eight he got up and said to the man he had addressed, 'I am going to the Revival at the Tabernacle. You ought to go with me.' The man replied, 'I feel a little depressed tonight. I shall have some rare fun. I will go with you.' They got up and put on their coats, and as this good man told me months afterwards, not a word was spoken from the hotel to the Tabernacle, but if ever he prayed in his life, he prayed every step he took that night that God would open that man's eyes. The chapel was crowded when they entered, and they sat by the door. An aged man was praying earnestly. 'Lord, bless some one that is here tonight. It may be he has just come in, but he is an enemy of Thine.' When he finished, a young woman struck up in the gallery the familiar hymn, 'Tell mother I'll be there.' The words pierced that man's heart, and he turned suddenly pale, and turning to the other said, 'Nobody will tell my mother I'll be there. She died, I understand, broken-hearted because of me.' And then he added, 'What shall I do? I know I am the greatest sinner in this chapel tonight. I have broken every commandment but one, and that is murder.' The good man felt that his prayers had been already answered, and he told him to 'Go forward and tell the people how you feel, and God will give the answer.' He went forward and stood before the large congregation, and with uplifted hand he asked, 'Is there salvation for one who has broken every commandment but one?' Replies came from every part of the chapel, all culminating in 'Him that cometh to me, I will in no wise cast out.' The man, thoroughly overcome, went on his knees and offered a prayer of sobs and tears with broken words. Afterwards he seemed calm.

Months later he came to Tabernacle seeking to conduct a meeting with three others. They were the same blasphemers from the hotel, who had found Christ. Wherever they went they told of their conversion and were the means of salvation of many others.[4]

The two gamblers

The next example comes from the Rhondda Valley:

> Two gamblers, well-known characters, were in the services on Sunday night, January 27th. Both were convicted, and each felt he would like to yield and stay to the after meeting, but out they went. Then one said to the other, 'I had an awful shaking tonight.' Said the other, 'If you had more of a shaking than I, you had a good one.' Both have been in a terrible state ever since fighting against the striving of the Spirit. But the victory was won over the power of darkness last Saturday . . . They were on their way to the Palace Theatre at Porth, two miles away, but after going more than half-way they were compelled to turn back and come to our Prayer Meeting. We had a glorious meeting and when I tested the meeting, asking if there was anyone present who would accept Jesus, one of them put up his hand. I shouted 'Praise the Lord. Here is one.' The other went down on his knees crying for mercy, thanking the Lord that He had brought them there.[5]

The man who would not say yes

When I sat with him in his cottage opposite the old railway station Richard Williams had been a faithful chapel man and respected villager in Nantlle Valley since the day he described in these words:

> Many in our village went to chapel but never asked to become a member —some because they were going to the Halfway Inn. They went to chapel because there was nothing else to do but that and read the *Herald* . . .
> I went to a revival meeting at Llanllyfni. I kept on saying 'I'm not going to change tonight', but I still went to the meeting. I was sitting in a gallery full of lads. The missioner would say, 'What are *you* going to

do?'—pointing his finger right round the circle. Then the finger stopped right in front of me and I went out at once into the street, stricken. As I was going down to the foot of Llanllyfni hill, I was sweating and yet nothing had happened. When I got home I said nothing, telling myself, 'It's my business.'

Later I went to Capel Hyfrydle and heard William Hughes speaking and a voice inside me was saying, *'Wyt ti am aros heno?'* ['Are you going to stay behind tonight?'] Some man was saying that he had once had that experience and had done nothing about it, so he had never been touched by the Spirit. Well, I knew that story but I still told that voice, 'No, I don't think so.' I took no notice of the preacher who was sweating with his efforts. He reminded me of another evangelist who almost pulled his hair out in desperation at failing to convince me and alter my ways lest I took myself to hell.

When it came to the evening service, the voice said once more, *'Wyt ti am aros heno?'* I said, 'No.' Again, *'Wyt ti am aros heno?'* 'No.' A third time, *'Wyt ti am aros heno?'* And now I said, 'Yes, Lord', and that was that. I stayed on to the after service and waited until the minister would shake my hand. Looking back after all this time I can see that I was being pursued even though the workers did not bother me and no one had come anywhere near me at the door.[6]

The deceiver

Though the names are probably fictitious there is no reason to doubt the general accuracy of Mrs S. M. Saunders's story of 'Harriet' who was guilty of deception and of stubborn resistance to the Spirit:

One evening in March, 1905, a very strange meeting was held in our chapel. No testimonies that night. Nothing but very earnest praying for the presence of the Lord in our midst. After spending two and a half hours like this, Mrs Powel stood up,—'We have been here since seven o'clock,' she said, 'asking for the Lord's presence. Our prayer has been answered, this place is full of the Divine Presence. There is no longer any need to ask him to come, He is here. Let us now forget ourselves, and forget our needs, and pray for the Spirit to trouble souls outside the fold; there is no need for us to name them, for the Lord knows them, but let each of us pray very urgently for the salvation of a particular person, and let us stay here to *await the answer.*'

In a moment someone is on his feet praying for his master; elsewhere another is interceding for his servant; a young girl is on her knees asking the Lord to save 'a young man I know'. Almost everyone was praying for a neighbour, a relative, an enemy, and Mrs Powel was sitting with her head in her hands whispering, now and then, the same word 'Aceldama.'

At some stage the chapel door was opened and two or three came in, but no one raised his eyes. After some time,—perhaps an hour, I do not rightly know,—there was a sudden silence, not one voice to be heard anywhere,—and in the midst of the hush, behold a new voice, a voice strange to us,—'Lord, I am very weak. Help me to tell the truth, in spite of the world, the flesh and the devil.' There was a sound of someone moving up towards the big seat, and in a moment we saw Harriet Harris standing straight in front of the congregation.

'Brothers and sisters,' she said in a broken voice, 'I want your attention for a little while. You know me as Harriet Harris, but the truth is that I am Hannah Harris,—I told a lie in order to get hold of a little farm and a sum of money. After I received the money, and returned to America, I tried to use it in different ways, but the same word was repeated constantly in my ears—"Aceldama",—the field of blood. At last I determined to give all the money to good causes. I made arrangements to transfer it; but as I was going to write my name at the bottom of the document, the word "Aceldama" sounded like thunder in my ear. I dared not write my name, but I ran out as if there were ferocious beasts after me, out, out anywhere; and yet the word followed me. At last, when I was in very dire straits, I cried out,—"O God, be merciful to me." And the face of my sister Harriet came before me. For long weeks I tried to find her,—America is a vast country, and it is very easy for one to get lost there. But at last I found her . . . She is here tonight, and I want you all to hear my confession. I am a thief,—I was willing to take my sister's possessions, but for that word "Aceldama" standing in my way. I took the trouble to search for Harriet; yes, but why? In order to be rid of the curse. I knew Harriet would be prepared to give me a share of everything . . . But fear and terror have overcome me. There is something terrible in this place! I have been for years seeking to deny to myself that there is a God, but tonight I feel His presence! I am afraid of Him! Afraid of His face! Afraid of His eyes! What shall I do? Is there a place of safety anywhere?'

'Yes,' said Mrs Powel, 'in the wounds of the Lamb. You may look into the face of God from the wounds of the Lamb' . . .

'Pray for me,' said Hannah, ' . . . The Lord has broken my heart, but it is as hard as ever.'

'Lord,' said Mrs Powel, 'melt this hard heart tonight, through the warmth of your love. Melt her heart here now!'

Hours went by as they prayed for Hannah Harris. By this time it was two o'clock in the morning and the lamps had gone out in the chapel. Someone volunteered to go for candles, and the meeting went on. Shortly afterwards Hannah found release:

> The congregation began to dance and sing; I found myself standing on one of the seats, nursing the baby and shouting at the top of my voice,—'Blessed! Haleluia!' Hannah Harris was dancing like a young girl, up and down the chapel, and no one was surprised. After a while, she went on her knees, and began to speak aloud to God. I do not know what she was saying, but her face was like Stephen's! The candles were not giving much light, but there was enough to see the face of Hannah Harris, and the Divine glory shining upon it![7]

The saint's rebel son

Martha Howells of Bethel Chapel, Aberdare, was a faithful worshipper who never doubted God, even in bitter poverty. She encouraged the minister by prayer, and members by her cheerful faith. She went on praying every day for her rebel son, Tom, for eighteen years without result. She died in 1893 with her son, who had forsaken religion and become bitter, hard and violent, still unsaved. Then, on a Saturday night in November 1904, Tom Howells made his way to the Stag Hotel in Trecynon. His colleagues were absent, and in an increasingly morose frame of mind, he realized they were in a revival meeting. He began to reason with himself aloud, and then, vowing to change his ways, he turned from his drink:

> After he had gone out into the street the soliloquy became living memories of his mother's prayers . . . Back to his memory came the prayers offered by her at his bedside, and those offered on her knees on the loft floorboards, and on the mat on the hearth in the firelight on many a long winter's night. The store of recollections brought a storm to his mind—its whirlwind went with a sudden rush into his conscience, and he hastened his footsteps to the direction of the crossroads, and to the chemist's shop to buy sweets to remove the smell of the drink from his lips: for his heart and face were now set on Ebenezer . . .
>
> There he makes his way slowly and meekly through the crowd on its feet in the aisle. Hush! He hears the voice of some lady singing under the gallery opposite where he stands. It is his sister Lizzy! She leads the crowd in prayer! A prayer for her brother Tom! who she thought would be in his cup as usual, wasting his money and destroying his soul! . . .

He went home that night weeping, and was kept awake till morning by the pangs of a guilty conscience.

Next day, Sunday, November 20th, a Young People's Meeting was held in Ebenezer Chapel. Who should come in with a child in each hand but Tom Howells . . .

As the meeting became more passionate, a cry broke out and drowned all else, and a man whose hair was beginning to grey fell almost full length on the floor. His children were afraid and weeping, imagining something strange had possessed him. It was Tom calling for God's forgiveness.

The sound of his prayer was almost lost in the volume of rejoicing of the congregation at the sight before them. The passing years were to show that this transformation was no temporary phenomenon:

From that day no drop of drink passed his lips, and no oaths or curses slipped out either. His pony could testify that his language had changed, and the rocks that his speech was new, and his wife and children could tell of a change in his spirit and nature, and the neighbourhood could tell of a change in his habits.[8]

The psychologist and sociologist, J. Rogues de Fursac, tried to explain all such events in his own humanistic terms. After telling several stories he wrote:

Beneath the surface operations of the conscious life, a second process is developing which is intimately linked with the first. It is much more active as well as inaccountable and it is susceptible of going silently on for a very long time. However a day comes when the changes it has forced upon the personality will manifest themselves in a sudden explosive way, not showing their origin but leaving the man under the illusion that these have been produced by powers outside his own ego.[9]

Such an explanation ignores the divine factor altogether and leaves no room for the Spirit. It is not adequate even for the rebel cases, let alone the ruined derelicts of the next chapter. It would be safer to trust the instincts of the converts themselves, who somehow saw clearly that it was not from within their souls but from the dynamic pressures of saving grace that they had come to the end of their rebellion. Some of their well-remembered prayers show this understanding clearly:

The devil is sure to set his nets to try to trap and bring back into his lair those he has lost. With the help of God, let us take care to avoid his treacherous deceits.

O Lord, thank you for putting a sprag on the wheels of the coach which was driving me fast to destruction and ruin.

You have felled me again tonight, dear Lord! Thank you, Oh! thank you!

Go after them, Lord. No one is too far away from you.[10]

The language and imagery of these people differ, but the experience is the same. They all know that it is God who has taken the decisive action. 'Not of works, lest any man should boast.' That other persons sometimes apply pressure in no way alters this essential feature. This is equally true of our last and most astonishing scene, when a great crowd of rebels surrendered unconditionally. Again we go to Port Dinorwic in January 1905. There a young man attended a meeting on Sunday evening at the beginning of the 'week of prayer', held traditionally during the first week of January. He seemed content to watch his contemporaries going forward to confess, but claims he did not really want to be committed. The account, taken from a letter quoted earlier, continues:

After the singing—I think it was then that a young man . . . in the gallery stood up, with an agitated look on his face, trembling with emotion and anxiety. His conscience had been awakened. He referred to some hideous sins which he was conscious of, and he said that his former life was nothing but hypocrisy, though he had professed religion. He marvelled that he was still alive, and he pleaded for mercy that night, there and then, before it had gone too late and lest he might not live to see the next morning. He WAS in earnest. Then he sat down, crumpled and crying. This scene was rather unexpected and astonishing to the congregation.

It was now long after ten o'clock. There was singing; and at the same time W. R. O[wen] was seen hastening towards him from the big seat. He sat beside him in the gallery and talked with him . . . Afterwards, W. R. O[wen] stood up on the edge of the gallery and said that a terrible tragedy had taken place in the life of that young man. He had not heard of anything greater having occurred during the entire Revival, and it had ended in the salvation of a soul. He was just about to say something about the nature of his conversion, but his words were

233

immediately drowned by the force of the people singing *'Diolch Iddo'* ['Thanks be to Him'], etc., over and over. It seems that this man had been very hostile to W. R. O[wen], and had insulted him in words and through rude letters over a matter of church discipline, &c. It was this which accounted for W. R. O[wen] going over to him and talking and shaking hands.

Next a young man confessed all kinds of sin and ungodliness, but the burden of his new prayer was that 'the Lord would really bend him, . . . and save him totally, and keep him from returning to his old sinful paths, because he felt so weak'. It was this rebel who began to name other young men and plead with them, shouting out his pleas with great emphasis. The scenes that followed were remarkable. He continued, crying now to God, now calling directly upon them and warning them of their danger. He urged a friend to come to his side, and together, with arms across each other's shoulders, they begged God to save their companions. Then they turned and urged the crowd of young men to come and kneel beside them and cry for mercy, acknowledging their sin:

From various parts of the chapel young men began to pour into the big seat; sometimes two at a time, with others waiting their turn. This went on until midnight. They were on their knees in a row, and some were around the square table inside the big seat. The elders and the old supplicators who were there were obliged to vacate it and find room elsewhere, and even W. R. O[wen] had to retreat into the pulpit.

The lads stayed there instead of going back to their seats, until two or three had to rise and go out of the big seat when it became too full. I was under no small disadvantage in trying to appreciate and remember purposefully all that was said, because I knew only very few of them. I will relate a few things here and there. It was their own sins that chiefly troubled these lads. They talked of 'I' all the time; and then they prayed seriously and earnestly for relatives and friends who had a large place in their intercessions. Some prayed for those they knew to be present, and to be wicked, naming them in a list, and others naming the same ones, and some of these could be seen coming forward hurriedly immediately afterwards, as if some invisible power were pushing them from behind. They fell on their faces in the seat as if they had received some kind of relief by pouring out their thoughts, and no doubt that is how it was for a number of them. Some among the supplicators half embraced their friends, at the joy of being united with those who had been pleading for them.[11]

Before we proceed with the account contained in the letter, it is necessary to say that revival leaders were often uneasy about this kind of mass surrender in these circumstances. After the hours of high emotion and repeated pleas aimed at named people there was strong chance of seed falling in shallow soil.

The following Tuesday saw the second great climax of the revival at Port Dinorwic. The proceedings began with events that were more ordinary, such as a man thanking God for saving him, 'the biggest swearer' in the town. There was a rather entertaining dialogue between two repentant railway workers and their godly station-master who had sat there listening, full of joy over so evident an answer to his prayers:

> He was giving thanks warmly and pleading for them that they might be kept from all evil wherever Providence saw fit to plant them during life's journey.

After this it was once more the turn of the rebels, male and female. One man who had been earnest and specific in his request for another came to the end of his prayer. No sooner had he done so than the very man for whom he had been praying thrust through the crowd to plead for forgiveness. He in turn was followed by his sister in great distress. When she confessed her faults she felt greatly at ease and gave thanks that her brother was showing interest and seemed about to surrender. So it went on:

> There was a young man there who confessed that one of his faults was blaspheming and scoffing at ministers of the Lord, and scorning their words. Another confessed that his great transgression was fornicating, and that despite his mother's admonitions to beware . . . There were also some footballers thumping away at the same evils. Six new people came forward in that meeting, and five on Sunday night (January 1st). But the success of these meetings cannot be measured by these numbers, because all the indications are that almost all who took part were people who had not been saved, although they had ostensibly been church members.[12]

This letter also contains one or two anecdotes about reformed drunkards, but their story belongs to a different class of lost and desperate people. Not consciously unbelieving or rebellious, the bulk of those at Port Dinorwic had lived carelessly and, through slow backsliding, had landed helplessly in a pit from which only the grace of God could lift them.

15
Out of the Depths have I cried

*'He brought me up also out of an horrible pit, out of the
miry clay, and set my feet upon a rock,
and established my goings'*
(Psalm 40:2)

It does not require a national revival for men and women to be delivered
from their mental and emotional chains or lifted out of the gutters of
drunkenness, gambling and lust. By sovereign grace people are changed
every day from being aliens to being members of 'the household of
God', released from sin's servitude to become 'servants of righteousness'. Yet this record would be incomplete without the cries of repentant
prodigals and the sound of their first prayers. The broken voices of men
and women from all walks of life were in many respects the hallmark of
the revival:

> Here he is, Lord. You know about him; he has drunk lots of beer, but
> give him the Living Water now, that is much better than beer.

> O Lord, help me. I've only been a disciple of yours for some three
> months. They have been three blessedly happy months, but I have
> twenty-five black years behind them; and I cannot do anything about
> them. I'll have to leave you settle them.

> The devil gave me a fair go, as far as he had power to give it, but in
> exchange I had plenty of sorrow, a thousand times over.

> I was just like an old grandfather clock. The face was quite fair, but the
> machinery was out of order.

> I never thought God was so near me, until this Revival showed me He
> was at my side.

> Thank you, O Lord, for catching my hand like a little child when I was
> down and had no way to rise up.

236

Thank you, Lord, for keeping me alive when I was only a dry tree encumbering your ground.

Thank you, O Lord, for taking my name off the black list.[1]

The following selected testimonies are but a few of the stories of men and women ruined by sin and evil. Nothing more than a sample can be given of how God dealt with the worldly and the weak, with the wanderers and the wastrels.

The frantic seaman

Dr William Edwards, Principal of the Baptist College at Cardiff, told the following story:

> During the revival we used a large room here in the college, to which we brought the converts, and where we took care of them. We brought them up from the gutters sailors and so on with no home whatever and we had to feed them and clothe them and keep them. This room was open for a month or two, and my wife used to make soup for them, and so on, and by caring for them for two or three weeks they soon became quite changed men. For instance, there was a Swedish sailor whom we intercepted on the way. He had been to our meetings, but he gave up hope, and every penny was gone. He sent a letter thanking us for what we had done for him, and saying it was no use, and tomorrow he would be dead and out of his trouble. And he added, 'Search the canal for my corpse.' We sent a young man after him and waylaid him. They brought him here, and we cared for him for a week or two, and now he is one of the brightest Christians, and writes to me from every port.[2]

The prodigal son

At Tabernacle Chapel in Cardiff a repentant young man was reconciled to his parents from whom he had been estranged for some years. The father, Evan Owen, was a magistrate, the secretary of the Miners' Permanent Fund, and a deacon at the church. He led his son away from the big seat down the aisle to where the young man's mother was quietly praying for the restoration of her long-lost son:

> She was oblivious of everything around her, and looked up rather startled when she felt a touch on her arm. For a few moments she scarcely realised who was standing beside her husband in the aisle, then, with a shriek that rang with pain through the chapel and thrilled every soul

within it, she rushed from the pew, and, throwing her arms round her son's neck, showered kisses on him . . . The mother, scarcely able to stand, and still tightly clasping her son, accompanied him to the big pew, where the two, holding each other's hands, knelt together in prayer, the father looking on at the scene, and showing that he felt it was the supreme moment of his life.[3]

The trade unionist

Dr William Edwards also related the following:

Another man comes here every day, and has been coming for nearly two years. He was a great leader of the colliers, the most popular man in South Wales. They called him 'The Rocking-Stone Chairman', when they had their big gatherings. He became in time a drunkard and a wanderer on the face of the earth, and was imprisoned here and there, and was homeless, having left his wife and family. He came into our meeting one night, and no doubt was soundly converted. I have been in touch with him for the last two years. He is in this town now, and is at my house nearly every day. He is not able to do much work, but he has been doing a great deal of evangelistic work.[4]

Dafydd's story

Robert Ellis of Tŷ-croes, near Ammanford, told this story of one 'Dafydd':

On the threshold of my ministry I came to know Dafydd . . . Before the revival the Temples of Bacchus and the sinks of corruption were his milieu. One could easily have applied Tudno's picture to him: 'His two fiery lips were like a door into a hellish charcoal furnace. Put a lock on his mouth, O Lord God, lest it open.'

All his belongings were in the custody of the pawnbroker. He had wandered far into the wilderness, so far that many despaired of his ever coming back. But, on Christmas morning, 1904, when he was flat on his back in the desert of drunkenness, he felt the strong and tender arms of 'the gentle Shepherd from heaven' taking hold of him and sobering him in an instant. In his life, as in the lives of many others, a new calendar began. In the church where he became an elder, Christmas mornings were spent as 'Dafydd's Birthday Meeting' . . . I spent much time in his company; everyone on the rota to provide hospitality for visiting ministers invited Dafydd to have food with the preacher. How easy it was to praise the Saviour, having been in the company of one of the great miracles of his grace.[5]

The farmer from Anglesey

G. Wynne Griffith tells of the following occurrence during a revival meeting in Llangefni:

There was a strange stirring throughout the chapel, like the effects of an electric current on the great congregation, and I saw a fairly tall man, about sixty years or more, come forward quickly to the 'big seat' and throw himself on his knees there by the small pulpit. All the groups were silent in a moment as though some invisible hand had waved a magic wand over them. Everyone seemed to be holding their breath. I had no idea who the man was. But I learnt afterwards that almost everyone in the congregation knew him, because he was a well-known farmer in the county. He would be in every fair and market but he never went home from them without going on a spree. And these sprees had left quite a mark on him, particularly on his circumstances and on his countenance. In a silence which was almost overpowering he began to pour out his soul in more solemn pleading than anything I had ever heard. The Bible speaks somewhere of 'rendering the calves of our lips' . . . I felt those words described the prayer of this farmer who for so many years had sacrificed many a calf in the service of the god of lust. But now that was all over and he poured out his petitions with incomparable eloquence, if it is proper to speak thus of the passionate experience of a sinner in the melting-pot of salvation.

Suddenly I noticed that the minister who was sitting by my side in the pulpit was being contorted by some strange impulse. I could not understand what was the matter with him. It was as if strong voltages of electricity were coursing through his whole body. Suddenly he went on his knees in the pulpit, with his head stretched out over its edge. He put a hand behind his ear to be able to hear better the fervent prayer of the farmer who was sobbing beneath us in the big seat. Then he shouted out words and phrases as if to punctuate the sentences of the man's prayer. Never before or since have I heard such a duet. I cannot remember what the man in the big seat was saying, but I know he was blessing God for forgiving him, and praising his love and grace. But I can remember some of the minister's phrases; this is what he shouted at the top of his voice—'O! Arglwydd mawr, . . . diolch iti . . . am achub fy nhad' ['O great Lord . . . thank you . . . for saving my father']. For who should the repentant farmer praying in the big seat be, but the father of the minister who was in the pulpit!

It is good to be able to testify that that farmer was truly saved, and that the grace of God kept him to the end, as was the case with thousands of others who experienced the powerful influences during the 1904-5 Revival.[6]

A footballer's testimony

At Ferndale on 8 December 1904, simultaneous with a Welsh meeting led by Evan Roberts, an overflow English meeting was being led in a local school by Annie May Rees:

> A young man rose in the middle of the congregation, and said he had come all the way from Caerphilly to give his testimony. He could not be quiet, although his past conduct, to which he was about to refer, was such as made him feel heartily ashamed of himself. He was one of those who had been referred to as one of the converts at Caerphilly. He was a member of the Caerphilly Football Club, and—he regretted to have to say it—he not only played football, but wherever he went, in the train or otherwise, he used to take with him in his pocket a pack of cards, with which he used to gamble, frequently losing money which he ought to have given to his poor mother. He used to take about with him in his pocket also bottles of whisky, young though he was, and last Christmas, between the cards and the whisky, he lost 26s., and there was his poor mother in the house—and he broke down sobbing, and could not complete his narrative. The congregation fervently sang 'Diolch iddo, byth am gofio llwch y llawr' ['Thanks be to Him for ever remembering the dust of the earth'], and 'Songs of Praises' . . . Resuming his narrative, the young man said that last Monday night he was for three-quarters of an hour wrestling with the devil, but ultimately he found salvation, and hoped to be able to devote his energies to the work of telling young men of his own age all he could about the love of the Saviour. He said that after his conversion he handed to Miss Rees a dance card, 'for,' he added, 'he had also wasted valuable time in connection with dances' . . .
>
> In conclusion the young man . . . asked if there were any young fellows like himself in that meeting who had been foolish enough to do what he had used to. If so, he hoped they would do what he had now done, for he certainly could tell them that this week had been the happiest week in all his life.[7]

The strong man and the Holy Spirit

John Powell Parry could tell of the following remarkable conversion:

> I remember one man in particular; he was a notorious character living in the town. He was a superman and I remember him very well. His name

was Levi Jarvis and he was a pugilist of sorts. He and his two brothers were fighters—there was a lot of fighting in those days before the revival and it was a form of entertainment. This man was a terror to the town in particular; he was the biggest man in town. Yet now he was afraid of coming out of his house and he was afraid of going out to work with the crowd in the morning. So he used to get up and go out at four instead of five. He was afraid of the revival, he was striken with terror, and his wife was very concerned about him. She was afraid of him going out of his mind. There was talk of him in the town and there was praying in the church for him. I had heard them pray for Levi, that the terror of the Lord would fall upon him. Now he was afraid of everybody whereas everybody was afraid of him before this experience.

The revivalist went to see his wife, who was weeping in the house because he was at work. When the revivalist enquired, she said, 'Oh, I'm afraid he is going out of his mind! He can't eat; he can't sleep; I don't know what is going to happen to him.' And when the husband came home, his wife said to him, 'What do you think? R. B. Jones has been to see me today and has been enquiring for you, and they are praying for you.' Then he replied, 'Oh! let me have something to eat and let me wash and let me go to the mountain out of the way.' There's a little place not far from the mountain, about a mile and a half to two miles. So his wife gave him dinner and he slipped away up the mountain.

He *was* afraid but when he came back from that little place, the Lord had saved him on the mountain. Now he went to the chapel that very afternoon and they say that he came into the chapel with his two hands up, surrendering himself to the Lord. When he came into the chapel, he cried out and asked, 'Can the Lord Jesus save such a wretch of a sinner as me?' and the people started to sing and pray, and the minister said, 'Come along, brother', and he went into the big pew. He went on his knees in the big pew and he was saved. How wonderful! People said, 'Look! Look! that notorious drunkard and fighter, that nasty bitter man. Now he is like a lamb.'

After the revival he continued to the end. He was in his late forties when he was saved and he continued till he was eighty. He was always talking about his experience. I had many a chat with him in his old age, and he would say, 'Come here, John, let's talk about that time when the Lord saved me.'[8]

The bully of Bridgend

R. B. Jones described 'Brother Tom' of Ogmore Vale near Bridgend as the most striking example of how people sunk in vice and crime were changed into saints. Tom had a terrible record of drinking bouts, fights, violent revenges, hatred of the police; every magistrate knew of him. He was such a moral wreck that no woman would think of marrying him. Yet this man was brought by the Holy Spirit to a revival meeting where he was suddenly forced to his knees. In only a few days, the valleys were astounded to see Tom pleading with roughnecks and other wretches, and to hear him praying startling, rough-hewn prayers. Some years later he developed lung-disease and had to be cared for by his sister. Many a down-and-out came to that door to ask the way to Christ; many a believer went to hear his testimonies. On his last day he lay back wearily in his bed, told his sister not to be afraid, then said quickly and simply, 'Father, I am ready; are You?'[9]

The most precious gifts he left were his letters to friends which show such wonderful understanding of God's ways. Most of these letters bear witness to what God's amazing grace had done for him. The last of these letters reads as follows:

God commanded the Light to shine in my old heart most unworthy. I must tell you it is shining terribly there. A holy treasure in an earthen vessel. It is my delight. The whole temple is lit up. It was blessed, blessed, Alleluia. Is it not wonderful that this Light has nothing to do with darkness, absolutely nothing? I have nothing henceforth to look for but His promises. My breath has gone so excessive short if I exert myself. When it is dark and the path narrowing down, what a privilege it is to trust God. Happy is he that trusteth. I do wonder when I look back over this year. How our loving Father has cared for us. His promise has been fulfilled—Isaiah 66:13. My cause is a cause to make me jump and sing for joy. Another twelve months at the throne of grace, and in school. I must tell thee I have no riches, but God supplies all my needs, not my wants. He has kept me like a king's son. Praise His holy Name.

Thou art asking how I am. Well I will answer thee scripturally. 2 Corinthians 4, vv. 16,17,18. I would say our outward man does perish, but I am very glad to complete the verse . . . 'the inward man is renewed day by day'. The proof of the Bible lies in its own experiences. Praise be to God for it. God says, 'When thou goest through the waters, I will be with thee', and He does not stop there. There are also RIVERS. I have said many a time lately. I would have drowned if it were not for Thee. The river of bronchitis is a very thick one. Praise His Name that he sends His word daily. It does not matter the state; it heals beautifully; it is balm in Gilead for every wound. I feel exactly like Job. He has fenced wonderful; he has fenced up my way that I cannot pass. He hath set darkness in my path; (Isaiah 42:16) he will make darkness light.

I have been greatly met with in the column 'Home Worship' in the *Life of Faith*. Have faith in God. Often have I read it, but last night our precious Father lit it up for me, wonder of wonders, through those words, 'we all have our mountains'. Then the Father showed me in the twinkling of an eye how he had removed scores of mountains in the past. Not only removed them but we could not find a trace of them. Just like that wonderful scripture in Isaiah 44:22 about our sins removed like a cloud—blotted out. And that is how God showed me the mountains I saw these last seven or eight years. I did see a good many, but when I look back for them now, I cannot see any trace of them, like the cloud, disappeared for ever.[10]

This catalogue of accounts might be extended indefinitely. Of details and circumstances there would be endless variations—but all on one glorious theme, that of the immeasurable love of God commended in the death of Christ for sinners. They could all sing from the heart that well-known hymn:

> In loving kindness Jesus came,
> My soul in mercy to reclaim,
> And from the depths of sin and shame
> Through grace He lifted me.
>
> > From sinking sand He lifted me;
> > With tender hand He lifted me;
> > From shades of night to plains of light,
> > Oh praise His Name, He lifted me!
>
> CHARLES H. GABRIEL (1856-1932)

243

IV. REPERCUSSION

What proclaims the silver trumpet?
  Zion's King sends forth His call!
Who are thus invited by Him?
  All the children of the Fall;
Home, oh home! ye wandering children,
  Leave the empty husks of sin,
Comes to all the King's glad welcome
  To His feast to enter in.

Why, oh why the King invites us?
  Why, He is the God of love.
What about the evil in us?
  His own blood will all remove;
His long-suffering is boundless,
  And His patience passing great,
Let us bow and seek forgiveness
  Now when it is not too late.

Can the old in sin be rescued?
  Yes, from deepest guilt he can.
Who will be to him a Saviour?
  Jesus Christ—the God and Man;
Sinners vile with all uncleanness,
  Full of sin and crushed with doubt,
Come to Jesus, come and welcome,
  He will never cast you out.

v.1: John Williams ('Sion Singer'; c.1750-1807);
vv.2-3: Roger Edwards (1811-80);
tr. by William Edwards (1848-1929)

16
Resisting the Spirit

'Behold, ye despisers, and wonder, and perish:
for I work a work in your days'
(Acts 13:41)

This chapter is devoted to a consideration of various kinds of attack from outside the churches. There was surprisingly little physical attack upon the revivalists; certainly nothing like the rough treatment handed out to the Welsh Methodist pioneers of the eighteenth century. Only one story has been recorded of a gang of drunken ruffians invading Tabernacle Baptist Chapel, Cardiff, lifting a deacon up and threatening to throw him over the edge of the balcony. The refined pastor, Charles Davies, could only send a desperate cry to the Lord, and that was answered at once. Miss Annie Rees was prompted to sing, 'Tell mother I'll be there', and the drunken louts were subdued and sober long before she ended. They sat to worship, with tears in their eyes.[1]

One district which showed enmity to the revival for months was the town of Llangollen where certain gentlemen, ardent patrons of sport, were spreading false stories and accusations in order to arouse opposition. The local paper, the *Llangollen Advertiser*, published the following letter on 20 January 1905:

> Sir,—Regarding the Revival movement at present in progress in the town and elsewhere, however good some of the results may be . . . there is no question that some are deplorable . . . One of these has recently been forcibly brought to my notice, and I am induced to give publicity to it because, from conversations I have had with my friends, I find that my experience is also theirs . . .
>
> I am not disposed to criticise the methods adopted by those responsible for the conduct of the meetings so far as they do not affect my comfort or convenience—and this is the attitude those on whose behalf I write are disposed to adopt towards them. More than this we are ready to be tolerant with the perpetuation in the winter of scenes in our streets

that in other years have not persisted when 'the tripper ceased from troubling; and the residents might rest.' Apart, however, from any feeling which street demonstrations and processions cause, we now find it is impossible to induce our servants to keep regular hours and observe the conditions of their agreements, and the convenience of their employers is totally disregarded in order that they may participate in meetings . . .

This week, very reluctantly, I have had to dispense with the services of one of my servants for this very reason. She found it impossible to become sufficiently 'revived' in two-and-a-half hours nightly; invariably coming home an hour or so late. My friends tell me they have the same thing to face . . .

In all seriousness I would ask 'is this kind of thing likely to do good to the class I refer to?' If it is the cause of their losing employment, what are they gaining by it? I may be told that 'they are laying up treasures where neither moth nor rust can corrupt;' I may be told also, that, like Mary, 'they have chosen the better part.' I am afraid I cannot see the matter in this light; nor can I regard it as otherwise than a perversion of the Divine injunction to teach servants to disobey their masters . . . I am drawn to the conclusion, which is shared by many, that throwing together a numbers [*sic*] of young men and women, under the spell of potent emotionalism, for extended periods of time, to advanced hours, is an experiment attended with grave moral dangers. At any rate, I desire to protect my household from any undesirable object-lesson of the folly, shall I say, of misdirected enthusiasm; and on behalf of many who think with me, to enter a protest against the whole business. Apologising for trespassing so much on your space.

I am, yours faithfully, CHARLES TAYLOR

The Grange, Llangollen
Wednesday, Jan. 17th, 1905.

Of the well-educated men interviewed in Rhos near Wrexham, the hairdresser-tobacconist T. J. Davies, although having a great admiration for R. B. Jones, showed a dislike for the emotional behaviour of revival converts which could, it must be admitted, take strange forms at times. He claimed that he had opted out of the revival simply because he was a 'thinking man'. He told this story:

I had a definite experience of conversion when I was a young man, but I was very modest and controlled and not carried away, so I felt nothing at the time of the revival. I was never affected at any time, although I often saw processions passing the shop. A stranger came into my shop and asked where he could find the revival. He told me he was an officer of the Rechabites and that he thought this revival would be a good thing for his Society. But I told him not to waste his time, because no one could reason there when all the meetings were in confusion.[2]

Then there was the Ruabon schoolmaster, J. T. Jones, who was a youth of sixteen when revival came to his home village of Rhos. The noise, disorder and display of emotion he witnessed when he attended one of Evan Roberts's open-air meetings in Anglesey in the summer of 1905 left him with a great distaste for informal revival meetings, so that he and his friends would only attend more traditional services.[3]

These two, so different, so similar, were typical of a new kind of Welshman who used their Board School education to acquire far more knowledge by means of the Miners Institute Libraries, the Carnegie Lecture Halls, second-hand information manuals and a wide range of debating societies. There they were introduced to rationalism, atheism and other philosophies, which raised them above the 'simple believers'. It was these men who welcomed the general attack on the many stories of aerial lights, aerial choirs, flashes and visions. They may not have known about Fursac's theory that Mrs Jones of Egryn was having visions and voices because she had had so many emotional upsets in earlier life,[4] but they must surely have heard of Fryer's lecture. This was read to the Society of Psychical Research and tentatively suggested that the lights could be the result of a mental stimulus, not dissimilar to the way a sharp blow to the head causes one to 'see stars'.[5] Trained in such ways to distrust anything abnormal as a delusion, self-educated men turned their critical eyes upon the whole revival. What they could not disprove they denied or pushed aside as mere auto-suggestion.

An excellent example of the kind of passive resistance put up by some of the intelligentsia can be found among the narratives from correspondents printed in the appendix to A. T. Fryer's lecture to the Society for Psychical Research. A man from Treorci, writing in June 1905, explained that he had left his church four-and-a-half years earlier because he 'could not agree with them in certain dogmas':

> The Idea of God and the Spirit World were put aside, and I read as much as I could on the subject of Psychic Phenomena. I read the lessons of the American school of science, and a course from the Psychic Research Society and the New Thought. I read Prof. W. James and

249

Stout's books on Psychology; also books on Ethics by Mackenzie and Newman Smith. I read books on Freethought, Ingersoll, 'Saladin', Foote, and Cohen, and some of J. S. Mill's books, also Paine, etc. I also attended lectures on Freethought. It all led me to Agnosticism and Abstractive Idealism. I may here tell you that I kept myself from all immoral actions. I always tried to think the best and live the noblest. I and a few friends started an Ethical Society, . . . and spent a year splendid together. Then the Revival started here at T[reorci].

When friends and acquaintances began to talk about moral change, answered prayer and the like, he explained it away as thought transference or as imitative instinct. Deeply perturbed by seeing friends in agony or crying and fainting, he took refuge in the device of auto-suggestion to stop himself being affected. He received another shock when he found that as soon as he and other sceptics left a meeting, it would come alive with fervour, many would feel the power of the Spirit and, most astonishing of all, other rationalist friends would suddenly shout out that they had found the real thing. Four months passed before this young intellectual asked for 'an experience of God':

A few young men wanted me to believe in Christ, but I could not. I could not see any actual value in this belief, because I believed in Abstractive Idealism, and thought a better conception of truth could not be got. The Spiritual world was not a *reality* to me . . . I wanted an evidence to prove that the Spiritual world was a reality. They insisted that I should believe in Christ first then I should do what He told us to do (that is to pray to God through Him, and I should find out for myself the result). After a few months' time I decided that I should obtain this experience if it was possible. So, on the 25th February, I determined that I would take Christ as my ideal in life. I went to the meeting that night. It was overcrowded. I never was in such a meeting. The prayers in this congregation had an inspiring effect upon me, which caused a thrill through my body, causing great pain. I cried bitterly; why, I don't know.

For some days after this thoughtful young man remained in a state of intensified emotion and great pain of body. 'How and why I cannot explain,' he says, 'but it is true.'[6]

Not a few university dons and their students regarded this kind of collapse by thinking people, under the pressure of a mass meeting, as being like an epidemic disease spreading. In his memoirs the physician,

Ifan Huw Jones, gives his version of how his sisters became 'infected' with revival fever, and then his father too:

> Mass hysteria is a frightening thing, when some unseen wave upsets the nervous system of hundreds or thousands of people . . .
> Some of you remember the last great revival in our land. I was studying at Bangor at the time, and when the mental illness had reached its peak, I went home for the weekend.
> The late Rev. Dr Davies, a Baptist minister in Caernarfon, was staying at my home, and my father asked what was my opinion of the revival. My only answer was 'Mass Hysteria,' and then the old minister said, 'Fair play to him, he has every right to his opinion, and I'm not so sure that he is not correct.'
> One evening my sisters had been in Seion Chapel, Coed-y-Ddôl, for hours, and at midnight my father went there to bring them home. He went into the chapel, and the first thing he heard was one of the riff-raff of the village praying. He was using pure and sweet language, and was expressing the most holy matters in the most cultured way possible. From where, pray, did he receive this speech, and what moved him to use it?
> There my father remained until two o'clock in the morning, and when he came home his eyes were red and moist.
> Despite his common sense, he too had been swept off his feet by the wave of mass hysteria.[7]

Resistance to the Spirit and the revival was not always so restrained, especially if the protester had some personal axe to grind. There were widely publicized occasions when the protest was very audible. Long before Peter Price, whose attack will be considered later, entered the arena, Evan Roberts had faced two challenges by agnostics, at Tylorstown in the Rhondda and at Llansamlet near Swansea, the second of which caused him and his friends much pain.

The first clash came unexpectedly during a very notable meeting in the Rhondda Valley in December 1904, which an eyewitness described afterwards as 'the meeting of opposing forces'. A man declared that he was an infidel. Evan Roberts asked if he were prepared to state his opinion publicly:

> After some hesitation, the unbelieving young man got up, and declared publicly,—'I believe in my heart there is no God.' The congregation went aflame, and would have ejected the atheist if given permission.

But the Revivalist did not want that. With great self-possession he quietened the troubled and threatening sea. 'Pray for him,' he said, and then told the man himself to go to his room and in the solitude there think God out of existence. The wind of resistance had arisen, and it looked as though it would blow more and more until it became a wearisome crosswind. Two others now sent written questions to Dr Phillips. We understand they were professed Christadelphians, or disciples of Swedenborg. They asked how was it possible to sin against God, and was Christ truly God? Dr Phillips said the meeting was not a place to debate or expound theological questions, and he encouraged them to call at his home another time. But one of the questioners rose up to oppose the doctrine of the deity of the Saviour. In a flash, the Revivalist was on his feet asking all who believed Christ was the Son of God to stand. The whole multitude stood up except these two and the first opponent. When he asked the other side to rise, only one was bold enough to do so. One stood up and asserted that it had not been put fairly to the congregation. It was not the same thing to say that Christ is Son of God as to say that he is God. Then Dr Phillips jumped to his feet and asked all who believed that Jesus was infinite God to stand up. They all rose up with the same unanimity as before with only three seated. Immediately after this, the three pushed out through the throng.

That particular battle ended with the confession of a mocker and the conversion of a man who was 'pierced through and broke down in a flood of tears, declaring his readiness to receive the Saviour'. It was considered that the revivalist had dealt well with this challenge.[8]

Not so on the second occasion, in Llansamlet in January 1905, when Evan Roberts was so prostrated by the enemy that an older man had to take over. It all began with two agnostics entering the meeting and giving out a challenge that he should pray there and then for them to be saved: 'You ask the Power to save us and we will believe you.' There followed much agony of soul and passionate prayers and sorrowful hymns. Eventually the old saint, Dr F. B. Meyer, stepped up:

Dear brothers and sisters, I never meant to speak in this meeting. I feel it is like a school of the Holy Ghost, and I am only a little child, sitting on a low form, learning. Therefore, I am a little child and I have no right to speak, but there is one thing that I said to a friend, and I repeat it. St. John said that 'there is a sin unto death; I do not say that ye shall pray for it.' That is, there may come a time in a man's life when he says 'No' to God and passes the line, and I do not think that in this world we can

252

hope for him. I do pray that my two brothers there have not crossed that line and if an Englishman may speak to them with a brother's heart, I say, 'Dear brothers, God is even now fighting in your behalf against your proud self-will, but, mind you, He cannot save you in spite of yourselves. You must say 'Yes.' Don't try to feel earnest but say it: say 'Yes' to Him by an act of the will . . .'

Some little further time having elapsed, one of the two men inquired, 'How long a time have we to wait?'

Mr. Roberts sternly replied: Coram, Dathan, and Abiram had to wait until the earth swallowed them, and the 50 had to wait until they were consumed with fire.[9]

Personal resentment and bitterness were frequent causes of someone declaring openly he was an agnostic. Thomas Williams of Trecynon, Aberdare tells of a man who was intelligent yet ruined by drunkenness and humiliated by an awful stutter. When derided for his handicap he would revile men and blaspheme God. He had a deep hatred of religious hypocrisy and when he announced that he was going to a revival meeting, his wife pleaded with him not to go, since she feared the effect that his scoffing would have on the people present. However, he insisted on going, and as soon as he had taken his seat, he was approached by a young man whose intentions were good but whose manner he found offensive. The young man's persistence proved more than he could endure:

As he was advising him to join religion, telling him how pleased his *wife* would be to see him becoming a member, and showing him the comfort it would bring to his home, the suggestion became too much for his 'old nature' to endure and he said,

'W-wait a m-moment! Honour your wife as I honour m-mine, and you needn't w-worry about doing wrong. I have come here to l-listen this afternoon, and not to be b-bullied by you. So leave m-me in peace Sam, or I'll pick up my hat and go, and then I'll be l-left in peace.'

As he went to reach for his hat beneath the pew, behold an even younger girl bending down alongside him, and praying passionately on his behalf. When he heard his *name* being used by her so boldly in her prayer, he raged terribly, saying—'You can st-stop it, too, my g-girl. You are st-still a little too young for this business, and there's no point you praying on my behalf. It is wasted work, m-my girl. You needn't bother the Great King about me. I can speak with Him myself if I so wish, so get off your knees, and leave this foolishness and n-nonsense.'[10]

'The Diary of a Working Man' has great value as a mirror of the mind and heart of a thoughtful, independent-minded young man who had eagerly drunk in the rationalist 'truth' from his friend 'A', but could not receive revival truth, especially when converts and pastors and family were putting on the pressure. He was upset at first because his mining class was ruined through everyone going off to a revival meeting advertised at Aberdare. The growth of his personal opposition is shown in these diary entries:

> *November 20, Sunday.* I stayed home from chapel to help the wife. I heard at dinner time that the revival had 'broken out' in Tabernacle. In the morning the minister read from the Scripture and prayed, but as he gave out his text, he broke down, shut his Bible, and took his place in the 'big seat', after telling the congregation to take the service into their own hands. A young girl, L.M., got up and another, a teacher named L.E., after her, one leading a hymn and the other praying. Then a number of young men prayed, and soon everyone was weeping all out . . .

The diarist was favourably impressed by Evan Roberts and disagreed with those who alleged that he was trying to hypnotize them. However, he was not influenced by the appeals of the revivalist, and when, in one meeting, an hour of praising and praying and short addresses was followed by an appeal for everyone who wanted to declare for Jesus to stand on their feet, the diarist alone refused to stand:

> Before long, I noticed two or three of Evan Roberts's 'young ladies' crossing the front of the gallery by walking on the seats behind the people who were on their feet. In next to no time two of them were sitting at my side. One of them put her arm around my neck and asked, 'Are you a member?' Why wasn't I? Didn't I believe in Jesus? What was keeping me back? I didn't answer much, and then sat silently, everyone around me gaping at me, and the majority of course marvelling that I was 'outside'.
>
> The girls implored and pleaded upon me, with tears in their eyes, and begged me to stand up. I remained seated. Soon the minister came up to me, and asked in Welsh: 'Brother _, aren't you a member?' I answered: 'No.' Weren't you? Wouldn't you like to be? I did not reply. I felt sorry to have to resist his pleadings; he spoke so splendidly, so full of feeling, so sincerely, but I felt less willing, or at least as unwilling, to 'cross the line' than I had ever done. At last, he went on his way, but as he came back he tried to get me to promise to go and see him that night,

or to pray for myself after going home. I did not and could not promise. I need hardly say that I did not go to the evening service.

The entry for Sunday, 27 November, describes a painful visit from his father and another deacon who pleaded with him to 'give in'. His friend spoke of the revival in terms of a 'reign of terror' and 'persecution', and of Evan Roberts's power of 'human magnetism'. Further pressure was put on both of them and this made him angry and hardened his attitude. He vowed that he would never again go to chapel, at least until the tumult had died down:

> *November 28.* Went to the top station at four in the afternoon. A crowd there going to meet with the revival in other places, 'our minister' among them. I tried to avoid him, but he came up to me.
>
> 'Have you come any closer?' He talked of my using my will, 'the will to believe'. I'm afraid I answered him rather impolitely:
>
> 'How can I make myself believe what I don't believe? It's just as if I were to try and lift myself by the collar of my coat.'
>
> I went to the ladies compartment on the train to get rid of him. But another minister followed me there. He also asked had I come closer, and then added something of his own experience. He had felt nothing until the Friday morning in Caersalem; since then, he had been in heaven. Sunday morning he went to bed at four o'clock. He awoke at six; some power, he said, had taken possession of him, something like a divine electric battery shaking him the length and breadth of the bedroom, and him singing at the top of his voice, 'Thanks be to Him.' The feeling, he said, was beyond description and altogether blessed. I must admit that he made a great impression on me at the time.
>
> I went to relations in the Rhondda. On the way back I had to wait for quite a while on a full platform at Porth. It was rather dark but I noticed a great crowd of young men there from our village. I avoided their company. Before the train arrived they began to sing, 'Tell mother I'll be there.' Happening suddenly like that, it frightened me and gave my nerves a shock.

The entry for a Sunday in the following month reads:

> I went to chapel for the evening service. I was sorry afterwards. After the minister read from Scripture and began to address us, J. T. broke across him to pray and another followed with a hymn. Then another deacon praying and L. following him. Then everyone who confessed Christ was asked to stand. I did not do so. Soon L. came down the aisle

to plead with D. D. (who attended the chapel regularly though not a member); he did this for over half an hour. My wife suggested that he 'gave in' for the sake of peace. I was left alone.

Right to the end the diarist went on criticizing the actions of the revivalists, claiming that he had never been touched by the revival events he witnessed. Such opposition seems to be direct resistance to the Holy Spirit until one remembers that he had been exposed to some very unwise pressurizing by the spirits of men.[11]

One more striking example of scepticism concealing deep personal feelings and problems was given by Grawys Jones. It concerned a young man who had seen someone in the meeting whose opinion he valued. As the young man made his way to the other to seek his verdict on the revival, he thought he heard a voice reminding him that what God said was more important than what man said. He was immediately transformed, and his attempt to walk to the front of the chapel was dramatic.

I was sitting in the front facing the doors, and I can only describe his entrance as if you put in a hook and pulled him in. He . . . began to tell how real the revival was.

'This is a reality', he said. 'Whoever said it is a sham is making a mistake. The stamp of the Divine government is upon it, and I am giving myself entirely to the Lord.' As he said this, he began to quiver, and his body began to shake back and forth, and the most awful look came to his face . . . Soon the colour came back to his face . . . and he fell down on the seat.

It was later discovered that he had been bitter and quarrelsome and had played the hypocrite. His acrimonious dislike of the revival was just a cover for his own problems.[12]

*   *   *   *   *

Another line of attack on the revival came via the numerous journals of learned professions and societies, some of which had the ear of local newspaper editors. Psychological journals classified the converts' experiences as forms of auto-suggestion and self-induced states, and a few made references to textbooks on the psychology of religion. In the medical journal, *The Lancet,* contributors gathered up stories which suggested a link between revivalism and lunacy. There were sociologists, too, who treated the Welsh revival as an outbreak of repressed racial passions and hopes, which were later diverted into new political causes. Among the local newspapers *Y Celt Newydd* ('The New Celt'), published at Ystalyfera in the Swansea Valley, sounded a warning note about voices and visions and the danger they posed to true revival.[13] When so many different kinds of intellectuals were suspicious or scornful, it was easy to use words such as 'crazy', 'deluded', 'wild'. The bolder critics accused Evan Roberts of using clairvoyance and prediction to shock people, and said he was using the Spirit's name as though he were a Delphic oracle.[14]

Some of the hostile newspapers, such as *Llais Llafur* ('Labour Voice') in the Swansea Valley or the *Rhondda Leader,* just gave minimum coverage to the revival. The campaign in the *Aberdare Leader* started on 19 November with a report of meetings at Trecynon, the main centre of the revival in the area, which described Evan Roberts as 'pacing the "set fawr" [big seat] back and fore Bible in hand, wringing his hands impatiently as if he were a mere bundle of nerves'. Seven days later an editorial talks of 'midnight revelries, dislocation of trade and unseemly excesses', of 'coerced converts' and 'holy hysteria', alleging also that whenever a quieter meeting was conducted 'the religious Anarchists from Trecynon' would go away disappointed and claim that Satan was there. The critics had the support of the Aberdare Ethical Society who wrote to complain 'that the superstitious element in Christianity is more or less introduced (by the revival] and forced on the ignorant masses'.[15]

It was only natural that Evan Roberts himself came under attack as having such intense personal magnetism that he hypnotized those who sang for him and was now focusing his hypnotic eyes upon congregations. An alternative theory was that Roberts had unusually penetrative eyesight and could pretend to be guided to a person when in fact he had spotted his distress in a preliminary look around. There were three pointed questions asked of this hypnosis theory which it found impossible to answer:

a) How long could a hypnotic spell last, since Roberts had gone away long ago?

b) Who had hypnotized the people of Cwm-bach, since Roberts had never even been there and yet there were 300 converts?

c) Were Anglican vicars also in the habit of hypnotizing, since they also had won over so many revival converts in their services?

These astute arguments could not stop the magnetism-hypnosis theory spreading further and further because so many wanted to believe this explanation of something they feared. It tied up neatly with the parallel attack on the excitability factor in revival meetings.

This onslaught really worried the defenders of the Welsh revival, and it needed someone like the prominent Welsh Calvinistic Methodist, Eleazar Roberts, to give a thoughtful reply, especially after a Welsh minister had made a public attack on the revival as a fake and deception. At a special Christian conference in Liverpool in May 1905, Eleazar Roberts quoted extensively from Dr Chalmers, Professor Caird, F. W. Robertson and Dean Stanley in order to demonstrate that fervour, ecstasy, passionate devotions, bodily gestures, etc., have always had their proper and essential place, even if at times these have the appearance of wild excitement and intoxication.[16]

Just how much damage was done to the revival movement by the sceptics and rationalists and other opponents outside church life cannot be estimated, but they could not have inflicted wounds as serious as the attacks from inside chapel and church. It is to these that we now turn our attention.

17
Grieving the Spirit

'Ye do always resist the Holy Ghost: as your
fathers did, so do ye'
(Acts 7:51)

Some object to the beloved young man, whom the Lord has chosen to spread the heavenly fire and light abroad . . .

Some object to women taking part in public prayer, exhortation, testifying, or reading of the Word . . .

Some persons object to so much singing in the daily meetings . . .

Some object to the length of meetings . . .

Some object to the visions seen . . .

Some ridicule the idea that Mr. Evan Roberts was not allowed to go as he wished, and intended to go to Cardiff, as if Paul, who wished to go to Asia and Bithynia, had not been forbidden to go there . . .

Some object to the great evangelist's desire to have all the assembly —when inspired to it—to publicly worship the Lord together, or simultaneously as they are moved by the Spirit to do . . .

Some object to the Lord's messenger calling attention to the icy souls, whom his anointed eyes perceive in the congregation, who, as ice, create an unfavourable atmosphere, as if no Satan was to be rebuked, and as if the revivalist had no message to dark minds; stony, starchy hearts, and sleepy consciences.[1]

In these fiery and fearless words Mathry Morgan, the minister at Llan-non near Llanelli, summarized the different kinds of reaction inside the churches and chapels of Wales as the revival gained in power. His list of motives can serve as a kind of map of the battlefields: a leadership contest, a war of generations, set prejudices, reluctance to accept new challenges, and a sharp resentment on the part of those who had remained cold against those who had been set on fire by the revival flame.

Fursac, perhaps influenced by a retrospect of what had happened to Calvin, Menno Simons, and the Huguenots and Jansenists of his own nation, declared that a clash between enthusiasts and entrenched leaders could not be avoided:

> The most bureaucratic of all have always viewed mysticism with concern . . . This suspicion is not without some justification: like every institution, whatever it may be, a Church can only function if it is organised, if it is led by a hierarchical and disciplined line of command. The nonconformist churches, despite their democratic character, are no exception to this rule. Now any mystical movement, by virtue of its enthusiasm and spontaneity, is at least to some degree revolutionary. It tends to destroy the organisation, to overturn the structure of authority. It is, in a word, decidedly inimical to clerical discipline, and seeks to lead the religious community away from its usual paths.
>
> The almost anarchical form of the revival meetings, where ministerial authority counted for virtually nothing, the half-morbid quality of the excitement displayed in them, the danger of these assemblies ending late at night, young men and women departing from them in an unhealthy state of nervous elation, left unsupervised, having sometimes several miles' journey ahead of them before reaching home: all this alarmed some ministers.[2]

For reasons which might not be easily grasped today, chapel and church officers became very worried about meetings going on after midnight. A group of Baptist leaders in Gwent discussed a resolution in their Assembly protesting at this practice as unseemly and disorderly.[3] This is only one aspect of the deep distrust shown toward revival freedoms. It is fair to say that the statements of some prominent figures in the revival, or self-appointed messengers, combined with certain odd patterns of behaviour, must have given the leadership every reason to feel nervous. Cynddylan Jones and Elvet Lewis were champions of the revivalists, but both of them warned off the hotheads and prophets, accountable to no one, who spoke in the early hours of the morning. Many of them had heard the report of a zealous American evangelist saying at a revival meeting in the Rhondda Valley, 'Some people think this revival is the fizz of a bottle of pop. No, no: it is the fizz of a fuse, and the dynamite is at the end of it . . . God is going to save the masses, and He must do it in His own way. He has told the ministers to stand on one side and let Him have a try.'[4]

It was senior ministers and laymen in Pembrokeshire who were responsible for the early opposition of the Welsh Baptists there. The editor of the magazine *Y Piwritan Newydd* ('The New Puritan'), J. J. Evans, minister of the historic Rhydwilym church, announced that:

> We cannot go along with the mode in which some meetings are carried on. Anything that tends to cause young hearers to stay behind is sure to be working against Baptist principles.[5]

Another fervent Baptist minister at Llwydcoed near Aberdare split a revival meeting by telling it that baptism by the Spirit did not dispense with the need for water baptism. All the other denominational groups went to a different chapel to continue the meeting, but the doughty minister carried on his attack on the revivalists for preaching obedience to the Spirit yet not practising that virtue by being baptized themselves.[6] Unfortunately this kind of official disapproval was not confined to the Baptists, and one can find strong words from bishops and leaders in other denominations.

The *Llanelly Mercury* reported several incidents of clashes between ordained ministers and keen groups within their churches. It told of a minister due to preach at Ammanford who was questioned about his salvation by youths who visited, examined and prayed for him:

> They told him that they could not allow him to preach in the chapel that day, not being satisfied with his answers. Very properly the minister resented this impertinence, and told them that he received his instructions from the deacons.
>
> Soon afterwards he took his place in the pulpit and conducted the service. As he was about to commence his sermon, however, there was another interruption—this time from a lady in the congregation, who rose to her feet and forbade him preaching. This created a sensation in the sacred edifice, but peace was restored when the deacons told the lady to resume her seat and the preacher his sermon.[7]

Fursac was told of an aged minister whom the revivalists accused of sinning against the Holy Spirit. They 'treated him almost as an anti-christ, and the unfortunate man, seeing that he had lost the day, resigned.'[8] There were many other clashes of this kind.

Nantlais Williams never forgot the hard establishment attitude, from which he was himself destined to suffer in the 1922-4 debate over his denomination's Confession of Faith. For once this mild and gracious man allows the bitterness to break through:

In general the oldest church officers were reluctant to welcome the visitation, as at the time of Pentecost . . . Some good men, and brothers whom we regarded as godly, were seen looking very frowningly upon the children of the Revival, critically and reprovingly too . . . It is possible that one reason for this opposition was envy. Some leaders saw the sceptre leaving their hands, since the converts often took the meetings into their own hands. They would burst into song, or prayer, or testimony in the middle of a sermon, or sometimes from the start of the service so that the preacher could only listen. Anything which robs us like this of our authority is sure to arouse our opposition . . . The Revival exposed the dearth in the churches of leaders acquainted with the Holy Spirit's special modes of operation.[9]

Could this have been also, as suggested earlier, a war of the generations—youthful zeal versus the authority of the elders? It certainly began with sniping at the youthful worker teams and witness teams whose conduct was both novel and unusual. Eventually the arguments between converts and elders turned into a tragic war of words between young and old in the public press. The *Llanelly Mercury* included the following in its correspondence columns:

In the present revival, the Bible is ignored, and it is claimed that visions and new revelations are received . . .

In the Book of Acts it is said that Paul ordained elders in every church . . . It is clear to all who wish to see that it was the elders who were to rule in the churches . . .

Peter, in his First Epistle, divides the church into two . . . and it would be well for the young people in the churches at present to understand their position in the churches according to New Testament teaching, and to submit to its directions . . . I would say a little on that which is enjoined upon the second group in the churches, that is the young: 'Likewise, ye younger, submit yourselves unto the elder . . .'

In the present revival, the elders are condemned as heretics if they do not yield, and conform to the methods of the young. The officers of the churches are at present ignored, although they have been set apart in office by the churches; thus, the Apostles of the Lamb are ignored; the hand of God is ignored; the Holy Spirit is ignored, and that by some other spirit that has possessed our young people.

The response was as might be expected:

The spirit of many a professing man of prayer is soured because God has not directed the stream to flow along the channels they have made . . .

It is obvious that he [the writer of the previous letter] has not been in one of the revival meetings, and has no shadow of sympathy with them, although the revival carries in itself clear proof that it could have come from nowhere but God . . .

He is not the first of the descendants of the 'elder brother' to be envious . . . Does he deny that the present revival is a revival of young people?[10]

So accusations and counter-accusations were exchanged—of prejudice, hindering the truth, behaving in the spirit of Romanism. These were matched by claims and counter-claims.

Another criticism came from one 'Dryw Bach' ('Little Wren') who alleged that the young people had lost all sense of duty and responsibility by claiming that the Holy Spirit was prompting all their schemes:

One of them has said that he has enough of the Spirit of God in him to turn the churches of the land upside down. I believe there is much more need to turn him upside down, so that he may live a little nearer to what he professes, that is that he may live the Bible, yes, and love everyone.[11]

One of the charges levelled against the critics was that they were full of prejudices, and there is some evidence that seems to confirm this opinion. Almost from the beginning there were cries that the people of Wales were becoming disorderly and uncontrolled. In mid-November 1904, 'Veritas' of Loughor wrote a letter suggesting that Evan Roberts's 'power to attract the multitude that throng to Moriah Chapel, Loughor, . . . lies in the absolute disregard on Mr. Roberts' part of all conventionalism and decorum'. He continues:

Each meeting at Moriah Chapel commences from 6 to 7 o'clock. After a few preliminaries, it practically resolves itself into a singing festival . . . At times, while one section is singing a hymn, another section in the chapel starts off a wholly different one. This is interspersed with short, spasmodic addresses by Mr. Roberts, relating to visions he has witnessed. Singing is kept up hour after hour—the same tunes and words being interminably repeated—far into the early hours of the morning . . .

The inevitable result of the singing, coupled with the late midnight hour, is that young girls and women, fatigued with exertion, are strung up to a pitch of feverish excitement. Their emotions overpower them and they break out into wild cries and gesticulations. These effects, unfortunately, are put down as a manifestation of the Spirit. Some participants have since been confined to their homes with nervous prostration.

Mr. Roberts asserts that he opens his mouth in obedience to Divine inspiration, and that the Spirit speaks through him. What need of denominational colleges? What need of universities? What need of laboriously prepared sermons by ministers? If inexperienced youths and girls can be mouthpieces of the divine intelligence, then all our educational institutions connected with religion are superfluous.[12]

By Wednesday, 30 November, at Bethania Chapel in nearby Morriston, a 'coldness characterised the gathering' and a 'tone of indifference' prevailed. According to the newspaper report, 'There was an apathy, governing the major portion of the audience, which killed all emotionalism. It was as if a re-action had set in.' At that meeting 'the coughing was so incessant, so harsh and loud at times, that the speakers, unless they were gifted with strong voices, were but imperfectly heard'. Nevertheless, the meeting continued until 1.30 a.m.[13]

Looking back a few years later, David Hughes marvelled at the fuss people made about the length of prayers or the repetition of songs. He dismissed the common accusation of long hours with scorn:

There has been and is much questioning, judging and legislating with regard to how long a religious meeting should continue . . . During cold and formal periods these questions flourish to a painful degree. Other meetings are not judged and legislated upon in that way. Neither professors of religion nor anyone else are ever heard complaining that eisteddfods, games, dances and other meetings are too long.

But when Revival comes by, the complaint about length of religious meetings goes away . . . [During the last Revival] the spiritual world became so real, time could not be seen in its light. The blessedness of eternity was everything. I know in this case also that some neighbourhoods were troubled with undesirable consequences. We regret that. But it does not affect the issue under discussion—namely that . . . the length of a religious meeting is trivial when the Holy Spirit's influence rests heavily on the meeting.[14]

For others the most unwelcome new feature was the change the revival occasioned in the type of hymn which was sung. Grumblings about the inferior quality of the new revival hymns grew louder and louder as the months went by, perhaps because of the English-language songs brought over from the Torrey-Alexander and other missions.

David Jenkins of the Music Department of the University College of Wales, Aberystwyth, felt that the revival singing had benefited to some extent from the 'singing-festival' tradition and hoped that that tradition would benefit from revival fervour, but he wished that there were a greater variety and a better taste in the tunes chosen during revival meetings.[15] This observation was polite compared with that of Tudur Llwyd of Blaenau Ffestiniog who published this in *Y Glorian:*

> The revival of last year in Wales has added much to the nation's hymnal or religious poetry. One cannot decide today how many verses of this 'poetry' will still be alive in a few years' time, but one can be sure that a great deal of it will have died. And there is a certain comfort in thinking that it is possible for 'poetry', like plants, and trees, and man, to do such a thing as die. I have seen many items of late under a title such as
>
> **'Hymns of the Revival'**
>
> which had no charm or annointing near them. They were dead, wintry bodies, of the earth earthy. The work of pigmy poets, and selfish and self-centred men. They took profane advantage of a Religious Revival to make money and to advertise themselves. They could no more make a hymn than they could make an epic. By far the majority of their productions were rhymes made in a day and a night, and the trash of girls at a fair. They took advantage of the tenderness of feeling, and the religious kindliness of a nation warm at a time of revival, in order to sell notions of silt and poetry of the marsh. A Revival is sometimes needed to get rid of 'poets' as well as to bring some to light.[16]

A North Wales Presbyterian minister, J. H. Williams, whose bardic name was Canwy, admitted he had lost his temper one night when he saw an elder trying to force everyone to kneel down in pews which were far too narrow, the company including an arthritic old lady who could not kneel. Canwy had heard a story of a young man who had dared to pray very fervently for the soul of his own minister to be saved:

> Hugh Roberts [the minister] went up to him at the close of the meeting and, laying his big, kind hand on his shoulder, said: 'My boy, do not try to make trouble between me and the Great King, for I knew him before you were born.'[17]

This is very similar to an account from the Nantlle Valley where a too-zealous convert had to be restrained:

I was told that one young man challenged the godly Hugh Evans and accused him of putting out the Spirit and killing the revival, because he wanted to hold Sunday school, not prayer-meetings. His response was, 'Go on, my boy, flame away; but my fire has been red for years.'[18]

For some reason private meetings in rural cottages were out of favour. The cottage meeting was a very old institution, but now it was regarded as a place of extremes, as in this story:

> In one home in . . . Caernarvonshire, the husband was fired [by the revival], but the wife remained completely cold in the midst of the fire. A prayer-meeting was held in their home. The wife was governed by caution and reason and, as a rule, she would go to bed at the proper hour. Often she could not sleep because of the praying in the kitchen. One night she went to the top of the stairs and told them in no uncertain terms to go home and go to bed and rest, and told her husband to come to bed. This prompted one of them to pray for her, asking the Lord to open her eyes to see the fount of Salvation at the bottom of the stairs. But the truth is that she knew of the fount at the foot of the Cross before any mention of the 1904-5 Revival.[19]

The open criticism and the private grumbling caused such distress to the new converts that at last a respected minister spoke in defence of the irregularity and enthusiasm of the revival meetings. James Owen addressed a meeting on the theme 'Religious Excitement':

> There are some persons who are afraid of all excitement in religious gatherings; they are not afraid of it in political meetings, in temperance meetings, in business (that is, when the business is prospering); they are not afraid of it in the club banquet or the holiday excursion but they are afraid of it in religion . . . but when they begin to awake to the fact that they are sinning against God, that sin means death, and that Christ is bringing salvation to them, they must not be excited; excitement then is fanaticism, and earnestness then is madness. Rather I would welcome the excitement that lifts a man up from the mire of sin, to restore and renew him.[20]

One of the men who watched the revival in North Wales realized that there was a still deeper current of opposition in the churches. This current of resentment was not just because Evan Roberts and other revival preachers had emphasized such doctrines as full assurance and holiness, but because of the double challenge they issued to every member—to have liberty and joy in worship and to have purity and sincere love daily. In the words of Nantlais:

> The warmth of the children of the Revival of necessity exposed the coldness of the usual leaders, and condemned them. Electric lamps reflect unfavourably upon rush candles. The praises of the children in the Temple were intolerable to the ears of scribes and Pharisees.[21]

At a different level a great many chapel attenders resisted and criticized the testing of meetings in order to see who was totally loyal to Christ:

> I believe the churches [in Liverpool] had a shock when Evan Roberts came. His emphasis was on the spiritual character and condition of the hearer, *whoever he was*. Was he obedient to the Spirit's call? Was he stiffnecked and unwilling to bend? Did he or she believe that *because* they were 'members' they had no need of conviction of sin? For all that it was a marvellous adventure—to search among the Welsh people and see how many were negligent [in matters religion].[22]

Just how the expressions of resistance reached their final form is one of the themes of *The King's Champions* and is also touched on by Dr Eifion Evans. Old converts such as John and Rhys Penry of Gorseinon have spoken freely about the many misunderstandings which led to chapels abandoning open-air witness, disowning the worker teams and denouncing the very forms of praise which had been the great feature of the revival. No wonder they and many others broke away or were ejected as troublemakers, so that they were bound to set up mission halls all over Wales. Here again we can use a biased report from a secular newspaper in West Wales to see which way the wind was now blowing. It is a report of the opening services of a new chapel called Bryn Moriah, between Tre-lech and Hermon, near Cynwil Elfed.

> Locally the members of this chapel are called Pentecostals, and the other name given to them is that of Free Baptist. They number from 17 to 25, and up to two years ago most of them were members of Bryniwan Independent Chapel (built 1851). At the ordinary meetings they displayed a great deal of revival fervour, it being hardly possible to carry on the meetings in their regular orderly manner. These members would continually break forth with their shouts of 'Bendigedig!' ['Blessed!]

'Diolch Iddo!' ['Thanks be to Him!] etc. The majority of the Bryniwan members were averse to such outbursts interfering with the general conduct of meetings, but they took no action. However, these few members wrote to the church expressing their intention of leaving, and a new cause was thus formed. For the last two years they have carried on their worshipping in private houses . . . It was decided to build a new chapel, and the simple little edifice stands on Rhydhir land, in a very exposed position on the extreme boundary of Cilrhedyn parish, about 200 yards from the other chapel.

On Wednesday large crowds were attracted to the opening services from the surrounding districts. Strangers were refused stabling accommodation in many of the neighbouring farms by those who were opposed to the doings of this new sect . . . It is known that some time before they left Bryniwan Church they waited outside the chapel until the early hours of the morning shouting and praying. A respectable farmer from Cilrhedyn who then passed advised them to control themselves and to go home, but this only resulted in increasing their so-called intense fervour.[23]

Noel Gibbard mentions that at Tumble, near Llanelli, division arose in Bethania Congregational Chapel between the minister and those fired by the revival, with the result that they were shown the door. Each one received the following note, dated 24 November 1905:

At a Church meeting held at Bethania last Monday night, it was resolved to remove from fellowship a number of members because they are disregarding Church rules, of whom you are one.

Among those who received the note were the treasurer, Thomas Jenkins, the precentor, William Jenkins (father of the well-known Congregational minister, Emlyn G. Jenkins), and Edward Wilkins, who was to go on an evangelistic mission to South Africa. The evicted ones later built Bryn Seion Gospel Hall on land given by Thomas Jenkins.[24]

Founders of the Free Mission at Mill Street, Carmarthen, stated their desire to teach 'Full Assurance and the Second Coming of Jesus'. The founders of Pen-y-groes Gospel Hall wrote these doctrines into their first covenant.[25] One of the three Llanelli gospel halls was for people who had been ejected because they wanted to be baptized a second time on the grounds that their first baptism had been meaningless.[26] At Fforest-fach in Swansea, John Rees and D. J. Jones led out a group who had been filled with a spirit of praise at Calfaria and other chapels. Finding this spirit slowly stifled, they formed a mission which later developed along Brethren lines.[27] Many other halls in Glamorgan were for converts frozen out from chapels.[28] In his column in *Yr Efengylydd*, A. H. Rogers wrote:

> Since the last Revival there have arisen many Gospel Halls in South Wales in which are gathered those who experienced great and deep things when the Lord visited our land with the saving power of His grace in 1904 and 1905. If some churches had dealt fairly with the Revival, and had welcomed and succoured those who were awakened and blessed through it, some of these Halls would not be in existence today. Hard, cold churches resisting the Holy Spirit are accountable for the existence of so many of these places found today in parts of Carmarthenshire and Glamorgan. Not all these Halls, unfortunately, have stayed faithful to the gospel in its simplicity. We are sorry to say that some have opened the door to the 'strange tongues', and have turned from the great central road of the gospel of grace. Despite this, there are some to be had which are worthy of their title—Gospel Hall. Recently we had the privilege of spending some two days among the people of one of these Halls and of preaching the Word to them. The vast majority of saints in that Hall are fruit of the Revival, and the fire kindled at the time continues to flame in their hearts despite every effort of devil and man to quench it.[29]

There is little profit in cataloguing the scores of examples of this open and final rejection of the 'children of the revival', but it is important to understand the motivations, since this will help us to see the much-publicized clash between Peter Price and Evan Roberts in its proper setting. There are other reasons for understanding the volume of resistance inside and outside the churches which we shall consider in the next chapter, but it is evident that the Peter Price letter to the *Western Mail* on the last day of January 1905 is only the visible tip of a submerged volcano or rather chain of volcanoes. He was giving shape and thrust to the thoughts and feelings of hundreds of professed Christians. One can only give a digest here of the distasteful attack, the furious defence, and the considered verdicts of influential men.

Peter Price, an honours graduate of Queens' College, Cambridge, was a Congregational minister at Dowlais. Readers of his letter to the *Western Mail* of 31 January 1905 were left in no doubt as to his intellectual prowess—Price himself saw to that by listing his academic qualifications. His contribution to the correspondence columns stirred up a hornets' nest.[30]

In it he begins by expressing concern that visitors are seeing a shallow, noisy, exhibitionist revival, and that some are imitating the contortions and sighings of Evan Roberts, and repeating stock phrases such as 'The Spirit is not here', or, 'I have had a vision', when visitors are present. Then he goes on to ask if Evan Roberts thinks he is the fourth person in the Godhead or the commander and master of the Spirit since he dares to say, 'He must come', and speaks as though the Spirit is entirely within his grasp or as though the Holy Spirit were led by him. After suggesting that Evan Roberts and his girl-companions should go home because Dowlais has young colliers of greater intellectual capability and spiritual power than he, Peter Price came to his main charges of exhibitionism, frolics, vain trumpery and the creation of false fire. It is hinted that some of this is achieved by threats, complaints and incantations in which the whole team play their set parts because they understand each other thoroughly. In addition he accuses Roberts of going to where the fire was already burning. The result, he said, was that there were two parallel revivals—the true and the fake—the quiet, spiritual awakening and the unseemly tumults of the Roberts team. (Asked in 1926 for second thoughts on the revival, Peter Price repeated his claim that he had unique power to discern the falsities of the Evan Roberts revival.)[31]

The first batch of letters on behalf of the revivalist—Evan Roberts himself did not reply—present facts which contradict Price's accusations and interpretations, or accuse Price of denying Christ, or point to the wonderful results of Roberts's work. Some view the attack as 'the fate of all true disciples of Jesus'. One H. J. Blackmore of Blaen-garw sees it as a contest between a man of degrees and a man who has had to take up his cross daily. Keri Evans asked what were the criteria by which Price distinguished between true and false fire. The only deep, searching examination came from a Wesleyan minister from Merthyr, T. J. Pritchard, who thought that the Peter Price attack was 'a "subconscious incubation" due to the ruling passions of the old serpent, and to the extreme aversion of learned men to put up with the "foolishness of the Cross"'. In this way did the supporters of Evan Roberts leap to his defence.

His opponents were equally forceful and direct. Pedr Williams from Treorci and 'Cymro' claimed that Price had voiced 'the opinion of every true follower of Christ', who all deplored Evan Roberts's claims to commune 'with God face to face'. A Mr G. Gilbert of Cathays, Cardiff, added that thousands of sane, righteous people fully endorsed the opinions of Price. Vyrnwy Morgan said that many eminent, spiritually-minded pastors and laymen agreed with Price but had not the courage to speak up. A Congregational minister by the name of J. Gari Phillips, of New Tredegar, added that the methods and demands of the evangelists and some of their self-appointed helpers were causing pain, confusion and offence to thoughtful and reverent people, especially by the habit of 'praying at the unconverted who happened to be sitting or standing by them'. A different attack came from the left wing when Mr E. Jones of Llandovery called Evan Roberts's claims to direct Spirit guidance profane, and his visions blasphemous, because he was not, as were the Apostles, 'endowed with Spirit gifts, of which we have abundant proof in healing the sick, raising the dead, giving sight to the blind, speaking in unknown tongues, prophesying, &c. Let Mr. Evan Roberts produce similar evidence that he is possessed of the same power before he expects rational men to believe him.'

On 11 February appeared a three-column article from the Rev. J. Towyn Jones of Garnant near Ammanford who, in a conciliatory fashion, generously called both Evan Roberts and Peter Price spiritual men who were, after all, only fallible—'Elijah was a man, subject to like passions as we are.' Then he went to the root problem—the flouting by the press of Evan Roberts's wish to make people look only to the Holy Spirit, and their attempts to credit one man with the pentecostal fire and make him out to be indispensable. This contradicted Scripture and history and ignored the fact that at New Quay, Ammanford and Rhos, there had been other God-intoxicated souls.

As this correspondence continued it grew even nastier and intentionally hurtful. Whatever one thinks of the merits or demerits of the case, Peter Price's letter created a new party which was out to oppose and block the 'Evan Roberts Revival', as some still call it. Tragically a great many other people drew back or fell silent, and many a spokesman and writer now had second thoughts about the revival. Yet even this cruel wound was not fatal; the revival was not stabbed but strangled to death. How?

Welsh writers and preachers have been asked repeatedly why the country's spiritual life fell back from the heights and began to lose strength again so soon. The answer lies in measure in the rejection by the churches of all those who had the new fire. The testimony of Dafydd Jones of Aber-porth is crucial here:

Question: Mr Jones, did the women continue to take part in the weeknight meetings for long after the revival?

Answer: No, the deacons stopped that.

Q: What about the processions of the children and what about the young witnesses and gospel singers?

A: I don't remember them for long after then.

Q: What happened to all those young people? Were they killed in the Great War?

A: No, only a few went to the war because they worked on farms. Later, many of us went to work in England and I went away too.

Q: A great many of you were quite young when you were converted. Did you get used by your chapels to take services, etc.?

A: No. Only the 9.30 prayer-meeting on a Sunday, and that was also conducted by the minister. I do not remember any missions.[32]

That was the final tragedy: the eagerness of the church members, and their leaders in particular, to go back to the old traditions and to become normal and sober once more. No one was more angered and saddened by this than Nantlais Williams:

> Words often heard from the mouths of some during the first years of the Revival were, 'Oh, the Revival has ended now, everything has gone back to normal here.' For such people the Revival was nothing more than a sad misadventure which disturbed the peaceful quietude of church and country, and because they thought there was no good in it, or rather, they did not want to see any good in it, they rejoiced at the slightest sign that it was disappearing. Very often the words, 'Oh, the revival is dead', were nothing but the expression of a deep desire in the speaker's heart.
>
> To be sure, we cannot but feel grieved about the dangerous and harmful imitations that were to be had during the blessed visitation of 1904-5. The false found nurture in the revitalising of the true . . .
>
> But, however grieved we feel because of the very unfortunate aspects, we feel more aggrieved at those men who saw nothing but ill in the Revival. In Jeremiah 17:6, it is said of someone that he 'shall not see when good cometh'. Is this not a wretched state to be in? Blindness to God's goodness; and was not this true of many during 1904-5? They did not know the time of their visitation. When the Master rode so prominently through our land they did not recognize him; but like the Pharisees of old they attributed everything to the devil. Although they saw clear evidences of the saving work of the Holy Spirit, they refused to

acknowledge it as His work. Is not such a condition worse than anything that happened in the Revival? Is not wilful continuance in this blindness the sin against the Holy Spirit?[33]

It is this deliberate quenching of the Spirit which is the theme of our last chapter. For evidence of this we are dependent exclusively on the voice of eyewitnesses.

18
Quenching the Spirit

*'Having begun in the Spirit, are ye now
made perfect by the flesh?'*
(Galatians 3:3)

From the beginning to the end of the revival there was a hard core who fulfilled Stephen's prophetic words, 'Ye do always resist the Holy Ghost' (Acts 7:51). Dr William Morris, the influential Baptist minister from Treorci, wrote with angry sorrow about this group:

> They have not experienced the kiss of the tender breeze from Calvary, nor have they felt the strength of the mighty wind of this Pentecost. The splendid high tide has not yet reached the threshold of their door, and the flame has not touched a hair of their beards. They are entire strangers to the Spirit in these days. We marvel to hear them talk: we shudder with fear as we listen to their opinion of this heaven-born and heaven-sustained work.[1]

The undermining of the revival had to begin at that point, whatever further reasons one can find. Naturally enough, hundreds of men and women who had come under conviction, but had never moved on to the final stage of new birth, fell by the wayside. Then the untouched group had a great deal to say about 'nine days' wonder' and 'flash in the pan' and so on. Their views were echoed in the English periodicals and thus, according to the analysis of Dr Edwin Orr, an exaggerated picture of failure came into being.[2]

Those who disliked or were uncomfortable about the revival were soon drawing their own conclusions from the rapid withdrawal of so many who had been convicted but not born again. Some of the critics demanded the immediate use of family prayers and of moral instruction to help new converts. Some said loudly that the excessive pressure of the total abstainer groups was frightening away many converts who were not ready for such a step. Some put the whole blame on the extreme excitements of the revival which had led to a general distrust of 'emotionalism'.

They said that the non-stop activities and the long, late-night meetings had stretched people's feelings and minds to breaking point.

The King's Champions, companion volume to this book, enquired into the chronic failure to instruct and safeguard the converts, apart from the untiring efforts of one group. It also told the story of theological failure and tragedy as the religious press and most pulpits were infected with higher criticism and anti-supernaturalism. Visions, voices, spiritual promptings, inspired prayers withered and died in the new climate of religious thought. Those who did not venture to set up or join new gospel halls and missions were perplexed and discouraged, as their pastors and leaders offered philosophical and psychological explanations for what had seemed to them to be a holy and unforgettable experience of the Spirit's work. Doubt and scorn quenched the fires.

Dr Eifion Evans was perfectly justified in claiming that the biggest defection from the denominational chapels after the revival was not a defection from Christianity but the defection of the thousands who decided to move on to freedom within the new gospel halls.[3] After all, it was these people who had felt most acutely the spiritual collapse, had known betrayal, and had heard the mocking cries of 'sham', 'peculiar', and so on. Very gradually the others who stayed on in the denominational churches realized that the spirit of rejection was gaining ground and that church leaders were going to disavow the awakening of 1904-5 and also oppose any further signs and wonders. Nevertheless, there were encouraging gains in every denomination for some time, and both Mrs Penn-Lewis and R. B. Jones could hold that the spiritual effects of the revival did last for many years. That did not stop them examining the causes of spiritual poverty and loss. Those who had been witnesses and partakers of the blessing were encouraged to discern the deeper reasons why the Lord would not continue to bless Wales with his great mercies.

R. B. Jones and Nantlais Williams felt that the major causes of spiritual weakness were disunity, fragmentation, lack of balance. This is what R. B. Jones wrote on the subject in 1913:

> Our deep conviction is, that whatever or whoever is a stumbling-block to spiritual work in Wales today—and the hindrances are many and varied—it is in the power of those who profess the greatest spirituality to be more of an obstacle than anyone else. Satan has always succeeded in hindering the Kingdom of God more effectively by using God's children than by using his own . . . Oh that we might take this to heart to consider it earnestly. We are not blind to the state of the things in the churches

275

and the pulpits—it is heartbreaking. Yet a worldly and carnal church, and an unorthodox and unanointed pulpit can never obstruct the Holy Spirit as can and do the defects revealed in the conduct and spirit of those who take upon themselves to walk upon the heights of holiness . . .

There is nothing today which is half as effective as an obstacle to revival powers working in our land as the lack of unity which is to be found among the Lord's children. Is there not something terribly amiss when those born of the same Holy Spirit, who receive their life from the same Lord Jesus, and who pray to the same Heavenly Father, are unable to sit down together in the same place to worship? Whence have come these almost endless divisions now to be seen among the best fruits of the Revival? Is it from love and the Spirit of Christ? Can such bitter streams flow from such a sweet fountain? Have they not come about because we have more zeal than love; because we put stress on the circumstantial more than on the essential; on the gifts of God rather than the Giver; on signs rather than faith; on psychic and bodily experiences rather than the Word of God; on ecstasies in special meetings rather than upon simple, quiet and consistent obedience to the Spirit of the One who is in us? . . .

[Zeal] is nothing but a terrible renderer when there is not enough love to balance it . . .

Let us all earnestly seek to be baptized in perfect love for one another . . . that love which can embrace a brother even if he cannot agree on every point of faith; that love which considers another better than ourselves; that love which can never fall away.[4]

Nantlais, in 1924, identified the cause of failure in the following words:

Indeed, one of the sad effects of backsliding is to make us narrow. Once we lose the love of Christ it is not long before we show signs of narrowness in every direction. Narrowness in judgement, in doctrine, in conduct. And the result is that we are constantly living on the other side of the fence with everyone. A high bank has been raised not only between us and the world, but between us and our brethren in Christ Jesus . . .

Is it not here that we have lost out? We are unable to lift a foot over some stile. Somehow we have raised a fence between each other as children of the Lord; and we can never look over it! We have raised high walls between us and the world, and we have no desire to go outside them with the word of the Gospel . . . The Revival we desire is close by—just across the fence, if only we could gain enough love and courage to take the step over . . .

We know there is in the land today a great host of children of the 1904 Revival and others of the same spirit who have been brought to Christ since that year; and before then too. There are a great many in the churches of every denomination, and again in halls outside the traditional denominations who are totally loyal to Christ, and eager to grow in the spiritual life. Are we not called upon to draw closer to our Lord and to one another? We may differ very warmly on some things; but surely this is no time to raise barriers and stand on opposite sides of the fence.[5]

What Nantlais had in mind was some kind of league of intercessors for revival who would fast and pray together and spend time with God to call upon him. It did not happen in Wales for twenty years, but Dr Edwin Orr mentions a fellowship of this kind existing in the late thirties.

Charles Davies said people failed to recognize that the revival was a great demonstration of the principle, 'Not by might, nor by power, but by my spirit', and that the right response had been not just outbursts of prayer in chapels, houses, work-places and fields, but also outbursts of bold testimony to the saving grace of God:

> We are always in danger from self-sufficiency. That is the Laodicean temperament. 'I am rich, and have need of nothing,' is the utterance of this temperament. There is no place here for anything but putrefied and tragic selfishness. The spirit of prayer dies in such a poisonous atmosphere, and the thoroughfare between us and heaven closes up. We saw in the Revival that 'power belongeth unto God', and all else everywhere was but weakness compared with His power. We had proofs that He was calling whoever He willed to come and work for Him, and was clothing them with strength and wisdom which caused us to wonder, and to bless the name of the Lord.[6]

Cynog Williams was so distressed by what he had seen after the revival—hundreds lost every year, saints slothful and careless and indifferent to the state of the world, leaders discouraged and converts so few—that he wanted to call a conference of ministers to consider in the light of God's Word whether to expect a revival or the personal return of Christ. He denied that industrial recession had caused the prevailing spiritual malaise:

> The present period of backsliding began in the good times that were had before the end of the Great War. Materialism got a grip on the heart of the nation at that time. The ripe fruit of that harvest is the unrighteousness

and dishonesty, the deception and riot, the impurity and infidelity that are characteristic of the times. At that time the spirituality of religion was lost, and the holy Spirit of God grieved.

Some of Cynog Williams's sentences in 1928 are strikingly up-to-date:

We fear that a great number in our churches have never experienced any inward change. They were encouraged into the church, without any assurance of conversion being sought, nor testimony of a changed heart being insisted upon . . . They remained in the world, as far as their spirit and their nature, their habits and their pleasures were concerned . . .

A few years ago the cry rose up that the church should draw nearer to the world, and prepare entertainment for the young people. The cry of 'the young people' is raised as an excuse for all worldliness . . . A deluge of worldliness engulfed the church,—the spirit of the world came in like a flood, and the Spirit of the Lord has not lifted up a standard against it . . .

It is a mistake for the church to form itself on worldly lines to suit the age, instead of on the ideal of the New Testament. The nearer it is to the apostolic ideal, the more effective will the church be in meeting the need of every age. A church on New Testament lines is the fittest instrument for the operations of the Spirit of God.[7]

In 1925 Nantlais Williams provided a new interpretation, that many young Christians went astray in the 1904 Revival through ignorance of the Spirit's character. They were led into counterfeit experiences where people claimed bodily sensations rather than holy affections as indicating the presence and approval of the Spirit. Others tried to localize the working of the Spirit. People ought to remember the character of the Great Revivalist—he is Spirit and he is Comforter. Nantlais knew only too well that certain untaught people had

linked the Spirit with terrifying things which were felt, and done. A strange spirit came into some meetings, a spirit which scared the sheep . . .

Many times we played on the edge of a precipice; but we were pulled back from peril by the memory of the comfort of the Spirit . . .

If we are to benefit fully from another Revival we must learn to recognize the Spirit as Comforter.

And is not this feature in His character lovely, divinely attractive? Does not His character as Comforter create in us a longing to see Him come again in His fulness?[8]

Twice in that period from 1920 to 1930, high hopes were raised that revival had come again. First there were times of blessing in eastern and northern Britain in the early twenties. The *Life of Faith* was full of long, serious articles about how revival could be encouraged and safeguarded.[9] Then in 1928-9 there was a little revival at Gorseinon and Loughor again, to which Evan Roberts came with a powerful ministry for a while. Once more there was a note of urgency and hope.[10]

In that period, Evan Roberts gave out his own interpretation of how times of refreshing and awakening could come:

Lessons of the Revival

(i)   Any and every revival begins with God. Therefore, it is He who must and He who does burden the saints with prayer, choosing the special instruments who are to operate as means of blessing: and empowering every means used to cause the awakening, and during its continuance . . .

(iii) . . . Since conscience forms such a close relationship with the life that leads to revival, every believer ought to watch that he in no way disobeys the persuasions of his conscience, for this is bound to extinguish the Divine life in the spirit of the man.

God deals with **life** from day to day. Is there readiness? Co-operation with God is essential for the development of that life. Therefore be careful to observe what the Lord says about your life. Watch also for the Divine compulsion in your spirit (Romans viii. 5).

(iv) The years of revival are only a small portion of the years of the life of the church. Therefore, strive to **raise** her life to the highest level possible, while pleading together in prayer for a special outpouring of the Spirit of God . . .

(vi) Too much emphasis cannot be placed on this fact:– No matter how earnest and numerous they are, without faith, prayers cannot ensure powerful answers from God for an awakening. Therefore, watch and be careful that your faith corresponds to your prayers. The Scripture says that it will be to you according to your **faith**, but the prayers that are entwined with doubts receive **nothing** from God. May you have the faith of God, without wearying or losing heart.[11]

It was in this decade that Nantlais, who was editor of *Yr Efengylydd*, gave Wales one of the finest and most spiritual messages on how to return to a revival situation. Based on the warnings and promises in Isaiah, chapter 43, his exposition compared the Welsh churches with Israel in Babylonian bondage, without a testimony and without a new song or grace or power. 'There is a way from Babylon every step of the way to Zion,' he asserts. He called on the nation to confess it had forsaken God and lost its liberty and joy because of backsliding and inconsistency. Only then would the way be cleared for the 'new thing' God was willing to do:

> The new deliverance that the Lord promised His people in Babylon was a great deliverance when He said: 'Behold, I will do a new thing' (Isaiah 43:19). But at bottom it was a deliverance through forgiveness. Indeed, that is the deliverance to God's people in every age: a deliverance through forgiveness. It is through forgiveness that we came to God the first time; and through it we returned to Him from every backsliding. It is through it also that we always develop to a deeper experience of God . . . That is His way of leading His people.
>
> In order that we may be raised from the distant Babylon of our backsliding, we must have a deep conviction of sin, a conviction of which we must all partake. It is not only the public backslider or the hidden backslider who must submit, but everyone: the most warm, and the most faithful. Bringing the nation back from Babylon was to cost as much, if not more, to godly Daniel as to anyone. He took the burden until he cried under it: 'O Lord, hear; O Lord, forgive; O Lord, hearken and do; defer not, for thine own sake, O my God' (Daniel 9:19). He shared also in the general repentance, although he was so holy; 'And while I was speaking, and praying, and confessing MY SIN and the sin of my people Israel' (Daniel 9:20).
>
> Oh! that we had this same intense feeling over our sins! Yes, we, the children of the Lord—the children of the 1904 Revival, or any other Revival! If we were to humble ourselves to the dust once more in the spirit of Daniel under the acknowledgement of our own sins, and the sin of each other—the immeasurable depth of God's forgiveness would soon be revealed to us! and its sufficient ground in the anguish of the Garden and the Cross of Calvary! That is Revival—seeing ourselves hopeless; seeing Jesus sufficient! The Revival that is on its way to Wales is seeking channels to preach repentance and forgiveness of sins in His name.[12]

Select Bibliography

Mabel Bickerstaff, *Something Wonderful Happened* (1954)
Ilsley W. Charlton, *The Revival in Wales. Some Facts and Some Lessons* (1905)
Robert Ellis, *Living Echoes of the Welsh Revival* (1951)
Eifion Evans, *The Welsh Revival of 1904* (1969; third edition, with index, 1987)
D. Wynne Evans, *Yr Ysbryd Glan a Diwedd-Wlaw y Diwygiad* (1906)
S. Evans & G. M. Roberts (ed.), *Cyfrol Goffa Diwygiad 1904-1905* (1954)
T. Francis (ed.), *Y Diwygiad a'r Diwygwyr* (1906)
M. Holyoak, *The Afterglow: Gleamings from the Welsh Revival* (1907)
Brynmor P. Jones, *The King's Champions* (1968; second edition, with index, 1986)
Brynmor P. Jones, *The Spiritual History of Keswick in Wales* (1989)
R. B. Jones, *Rent Heavens* (1931)
H. Elvet Lewis, *With Christ among the Miners* (1906)
Jessie Penn-Lewis, *The Awakening in Wales* (1905)
David Matthews, *I saw the Welsh Revival* (1951)
J. Vyrnwy Morgan, *The Welsh Religious Revival 1904-5* (1909)
J. Edwin Orr, *The Flaming Tongue* (1973)
D. M. Phillips, *Evan Roberts, The Great Revivalist and His Work* (1923)
Thomas Prichard, *An After Reflection of the Late Revival in Wales* (1908)
R. D. Rowland (ed.), *Perlau'r Diwygiad* (1906)
W. T. Stead, *The Revival in the West* (1905)

Newspapers and periodicals containing useful material

The British Library (Collingdale Division), London, and the National Library of Wales, Aberystwyth, have information regarding the location of library holdings of newspapers.

Aberdare Leader
Baptist Times
Cambrian News
Cardigan & Tivy-side Advertiser
Haverfordwest & Milford Haven Telegraph
Life of Faith
Llanelly Mercury
Llanelly & County Guardian
Llangollen Advertiser

North Wales Guardian
Porth Gazette
Rhondda Leader
Rhos Herald
Seren Cymru
Seren Gomer
South Wales Argus
South Wales Daily News
South Wales Daily Post
Western Mail
Wrexham Advertiser

Y Cloriannydd
Y Cylchgrawn Efengylaidd
Y Drysorfa
Y Dysgedydd
Y Geninen
Y Glorian
Y Goleuad
Y Tyst
Yr Efengylydd
Yr Herald Cymraeg

Notes

ABBREVIATIONS

Diwygiad yn Rhos—[W. S. Jones], *Y Diwygiad Crefyddol yn Rhosllanerchrugog* (Rhosllannerchrugog: R. Mills, [1905]).

Jiwbili—the record *Jiwbili y Diwygiad* (BBC/Qualiton Recordings, 1954).

Phillips—D. M. Phillips, *Evan Roberts, The Great Welsh Revivalist and his Work* (London: Marshall Brothers, 1923).

Supplement—*The Religious Revival in Wales 1904* (a series of six booklets of newspaper reports collected from the *Western Mail*; the booklets were published by the *Western Mail* between December 1904 and May 1905).

Prologue: THE FIRST VOICES OF THE AWAKENING

1.   *Cyfrol Goffa Diwygiad 1904-1905*, ed. Sidney Evans and Gomer M. Roberts (Caernarfon: Llyfrfa'r Methodistiaid Calfinaidd, 1954), p.37; see also articles by John Thickens in *Y Drysorfa*, April 1961–December 1963.

2.   R. B. Jones, *Rent Heavens*, second edition (London: Pioneer Mission, 1948), pp.27-30, and *Western Mail*, 13 and 22 December 1904.

3.   *Yr Efengylydd*, February 1935, p.22.

4.   ibid., May 1929, p.105.

5.   As related to the author by J. Ellis Jones, who had heard the story from R. B. Jones himself; see B. P. Jones, *The King's Champions*, second edition (The Author, 1986), p.49.

6.   *Y Diwygiad a'r Diwygwyr*, ed. T. Francis (Dolgellau: E. W. Evans, 1906), p.217.

7.   E. Keri Evans, *My Spiritual Pilgrimage*, tr. T. Glyn Thomas (London: James Clarke & Co. Ltd., 1961), pp.63-4.

8.   Anecdote related in a letter in the possession of Mr Meurig Thomas, Llangeler, Dyfed. (Copy in the Evangelical Library of Wales, Bridgend.)

9.   Robert Ellis, *Living Echoes of the Welsh Revival* (London: Delyn Press, [1951]), pp.52-3. On W. W. Lewis, see also W. Nantlais Williams's article in *Y Goleuad*, 8 June 1938.

10. *Cyfrol Goffa*, pp.36-7.

11. ibid., p.34.

12. ibid., p.35.

13. Accounts of the revival in these areas are recorded in Chapters 5, 7 and 8.

14. J. Tudor Rees, *Evan Roberts, His Life and Work* (London, 1905); also D. R. Grenfell's conversation with Aneirin Talfan Davies on the record *Jiwbili y Diwygiad* (BBC/Qualiton Recordings, 1954).

15. Mabel Bickerstaff, *Something Wonderful Happened* (Committee of the 1904-5 Revival Memorial Fund, 1954), pp.65-7.

16. W. T. Stead, *The Revival in the West* (London: 'The Review of Reviews' Publishing Office, [1905]), pp.42-3.
17. Phillips, pp.122-3.
18. Supplement, 3:29-31.
19. *Jiwbili.*
20. ibid.; see also Phillips, p.137.
21. Phillips, p.161.
22. ibid., p.163.

Chapter 1: THE HERALD STANDS FORTH AT LOUGHOR

1. Phillips, pp.167-8.
2. *Jiwbili.*
3. Phillips, pp.243-4.
4. ibid., pp.235-6.
5. Cassette no. 102. (Copy in the Evangelical Library of Wales, Bridgend.)
6. In a letter and interview with the author, *c*.1963-4.
7. Cassette no. 100. (Copy in the Evangelical Library of Wales, Bridgend.)
8. Cassette no. 101. (Copy in the Evangelical Library of Wales, Bridgend.)
9. Cassette no. 103. (Copy in the Evangelical Library of Wales, Bridgend.)
10. Phillips, p.213.
11. ibid., pp.211-12.
12. Cassette no. 102. (Copy in the Evangelical Library of Wales, Bridgend.)
13. From an interview with the author conducted in a Christian Nursing Home at Swansea in October 1986.
14. Phillips, p.244.
15. *Cyfrol Goffa*, p.43; see also the article by David Hughes entitled 'Dechreuad Diwygiad 1904-1905, yn Mhont-y-cymer' in *Y Dysgedydd*, November 1906.
16. *Llanelly Mercury*, 17 November 1904; see also Supplement, 1:4-5.
17. *Y Drysorfa*, 1954, p.221.

Chapter 2: THE VOICE OF A CHRISTIAN JOURNALIST

1. T. Awstin Davies's obituary notice is in the *Western Mail*, 19 May 1934.
2. *Cyfrol Goffa*, pp.43-6.
3. Phillips, pp.201-6; David Matthews, *I saw the Welsh Revival* (Chicago: Moody Press, 1951), pp.33,37.
4. *Y Dysgedydd*, November 1906.
5. Supplement, 1:9,10.
6. ibid., 2:6.
7. Supplement, 2:13-14; see also John Evans, Abermeurig's notes on the revival in NLW, CMA 14851.
8. ibid., 3:2.
9. ibid., 3:15; see also Phillips, p.345.
10. Supplement, 3:26.
11. ibid., 4:7-8.

12. ibid., 4:12.
13. ibid., 1:27.
14. ibid., 2:7.
15. Phillips, pp.280-2.
16. Phillips, p.328; cf. *Baptist Times*, 27 January 1905.
17. Supplement, 1:27.
18. ibid., 3:9.
19. Phillips, p.214.
20. *Y Tyst*, 7 December 1904.
21. *Cyfrol Goffa*, p.72.
22. *Revival in the West*, p.39; quoted in Phillips, p.303.

Chapter 3: THE SINGERS OF THE DAWN

1. *Llanelly Mercury*, 1 December 1904.
2. *South Wales Daily News*, 1 December 1904.
3. Supplement, 1:25-6.
4. ibid., 1:25-6; 2:3,5,11,12.
5. ibid., 1:16.
6. ibid., 1:26.
7. ibid., 5:12.
8. Phillips, pp.266-7. Dr William Edwards's English translation of '*Dyma gariad fel y moroedd*'—'Here is love, vast as the ocean'—was published in the *Baptist Times*, 6 January 1905. His other translations of Welsh hymns which are reproduced at the beginning of each section of this book were published in the *Baptist Times* in January and February 1905.
9. *Jiwbili.*
10. *Llanelly Mercury*, 2 February 1905.
11. *Wrexham Advertiser,* 15 April 1905.
12. Cassette no. 102. (Copy in the Evangelical Library of Wales, Bridgend.)
13. ibid.
14. *Llanelly Mercury*, 12 January 1905.
15. *Y Cylchgrawn Efengylaidd*, September/October 1949, pp.17-19.
16. *Cyfrol Goffa*, p.95.

Chapter 4: HOLY SPIRIT REVIVAL IN SOUTH WALES

1. *Baptist Times*, 6 January 1905 and 2 December 1904.
2. ibid., 13 October 1905.
3. *Seren Cymru*, 11 September and 30 October 1903.
4. ibid., 26 February 1904.
5. ibid., 5 August 1904.
6. *Y Greal*, November 1906, pp.291-3 (reprinted from *Seren Cymru,* 15 July 1904; see also *King's Champions*, p.29, and *Diwygiad yn Rhos*, pp.2-4
7. *Y Drysorfa*, October 1954, pp.209-11.
8. Eifion Evans, *The Welsh Revival of 1904*, third edition (Bridgend: Evangelical Press

of Wales, 1987), pp.104-5.

9. *Y Diwygiad a'r Diwygwyr*, pp.376-96; see also Phillips, pp.264-5.
10. *Jiwbili.*
11. *South Wales Daily News*, 17 November 1904.
12. Phillips, pp.219-20.
13. ibid., p.230.
14. *South Wales Daily Post*, 28 November 1904.
15. *Llanelly Mercury*, 22 December 1904; see also *Llanelly & County Guardian*, 22 December 1904.
16. *South Wales Argus*, 29 December 1904.
17. ibid., 29 December 1904.
18. ibid., 30 December 1904.
19. *South Wales Daily News*, 14 January 1905.
20. Ilsley W. Charlton, *The Revival in Wales. Some Facts and Some Lessons* (London: Jarrold & Sons, 1905), pp.9-13.
21. Supplement, 1:23-4.
22. *Llanelly Mercury*, 29 December 1904.
23. *Baptist Times*, 13 January 1905.
24. ibid., 21 April and 5 May 1905.
25. J. Vyrnwy Morgan, *The Welsh Religious Revival 1904-5* (London: Chapman and Hall, 1909), p.135.
26. M. Holyoak, *The Afterglow: Gleamings from the Welsh Revival* (London: Marshall Brothers, 1907), p.71.
27. *Y Tyst*, 7 December 1904.
28. *Llanelly & County Guardian*, 2 March 1905.
29. *Y Dysgedydd*, November 1906.
30. *Diwygiad 1904-5. Tabernacl, Pontycymer. Hanes Blwyddyn o Dân* (Merthyr Tydfil: Joseph Williams, [1905?]), pp.53-6.

Chapter 5: REVIVAL MISSIONS IN RURAL WALES

1. See the Prologue.
2. *The Cardigan & Tivyside Advertiser* covers many villages and has a published index for the years 1866 to 1980. Other publications which may be consulted are *The Cambrian News*, *Y Negesydd* (Corris) and *The Merioneth News and Herald.*
3. Phillips, pp.238-9,243.
4. *Y Diwygiad a'r Diwygwyr*, p.54.
5. ibid., pp.52-3; see also *Cyfrol Goffa*, pp.35-6.
6. ibid., pp.54-5.
7. *Cambrian News*, 30 December 1904.
8. *Cardigan & Tivyside Advertiser*, 18 November, 16 & 30 December 1904.
9. *Y Piwritan Newydd*, April 1905.
10. ibid., April 1905.
11. ibid., January, February and March 1905.
12. *Haverfordwest & Milford Haven Telegraph*, 18 and 25 January 1905.
13. *Y Diwygiad a'r Diwygwyr*, pp.156-8.
14. NLW, CMA 28678.

15. *Rent Heavens*, second edition 1948, p.69.
16. *Y Goleuad*, 4 and 11 September 1957.
17. *Seren Cymru*, 17 March 1905.
18. *Cambrian News*, 9 December 1904.

Chapter 6: THE YOUNG CHRISTIAN WORKERS

1. Supplement, 1:13.
2. Cassette no. 102. (Copy in the Evangelical Library of Wales, Bridgend.)
3. *Afterglow*, p.71.
4. *Haverfordwest & Milford Haven Telegraph*, 18 January 1905.
5. Supplement, 2:3.
6. *South Wales Daily News*, 26 December 1904.
7. *Llanelly Mercury*, 8 and 15 December 1904; see also *Llanelly & County Guardian*, 15 December 1904.
8. Supplement, 1:13.
9. *South Wales Daily Post*, 29 November 1904.
10. *I saw the Welsh Revival*, pp.42,49.
11. *Western Mail*, 26 December 1904.
12. *Diwygiad yn Rhos*, p.21.
13. *Yr Herald Cymraeg*, 10 January and 7 March 1905; *Llangollen Advertiser*, 3 March 1905.
14. From an interview with the author in 1964.
15. Letter from Caradoc Jones to the author *c*. 1962 (now deposited in the National Library of Wales); see also Winifred M. Pearce, *Knight in Royal Service* (London: Pioneer Mission, 1962), pp.13-16.

Chapter 7: TWENTY WONDERFUL WEEKS IN CLWYD

1. *Y Greal*, November 1906, pp.291-3; *Diwygiad yn Rhos*, pp.2-4.
2. *Jiwbili*.
3. *Y Greal*, November 1906, pp.295-7.
4. *Diwygiad yn Rhos*, pp.6-8.
5. This picture is confirmed by John Powell Parry's recollections in a recorded interview with Paul E. G. Cook in which he says that people arriving from England on the local trains began to feel a special kind of atmosphere as they went up from Johnstown station.
6. *Diwygiad yn Rhos*, pp.18, 19, 22-4.
7. *North Wales Guardian*, 27 January 1905; *Wrexham Advertiser*, 1 April 1905.
8. Letter from J. T. Jones of Rhos to the author in 1961 (now deposited in the National Library of Wales).
9. *Y Cylchgrawn Efengylaidd*, April/May 1952, pp.24-5.
10. *North Wales Guardian*, 27 January 1905.
11. *Wrexham Advertiser*, 4 March 1905.
12. *Llangollen Advertiser*, 8 July 1905.

13. ibid., 17 February 1905.
14. Cassette 230 in the Oral History Project collection at the Clwyd Library and Information Services Headquarters, Mold.

Chapter 8: PRAYER-MEETING REVIVALS IN GWYNEDD

1. *North Wales Guardian*, 3 February 1905.
2. *I saw the Welsh Revival*, pp.106,110.
3. *Y Goleuad*, 3 November 1904.
4. *North Wales Guardian*, 20 January 1905.
5. ibid., 27 January 1905.
6. *Wrexham Advertiser*, 1, 8 & 15 April 1905.
7. *Cyfrol Goffa*, pp.37-8.
8. Part of a letter from Evan Jenkins to his wife published in *Y Glorian*, 17 December 1904.
9. *South Wales Daily News*, 2 December 1904.
10. ibid., 28 December 1904.
11. NLW, CMA 26512.
12. Notebook ZM 3829, Gwynedd County Archives, Dolgellau.
13. NLW, CMA 17394. Lewis Lloyd may well have been the visitor who triggered off the revival at Tre Taliesin in the Christmas holidays of 1904 (see Chapter 5).
14. NLW, CMA 17392.
15. NLW, CMA 17388.
16. Document XM/3329/3, Gwynedd County Archives, Caernarfon.
17. NLW, CMA 17395.
18. *Y Drysorfa*, October 1955, pp.212-13.
19. *Yr Efengylydd*, January and February 1932, pp.6,7,24,25.
20. From notes made by the author in 1964.
21. *Y Diwygiad a'r Diwygwyr*, pp.144-6.
22. *Yr Efengylydd*, November 1932, p.203.
23. ibid., January 1933, pp.5-6; February 1933, p.25.

Chapter 9: THE VOICES OF THE VISITORS

1. The exceptions are Awstin, Jessie Penn-Lewis and J. Edwin Orr.
2. Ferrier Hulme also followed Evan Roberts's missions in North Wales and remained a close friend for over twenty years.
3. *Baptist Times*, 16 December 1904.
4. ibid., 2 December 1904.
5. ibid., 6 January 1905.
6. ibid., 13 October 1905.
7. *Diwygiad yn Rhos*, p.20.
8. NLW, CMA 17384-17387.
9. *Baptist Times*, 24 February 1905.
10. Supplement, 1:19, 2:13, 3:21-2, etc.
11. ibid., 2:30.

12. ibid., 2:32.
13. ibid., 3:4; cf. 4:18.
14. ibid., 1:19; 2:16,18,20.
15. ibid., 2:16; 3:8,14,15; 4:4.
16. *Diwygiad yn Rhos*, pp.19-20.
17. Edwin Orr, *The Flaming Tongue* (Chicago: Moody Press, 1973), p.47.
18. *Baptist Times*, 3 February 1905.
19. ibid., 13, 20 and 27 January; 24 March 1905.
20. ibid., 17 February 1905.
21. Supplement, 5:2.
22. ibid., 1:15; 2:16; 4:10.
23. *Baptist Times*, 13 January 1905.
24. Supplement, 3:15,18.
25. *Baptist Times*, 31 March 1905.
26. ibid., 21 July 1905.
27. *Seren Cymru*, 2 February 1906.
28. *Cyfrol Goffa*, pp.99-100.
29. Jessie Penn-Lewis, *The Awakening in Wales and Some of the Hidden Springs* (Poole: Overcomer Literature Trust, n.d.), p.67.
30. *Revival in Wales*, pp.17-23.
31. H. Elvet Lewis, *With Christ among the Miners* (London: Hodder and Stoughton, 1906). Lewis was a poet, hymnist and famed preacher.
32. The novelist evaluated the revival in a New Year's Eve message in the *Western Mail* (31 December 1904).
33. J. Rouges de Fursac, *Un Mouvement Mystique Contemporain* (Paris: Félix Alcan, 1907).

Chapter 10: THE SOUND OF VICTORIOUS PRAISE

1. *I saw the Welsh Revival*, p.29.
2. T. Williams, *Adgofion am Ddiwygiad 1904-'05 yn Nhrecynon* (Dolgellau: E. W. Evans, 1913), pp.55-6.
3. *Yr Efengylydd*, May 1909, pp.76-7.
4. *Llanelly Mercury*, 15 December 1904.
5. ibid., 29 December 1904.
6. *Llanelly & County Guardian*, 24 November 1904.
7. *Llanelly Mercury*, 15 December 1904.
8. *Wrexham Advertiser*, 1 April 1905.
9. *Yr Efengylydd*, October 1932, p.188.
10. *Adgofion*, pp.83-6, 67-9.
11. *Yr Efengylydd*, July 1935, pp.128-9
12. *Wrexham and North Wales Guardian*, 10 March 1905.
13. *Llanelly Mercury*, 5 January 1905.
14. Document NDX/517/19 in the Pembrokeshire Record Office, Haverfordwest.
15. *Y Greal*, November 1906, p.292 (reprinted from *Seren Cymru*, 15 July 1905).
16. *Yr Efengylydd*, May 1909, p.77.
17. *Y Glorian*, 14 January 1905.

18. NLW, CMA 17388.
19. Document ZM 3829 in Gwynedd County Archives, Dolgellau.
20. John Powell Parry in a recorded interview with Paul E. G. Cook
21. *Y Diwygiad a' r Diwygwyr*, pp.146-7.
22. *Baptist Times*, 4 August 1905.
23. Y *Glorian*, 7 January 1905.
24. *Adgofion*, pp.59-60.
25. Document ZM 3829 in Gwynedd County Archives, Dolgellau.
26. *Cyfrol Goffa*, pp.93-4.
27. Supplement, 3:7.
28. ibid., 1:28-9.
29. *Diwygiad yn Rhos*, p.22.
30. *Baptist Times*, 6 January 1905, article by J. W. Ewing entitled 'Impressions of the Welsh Revival'.
31. Supplement, 3:8; 2:12.
32. *Yr Efengylydd*, May 1909, pp.77-8.
33. *Afterglow*, p.26.
34. *Adgofion*, pp.75-6.
35. *Llanelly Mercury*, 5 January 1905; see also Supplement, 3:19.
36. In a recorded interview with Paul E. G. Cook
37. *The Revival in the West*, W. T. Stead, p.40.
38. *I saw the Welsh Revival*, pp.32-3.
39. Document ZM 3829 in Gwynedd County Archives, Dolgellau.
40. *Yr Efengylydd*, May 1909, p.76.
41. *Adgofion*, pp.101, 103, 111-12, 115-16.
42. *Yr Efengylydd*, April 1930, pp.75-6.
43. ibid., July 1924, p.146, article by Daniel Jones. This meeting was still being held in Cardiganshire in the 1970s.

Chapter 11: THE CALL OF THE MASTER

1. *Seren Gomer*, March 1905, p.60. 'Bord Gron' was the title given to a number of articles that appeared in that publication.
2. *Y Cylchgrawn Efengylaidd*, Autumn-Winter 1957, pp.5-6.
3. From an interview with the author in 1962. His voyage to South Africa is narrated in a Welsh book, *Profiad yn nhyd a Hanes Taith Edward Wilkins o Cross Hands, Llanelli, i Cape Town, Deheudir Affrica* (Llanelli, 1910).
4. *Cyfrol Goffa*, p.70; see also J. Rogues de Fursac, *Un Mouvement Mystique Contemporain*, p.145; *Journal of the Society for Psychical Research*, December 1905, article by A. T. Fryer entitled 'Psychological Aspects of the Welsh Revival: 1904-5', pp.96-107; NLW, CMA 17391 (letter from Mary Jones, Egryn, to D. M. Phillips, from Pencoed near Bridgend in July 1905); *Wrexham Advertiser,* 15 April 1905.
5. *Llangollen Advertiser*, 6 January 1905; *Y Glorian*, 14 January 1905.
6. *I saw the Welsh Revival*, p.68.
7. *The Efengylydd* printed regular reports on Francis's work from 1920 to 1922. The author has documents relating to his later ministries.
8. Recorded statement loaned by Mr J. Cudmore of Merthyr Tydfil.

9. *Y Drysorfa*, May 1951, p.117.
10. *Cyfrol Goffa*, pp.89, 89-90, 90, 90-1.
11. Phillips, pp.231-2.
12. *Cyfrol Goffa*, pp.67-8.
13. *Welsh Religious Revival*, pp.261-2.
14. *South Wales Daily Post*, 2 December 1904.
15. *Y Drysorfa*, October 1954, pp.227-8.
16. ibid., October 1955, p.211.
17. *Adgofion*, p.86, drawing on a testimony in *Y Diwygiwr*, July 1906.
18. S. M. Saunders, *Y Diwygiad ym Mhentre Alun*, (Wrexham: Hughes a'i Fab, 1907), pp.15-16.
19. ibid., pp.7-11.
20. Cassette no. 100. (Copy in the Evangelical Library of Wales, Bridgend.)
21. Cassette no. 102. (Copy in the Evangelical Library of Wales, Bridgend.)
22. *Y Diwygiad ym Mhentre Alun*, p.vi.
23. Supplement, 2:14.
24. *Afterglow*, p.28.
25. NLW, CMA 28678.
26. *Y Cylchgrawn Efengylaidd*, April/May 1952, pp.25-6.
27. NLW, CMA 17669.
28. Evidence submitted as part of Fryer's report, *Journal of the Society for Psychical Research*, December 1905, pp.141, 95.
29. *Y Drysorfa*, October 1955, p.218.
30. From an interview with the author in October 1989.
31. *Y Geninen*, April 1905, p.114—article by Dr William Morris, Treorci, entitled 'Chwyldroadau y Diwygiad' ('The Revolutions of the Revival').

Chapter 12: THE PUBLIC WITNESS OF CHURCHES

1. St Mary Street Baptist Church, Stow Hill, Newport, *The Monthly Visitor*, June 1905, p.3.
2. Phillips, p.442.
3. Supplement, 4:4,6,7; 6:13,24.
4. Phillips, p.321.
5. Supplement, 6:13.
6. *Y Llan*, 27 January 1905; see also 6 and 20 January 1905.
7. *Llangollen Advertiser*, 27 January 1905.
8. *North Wales Guardian*, 27 January 1905.
9. *Wrexham Advertiser*, 17 June 1905.
10. *Y Greal*, November 1906, pp.297-8.
11. *Diwygiad yn Rhos*, p.28.
12. In a recorded interview with Paul E. G. Cook.
13. *Diwygiad yn Rhos*, pp.21-2. A similar incident took place in Tonypandy when the colliery pump broke and the colliers went to a chapel vestry to join in the prayers (*Western Mail*, 18 December 1906).
14. In a recorded interview with Paul E. G. Cook.

15. From notes of a conversation between the author and Mrs Emmelina Morgan in Rhos, 1963.
16. *Y Glorian*, 14 January 1905.
17. *Afterglow*, pp.74-5.
18. *Western Mail*, 2 February 1905.
19. *Baptist Times*, 3 and 10 March 1905.
20. *Y Drysorfa*, May 1951, pp.117-18.
21. *Afterglow*, pp.32-3.
22. From notes of a conversation with the author in 1963.
23. George Griffiths, *What God Hath Wrought* (1962), pp.4,6. This little booklet tells the story of Tro'r Glien Mission, Cwm-twrch.
24. *Afterglow*, pp.60-1.
25. ibid, p.34.
26 Robert Ellis, *Living Echoes*, p.93.
27. *King's Champions*, p.80.
28. ibid., pp.107-15.

Chapter 13: SOCIAL AND CULTURAL OVERTONES

1. *I saw the Welsh Revival*, p.58.
2. In a recorded interview with Paul E. G. Cook.; see also *APC News*, 7 (February 1991), p.4.
3. *Llanelly Mercury*, 24 November 1904.
4. From personal conversations with the author in 1963.
5. *Rent Heavens*, second edition 1948, p.60.
6. *Chwalfa* by T. Rowland Hughes. An English translation of the novel, under the title *Out of their Night*, was published in 1954.
7. *Y Diwygiad a'r Diwygwyr*, pp.145-6.
8. *Rent Heavens*, p.63.
9. *Y Glorian*, 11 February 1905.
10. *Rent Heavens*, p.63.
11. *Cambrian News*, 23 December 1904.
12. *Rent Heavens*, pp.66-7.
13. *North Wales Guardian*, 20 January 1905.
14. *Perlau'r Diwygiad*, edited by 'Anthropos' (Caernarfon, [1906]), pp.19,27,22. 'Anthropos' was the pen-name of the Caernarfon minister and author, R. D. Rowland (1853?-1944).
15. *Diwygiad yn Rhos*, p.31.
16. *I saw the Welsh Revival*, p.50.
17. David Smith & Gareth Williams, *Fields of Praise* (Cardiff: University of Wales Press, 1980), p.126.
18. *Y Greal*, September 1905, p.242
19. *Wrexham Advertiser*, 6 May 1905; see also 3 June 1905.
20. *Seren Gomer*, March 1905, pp.69-71.
21. *Welsh Religious Revival*, pp.254-5.

Chapter 14: THE CRY OF THE REBEL

1. *Y Cylchgrawn Efengylaidd*, September/October 1949, pp.18-19.
2. *Y Drysorfa*, October 1954, p.227.
3. *Western Mail*, 11 February 1905.
4. *Afterglow*, pp.82-4.
5. ibid., pp.52-3.
6. From an interview with the author in 1963.
7. *Y Diwygiad ym Mhentre Alun*, pp.52-8.
8. T. Williams, *Adgofion*, pp.96-8.
9. *Mouvement*, p.68.
10. *Perlau'r Diwygiad*, pp.36,39,23,28.
11. *Yr Efengylydd*, November and December 1932, pp.204,229-30.
12. *Yr Efengylydd*, February 1933, pp.25-6.

Chapter 15: OUT OF THE DEPTHS HAVE I CRIED

1. *Perlau'r Diwygiad*, pp.21,29,33,35,39,40,41.
2. *Afterglow*, p.82.
3. Supplement, 2:26.
4. *Afterglow*, p.82.
5. *Y Drysorfa*, October 1955, pp.209-11.
6. ibid., pp.213-14.
7. Supplement, 1: 29-30.
8. In a recorded interview with Paul E. G. Cook.
9. Brother Tom's story is in *Rent Heavens*, pp.48-9, and in *Cyfrol Goffa*, pp.68-9; see also *Y Darian*, 20 February 1930.
10. *Yr Efengylydd*, 'Life and Letters of Brother Tom', vol.I, p.99—vol. IX, p.141 (1914-17).

Chapter 16: RESISTING THE SPIRIT

1. J. Williams Hughes (ed.), *Charles Davies, Caerdydd* (Cardiff, 1933), p.66-7.
2. From an interview by the author with T. J. Davies of Rhos, conducted in 1963.
3. Letter sent to the author by J. T. Jones of Rhos in 1961 (now deposited in the National Library of Wales).
4. *Mouvement*, pp.144-8.
5. *Proceedings*, vol. xix (December 1905).
6. ibid.
7. Ifan Huw Jones, *Mygyn gyda'r Meddyg* (Liverpool: Gwasg y Brython, 1948), pp.58-9.
8. *Y Diwygiad a'r Diwygwyr*, pp.112-13; cf. Supplement, 2:5.
9. Supplement, 3:10-11.
10. *Adgofion*, pp.63-4.
11. *Y Dysgedydd*, March-April 1953.
12. *Afterglow*, p.29.
13. *Y Celt Newydd*, 16 December 1904.

14. *Llanelly Mercury*, 2 March 1905.
15. *Aberdare Leader*, 19 and 26 November 1904.
16. *Monthly Treasury*, September 1905, pp.198-9.

Chapter 17: GRIEVING THE SPIRIT

1. *Llanelly Mercury*, 16 March 1905.
2. *Mouvement*, pp.115-16.
3. Minutes of Gwent English Baptist Association, *Western Mail*, 1 December 1904.
4. Supplement, 2:6.
5. *Y Piwritan Newydd*, January 1905.
6. *South Wales Daily News*, 25 November 1904; see also *King's Champions*, p.93.
7. *Llanelly Mercury*, 1 December 1904.
8. *Mouvement*, p.117.
9. *Cyfrol Goffa*, pp.86-7.
10. *Llanelly Mercury*, 26 January and 2 February 1905.
11. ibid., 20 April 1905.
12. *South Wales Daily Post*, 15 November 1904.
13. ibid., 1 December 1904.
14. *Yr Efengylydd*, May 1909, p.77.
15. *Y Glorian*, 25 March 1905.
16. ibid., 17 February 1906.
17. *Y Drysorfa*, October 1954, p.219.
18. From an interview by the author with Mr Robert Williams in 1963.
19. *Y Drysorfa*, October 1954, p.219.
20. *Llanelly Mercury*, 15 December 1904.
21. *Cyfrol Goffa*, p.87.
22. *Y Drysorfa*, October 1954, p.223.
23. *Cardigan & Tivy-side Advertiser*, 7 November 1913.
24. Noel Gibbard, *Hanes Plwyf Llan-non* (Cyngor Cymuned Llan-non, 1984), p.57.
25. Details supplied by Mr Meurig Thomas, Llangeler, Dyfed.
26. ibid.; further details from Miss Morfudd Jones, Tŷ-croes, Dyfed.
27. Details supplied by Mr Daniel Roberts of Fforest-fach, Swansea.
28. Information from Mr Lewis of Brynaman and Mr Idris Davies, Ammanford.
29. *Yr Efengylydd*, January 1929, p.13.
30. Correspondence Columns, *Western Mail*, 1-6 and 11 February 1905; J. V. Morgan, *Welsh Religious Revival*, pp.141-62.
31. *Seren Cymru*, 21 May 1926.
32. Interview with the author in October 1989.
33. *Yr Efengylydd*, October 1915, p.147.

Chapter 18: QUENCHING THE SPIRIT

1. *Y Geninen*, April 1905, p.114.
2. J. Edwin Orr, *The Flaming Tongue,* pp.26-8, 189.
3. *Welsh Revival of 1904*, p.186.

4.   *Yr Efengylydd*, June 1913, pp.82-3.
5.   ibid., May 1924, pp.95-6.
6.   ibid., June 1925, p.109.
7.   ibid., September 1928, pp.198-9.
8.   ibid., April 1925, pp. 63-4. This is part of a series, continued in May and June, entitled 'Cymeriad yr Yspryd' (The Character of the Spirit').
9.   *Life of Faith*, 1922. (Complete file at the British Library, London.)
10. See article by Alun Gibbard in *Y Cylchgrawn Efengylaidd*, August/September 1980, p.17.
11. *Seren Cymru*, 21 May 1926.
12. *Yr Efengylydd*, May 1922, pp.85-7.

Index

1. Persons

296

Webb-Pebloe, 151
Webster, F. S., 144
Wesley, John, 137
Wilkins, Edward, 184, 268
Williams, Edgar, 212
Williams, Elizabeth, 119-22
Williams, Evan, 106, 203
Williams, J. Cynog, 103, 200, 277-8
Williams, J. H. ('Canwy'), 265
Williams, John, 60-61, 132, 138

Williams, Mary, 199
Williams, Nantlais, 66-8, 103, 136, 187-9,
   200, 261, 267, 272, 275, 276-7, 278,
   279-80
Williams, Peter ('Pedr Hir'), 168
Williams, Robert, 132
Williams, Richard, 228-9
Williams, T. Charles, 138, 169
Williams, Thomas ('Parcwyson', 159,
   163, 169, 175, 178, 190, 253

2. Places

3. Subject

Books on revival and related subjects from the Evangelical Press of Wales

*   *   *

Revival Comes to Wales
by Eifion Evans

A moving and thrilling account of the mighty working of God the Holy Spirit in Wales at the time of the 1859 Revival.

The Welsh Revival of 1904
by Eifion Evans

A well-documented but very readable study of the 1904 Revival, with a foreword by D. Martyn Lloyd-Jones.

Howell Harris and the Dawn of Revival
by Richard Bennett; introduction by D. M. Lloyd-Jones

A detailed account, based on the diaries of Howell Harris, of the first three years of his spiritual pilgrimage—a crucial period in the origins of the Great Awakening of the eighteenth century.

The Christian Heritage of Welsh Education
by R. M. Jones & Gwyn Davies

A bird's-eye view of Christian education in Wales down the centuries, which demonstrates its close inter-relationship with revival.

'Excuse Me, Mr Davies—Hallelujah!'
by Geraint Fielder; foreword by Lady Catherwood

The absorbing story of evangelical student witness in Wales in the twentieth century, a story which includes periods of quite remarkable spiritual blessing.

Further titles
from the Evangelical Press of Wales

Christian Preachers *by Nigel Clifford*
The lives and achievements of 31 of some of the outstanding men of the Christian Church, from Chrysostom and Augustine to Tozer and Martyn Lloyd-Jones. It is also a book about preaching itself and offers a bird's eye view of some facets of the history of the church.

Christian Handbook *by Peter Jeffery*
A well illustrated and straight-forward guide to the Bible, church history and Christian doctrine. Over 90 illustrations, including maps, charts, drawings and photographs.

Covenanting with God *by Gwyn Davies*
A study of the spirituality of the past, focusing attention on covenants between individuals and God and on church covenants binding members to one another and to their Lord. As well as including examples from Wales, it deals with the role of covenanting in the lives of such figures as Matthew Henry, Jonathan Edwards and C. H. Spurgeon.

Glory Over Calvary *by Peter Trumper*
A book which retells the 'old, old story' of the Cross in a fresh and vivid way, through the eyes of those who were actually there outside the walls of Jerusalem.

What is Truth? *by Bryan A. Williams*
68 pages which cover the whole spectrum of 'Bible basics', a very readable primer in Christian theology.

Jesus—Power Without Measure *by Douglas MacMillan*
An illuminating study of an aspect of truth which is rarely considered, the work of the Holy Spirit in the life of our Lord.

I Want to be a Church Member *by Eric Lane*
'There is nothing else which within so brief a compass describes as helpfully the procedures and privileges of church membership.'—Geoffrey Thomas.

An Angry God? *by Eryl Davies*
What the Bible says about the wrath of God, final judgment and hell.